THE ANIMAL
IN
HOLLYWOOD

THE ANIMAL
IN
HOLLYWOOD

Anthony
Fiato's
Life
in the
Mafia

John L. Smith

Barricade Books, New York

Published by Barricade Books Inc.
150 Fifth Avenue
Suite 700
New York, NY 10011

First Edition

Library of Congress Cataloging-in-Publication Data

Smith, John L., 1960–
    The animal in Hollywood : Anthony Fiato's life in the
Mafia / by John L. Smith.
        p.   cm.
    ISBN 1-56980-126-6
    1. Fiato, Anthony.   2. Gangsters—California—
Los Angeles—Biography.   3. Mafia—California—
Los Angeles.   I. Title.
HV6452.C29S65 1998
364.1'092—dc21
    [B]
                                                        98-16584
                                                        CIP

For my brother, Jim.

And for Anthony's brother, Larry.

"What are you, a tough guy? Well,
let me tell you something. All the tough
guys are dead. We do away with them all."

—Larry Baioni,
chief enforcer for the Boston Mafia

"What are you going to do, kill me?
Everybody dies."

—John Garfield,
Body and Soul, United Artists film, 1947

CAST OF CHARACTERS

Angiulo, Donato: ("Danny") New England mob figure.

Angiulo, Gerardo: ("Jerry") Bookmaker, street boss in New England mob.

Anselmo, Joseph: ("Joe Burns") Boston Mafia underboss.

Aron, Leonard: Implicated in $1 million bond scam.

Barboza, Joseph: ("Joe the Animal") Boston Mafia associate, killer of more than 20 people. Deceased.

Bayden, Leonard: Los Angeles-based bookmaker.

Bayless, Earl: Bookmaker, resides in Southern California.

Betts, Alan: Career criminal, convicted of murdering Frank Christi.

Bianco, Nicky: New England mobster. Deceased.

Blitzstein, Herbert: ("Fat Herbie") Bookmaker, Chicago mob associate. Deceased.

Bompensiero, Frank: ("The Bump" and "Frankie Bomp") Los Angeles Mafia underboss. Deceased.

Branco, John: Los Angeles Mafia associate, loanshark, bookmaker. FBI informant in murder of Herbie Blitzstein.

Bulger, James: ("Whitey") Boss of the Winter Hill gang. Currently in hiding after being revealed as an FBI informant.

Caan, Jimmy: Actor with numerous starring roles. A longtime associate of mob figures, Caan once put up his house as collateral for hoodlum Joey Ippolito.

Caan, Ronnie: Younger brother of James Caan.

Caci, Charles James: ("Bobby Milano") Singer, Mafia soldier. Formerly married to Keely Smith.

Caci, Vincent Dominic: ("Jimmy") Los Angeles Mafia lieutenant.

Carrol, Bill: Mustang strip club owner. Convicted felon. Survived murder attempt by Mike Rizzitello.

Cassesso, Ronald: ("Ronnie the Pig") Boston Mafia soldier.

Catain, Jack: Los Angeles businessman, longtime Mafia associate.

Cataldo, Carl: Los Angeles crime family associate.

Cincotti, John: ("Fat Johnny") Boston Mafia soldier.

Cino, Steven: ("Fat Steve" and "The Whale") Los Angeles Mafia soldier, associate of Buffalo mob. Convicted felon. Suspected conspirator in plot to murder Herbie Blitzstein.

Coe, Ronald: Criminal, convicted of murdering Frank Christi.

Coe, Donald: Brother of Ronald.

Cohen, Mickey: Los Angeles crime boss. Deceased.

Costanza, Nicky Sr.: Chicago mob associate.

Costanza, Nicky Jr.: Mob associate, drug dealer. Deceased.

Craig, Bobby: Bookmaker.

D'Agostino, Dino: Chef, Mafia associate, convicted drug dealer.

D'Amore, Patsy: Restaurant owner, friend of Frank Sinatra. Deceased.

DeCiccio, Vincent: ("Vinny Jackson") Boston Mafia soldier, partners with J.R. Russo.

De La Mantaigne, Vince: FBI undercover agent.

Dellacroce, Aniello: ("Mr. Neil" and "The Lamb") Gambino crime family underboss, confidant of Mike Rizzitello.

DiGiacomo, Biaggio: Sicilian-born Mafia soldier.

DiMattia, John: Los Angeles and New Jersey Mafia associate.

Dragna, Jack: Los Angeles Mafia boss. Deceased.

Dragna, Louis Tom: Los Angeles acting boss in 1970s, cooperating witness.

Durosia, Rocky: Los Angeles Mafia associate.

Esposito, Michael: Lucchese crime family associate. Pornographer.

Ferrara, Vincent: ("Vinny Nip") College-educated Mafia soldier. Suspect in numerous hits.

Fiato, Anthony: ("Tony Rome," "Anthony Fortunato," "Tony the Animal") Mobster, undercover informant. Fiato was an enforcer and street boss in rogue family run by Mike Rizzitello and in Los Angeles family headed by Peter John Milano. Suspected hit man. Testified in the murder case of O.J. Simpson. Now living under an assumed name as a relocated federal witness.

Fiato, Larry: Mob collector and bookmaker, undercover informant. Anthony's younger brother, Larry also testified in the Simpson case. Now living under an assumed name as a relocated federal witness.

Fiato, Johnny: Bartender. Father of Anthony and Larry Fiato. Deceased.

Fine, Jack: Los Angeles-based con artist, associate of Mike Rizzitello. Deceased.

Finkel, Steve: Los Angeles Mafia associate.

Flemmi, Stephen: ("Stevie the Rifleman") Boston Mafia enforcer, FBI informant.

Fopiano, Willie: ("Floppy") Boston Mafia associate, once the protege of Larry Baiona. Deceased.

Fratianno, Aladeno: ("Jimmy the Weasel") Mob hit man, government informant. Deceased.

Freedburg, Norman: ("Norman Cole") Actor, bookmaker, suspected drug dealer. Living in Palm Springs.

Gallo, Ernest: ("Blackie") Career criminal, mob associate, leader of Halifax Gang, he bragged of working a straight job only one day in his life. Currently living in California.

Gallo, Joseph: ("Crazy Joe") Mob killer associated with Colombo crime family, attempted family takeover. Deceased.

Gelfuso, Luigi: Los Angeles Mafia lieutenant, convicted drug dealer, murder suspect.

Gelfuso, Michael: Los Angeles Mafia associate.

George, Johnny: Casino boss, Chicago mob associate. Deceased.

Giglio, Salvatore: ("Harry Leonard") Bonanno crime family member. Currently residing in Florida.

Giso, Nicola: ("Nicky") Boston Mafia soldier who reported to Paul Intiso, operator of the Coliseum nightclub, ostrascized by family after he began dating a teen-age girl. Deceased.

Granito, Sam: Boston Mafia lieutenant. Deceased.

Hamer, Robert: FBI Agent.

Hampshire, Russ: Pornographer.

Henderson, James: Top prosecutor for Los Angeles Organized Crime Strike Force. Currently in private practice.

Holden, Gene: Bookmaker, loanshark. Loanshark partner of Anthony Fiato, Robert Zeichick.

Intiso, Paul: ("Paulie") Boston Mafia street boss.

Ippolito, Joseph: New York mobster and drug dealer. Moved to Los Angeles, later became a government informant.

Isgro, Joseph: Los Angeles mob associate, independent record producer, distributor.

Jones, Charles: FBI Agent.

Kessler, Robert: Los Angeles Mafia associate, FBI informant. Deceased.

Kreiner, Mark: Limousine driver.

Lamattina, Ralph: ("Ralphie Chiong") Boston Mafia soldier, implicated in crimes ranging from armed robbery to murder.

Lange, Tom: Los Angeles Police Department Robbery/Homicide Detective.

LaPrieda, Pat: ("Pat the Priest") Hit man for Los Angeles mob. Deceased.

Licata, Nick: Los Angeles Mafia boss after Jack Dragna.

Liszt, Mike: Los Angeles Mafia associate.

LoCicero, Jack: Los Angeles crime family consigliere. Deceased.

McClain, Enoch: ("Mac") Los Angeles Police Department Robbery/Homicide Detective.

Mack, Joseph: Boston drug trafficker.

Manarite, Sam: ("Springfield Sam") Genovese crime family member, career criminal. Currently incarcerated.

Mangiapani, Joey: Boxing trainer and manager, mob associate.

Matricia, Jerry: Boston Mafia associate and drug dealer. Now a cooperating witness.

Mondavano, Danny: White-collar criminal, associate of Mafia families in Boston and Los Angeles.

Mercurio, Sonny: New England mobster, FBI informant, involved in setting up Mafia induction ceremony that was recorded by law enforcement.

Milano, Carmen: ("Flipper") Former attorney, Los Angeles Mafia family underboss.

Milano, Peter John: Los Angeles Mafia boss. Currently living in Southern California.

Monaco, Steven: ("Blockhead Steve") Los Angeles mob associate.

Motto, Jack: Los Angeles Police Department Administrative Vice detective. Organized crime, gambling expert.

Munichiello, Steve: Los Angeles crime family associate.

Napolitano, Joseph: ("Joe Nap") Boston Mafia associate. Deceased.

Nelson, James: FBI Agent.

Nunez, Albert: ("Albie") Los Angeles mob associate, convicted felon.

Patriarca, Raymond Sr.: New England Mafia boss of bosses. Deceased.

Patriarca, Raymond Jr." ("Jr.") Assumed leadership of Boston Mafia over objections of longtime members, who believed he was too soft for the job. Demoted after entering prison.

Pellegrino, John: Los Angeles restaurateur, Mafia associate.

Piscopo, Luigi: ("Dago Louie") Los Angeles Mafia soldier. Deceased.

Pisello, Sal: Gambino crime family member associated with major entertainment company.

Polosi, Sonny: Boston Mafia associate and drug dealer. Deceased.

Raffone, Dominic: ("Dominic the Pig") Los Angeles mob associate.

Ricciardi, Thomas: ("Tommy") Los Angeles Mafia soldier. Deceased.

Richichi, Natale: ("Big Chris") Gambino crime family capo, adviser to John Gotti.

Rizzitello, Michael Anthony: ("Mike Rizzi") Mob hit man. Born in New York, Rizzitello survived the "Gallo War" and rose to prominance in Los Angeles. Currently in prison for attempted murder of strip bar owner Frank Carrol.

Romanowski, Ronald: ("Ronnie Rome") Boston and Los Angeles Mafia associate.

Rooney, Pete: Bookmaker.

Rosenthal, Harvey: ("Harvey Ross") Small-time criminal who participated in the murder of Frank Christi.

Rosselli, John: Mobster with influence in Hollywood and Las Vegas. Corpse found in oil drum floating off Florida coast in 1976.

Russo, Joseph: ("J.R.") Boston Mafia lieutenant. Died of cancer in 1998.

Sacco, Felipo: (See Rosselli, John)

Sandrelli, Anthony: ("Tony Canadian") Boston Mafia boss. Deceased.

Salemme, Frank: ("Cadillac Frank") Boston Mafia soldier, sought status as head of the family after gaining release from prison.

Sandrelli, Michael: ("Mikey Sands") Former boxer, Los Angeles Mafia associate.

Santone, Joseph: Los Angeles mob associate. Deceased.

Scibelli, Frank: ("Frankie Skyball") Genovese crime family lieutenant.

Sciortino, Sam: Los Angeles Mafia soldier. Deceased.

Strauss, Jack: ("Treetop") Professional poker player, mob associate, suspected drug trafficker and money launderer. Deceased.

Selvitella, Henry: ("Henry Noyes") Former boxer, mob hit man and boss.

Sica, Fred: Bookmaker, Los Angeles organized crime figure.

Sica, Joseph: Bookmaker, Los Angeles organized crime figure.

Silverio, Al: ("Skinny Al") Boston mob associate.

Spilotro, Anthony: ("Tough Tony" and "The Ant") Chicago Mafia soldier assigned to Las Vegas. Deceased.

Stevens, Walter: Bookmaker, loanshark. Enemy of Mike Rizzitello.

Taccetta, Martin: Lucchese crime family soldier. Pornographer.

Teresa, Vincent: ("Fat Vinny") Boston Mafia associate, government informant. Deceased.

Terry, Mike: Detective, Torrance Police Department.

Tracy, David: ("Cowboy Dave") Los Angeles Mafia associate.

Urgitano, Angelo: ("Cheesecake" and "The Jet") Lucchese crime family soldier. Deceased.

Vannatter, Phil: LAPD Robbery/Homicide Detective.

Vaccaro, John: Los Angeles Mafia soldier. Currently incarcerated.

Wacks, Michael: FBI Agent with undercover experience in BRILAB case in Louisiana. Case agent in "Rising Star" investigation.

Weichert, William: FBI case agent on "Operation Rising Star."

Wekar, Milton: Illegal bookmaker associated with Genovese and Lucchese crime families.

Zangari, Rocco: ("Rocky" and "Big Foot") Los Angeles Mafia soldier.

Zannino, Ilario (Larry Baioni): Underboss of Boston mob, top hit man in New England's version of Murder, Inc. Deceased.

Zappi, Etore: ("Terry") Gambino crime family soldier, pornographer. Deceased.

Zeichick, Robert: ("Puggy") Los Angeles loanshark.

Zemer, Jacob: Implicated in stolen bond scam.

AUTHOR'S NOTE

In my life as a Las Vegas newspaperman, I've met numerous members and associates of organized crime and viewed their ways with the kind of fascination otherwise reserved for the zoo's exotic carnivores. No matter how colorful the tale, I have always approached their stories with extreme skepticism. It was that way when I encountered Craig Anthony Fiato.

The evidence gathered by Fiato, the top mob enforcer-turned-government informant, led to the conviction of at least 60 Mafia men from Hollywood to Boston. Fiato played an integral role in nailing the killers of *The Godfather* actor Frank Christi, and he testified in the O.J. Simpson murder trial. The fact that he put so many criminals in the penitentiary was a testament to his credibility in legal circles, but in my experience Mafia turncoats lied almost as often as the men they were betraying. And so as this project developed I took nothing Fiato said at face value.

Instead, I read hundreds of pages of transcripts from the telephone wiretaps and body recordings illustrating Fiato's role in the FBI's "Rising Star" organized crime investigation. Culminating in 1988, "Rising Star" devastated the Los Angeles mob, otherwise known as the Peter John Milano crime family. Thanks to Fiato, Mike Rizzitello's dream of running his own family also was shattered.

I also listened to the tapes the government had made of Fiato prior to his turning informant and quickly realized how he came by his nickname, "The Animal." In the early 1980s as Mike Rizzitello's top lieutenant and enforcer, Anthony Fiato brought a brand of violence to the streets of Los Angeles that the city had rarely seen outside the silver screen.

For more than a decade, Craig Anthony Fiato was a two-legged carnivore who prowled the streets of Hollywood and feasted on its hedonistic excesses. He ate at the most expensive restaurants and mixed with the movie industry's stars. Top actors and entertainers sought his company. Models and starlets crossed crowded rooms to meet him. While they were admiring him, Fiato was sizing them up for his next score as Southern California's strongest street mobster. In his prime, he was positioned like a hungry wolf in the heart of the American dream machine and terrorized bookmakers and moneylenders throughout Los Angeles, generating more than $50,000 a week for himself and his people.

Nominated for membership in the Rizzitello and Milano Mafia families, ruthless Anthony Fiato was the mob's rising star. When he went undercover for the FBI, the Hollywood mob would never be the same.

Anthony Fiato's candor is a bit unnerving. His recollection of his career in the mob and his work for the government is eerily precise, as if a movie of his life in the Mafia plays in his head. In time I discovered, as will the reader, that the image of the American gangster affected Anthony Fiato's life in many ways. It is my belief that, for many mobsters, life imitates art.

As to the issue of homicide, law enforcement sources suspect Fiato in up to a dozen murders. On FBI surveillance tape, he was recorded ordering numerous hits, which fast-acting federal agents made certain were not carried out. Over the years, Fiato has been interviewed about his insider's knowledge of more than 50 gangland slayings. Although some of Fiato's victims are not heard from again, the reader will note that for all his violence he commits no murder in these pages. Nor did he share with me any such incriminating information. Anthony Fiato is a free man today in no small part because he chooses his words even more carefully than his friends.

At various times in his life, Fiato has been known as Craig, C. Anthony, Tony Rome, Tony Fortunato, Tony the Animal, and just plain Anthony. To make it easy for the reader, Fiato is referred to as Anthony or Fiato throughout this book.

Anthony Fiato goes by another name these days, but that identity will remain confidential.

PROLOGUE

In the beginning, there was a boy's dream on Hanover Street.

Anthony Fiato was a child from Boston who found himself standing on the most famous thoroughfare on the North End. It was the early 1950s. Cutting through the tangle of produce vendors and merchants in aprons, Anthony accompanied his grandfather, Atillio Sceppa, for a morning of shopping. Hanover buzzed with activity and a mixture of Italian and English filled the air.

Ahead, the crowd parted and went strangely quiet. Three men in overcoats walked past. Shopkeepers acknowledged them. A fruit vendor said nothing when one of the men helped himself to an apple. In a moment, the three disappeared down the sidewalk. Atillio had seen many such men most of his life and could only shake his head. Young Anthony was impressed not only by the cut of their expensive clothes, but also by the way the people on the street showed them respect. Surely these were important men.

Anthony drank in the sights on Hanover Street and many times saw the way citizens feared and admired members of the neighborhood Mafiosi. And the North End was awash in these characters. Phil Buccola had been deported in the 1940s, but even now, the mention of his name was enough to silence grown men. There was Anthony "Tony Canadian" Sandrelli, Henry "Noyes" Selvitella, Raymond Patriarca, Joe Lombardo, the Angiulo brothers, and countless lesser players. In the 1950s, New England was

teeming with dangerous men. Its mob had two hearts: one beat on
Federal Hill in Providence, Rhode Island; the other on Boston's
North End.

"These guys were like gods, or at least popes, on the streets,"
Anthony Fiato recalled years later. "There I was a kid with holes
in his shoes on his way to growing up to be a bartender like my
father, and these guys wore the best clothes, tailored suits and
cashmere coats, silk shirts and Italian shoes that cost more than
most people earned in three months. They had everything. The
cars, the prestige, and most of all the fear and respect. They had
real power.

"Raymond Patriarca controlled not just the street rackets but a
fair number of politicians and cops. He had strength in commu-
nities outside the North End, and friends who were Jewish and
Irish. I watched his lieutenants and soldiers the way most kids
would watch Ted Williams or Yaz. I imitated their style, wanted
their clothes. By the time I was old enough to take my first Holy
Communion, I knew what I wanted to be when I grew up."

A gangster.

Other influences appeared every Saturday after shopping, when
Fiato accompanied his grandfather to the movies. There on the
silver screen was everything a kid needed to know about walking
and talking like a tough guy in the form of Lawrence Tierney in
Dillinger and James Cagney in *White Heat*.

"My grandfather used to take me to all the gangster movies,"
Fiato recalled. "I'd go with him and we'd buy groceries on
Saturday and we'd sneak off and see a movie. He loved gangster
movies. He spoke broken English and was a square guy. He
worked as a foreman at a shoe factory.

"He wouldn't miss a John Wayne movie. He loved John
Wayne, and so I did, too. Humphrey Bogart, Edward G. Robinson,
John Garfield. He thought they were all the greatest. I liked all the
tough guys. I remember one movie with Robert Mitchum, *The
Night of the Hunter*. I was used to seeing him as a gangster or a
gumshoe, but in this movie he was a preacher. And he was

absolutely evil. He dressed as a good guy, but he was bad. In my neighborhood, the men I admired most were bad guys, but to me they were good guys. I was an altar boy, but I longed to be like those important men in the neighborhood.

"When my dad announced we were moving to California and he was taking a job as a bartender at a famous Hollywood restaurant, the Villa Capri, thanks to his friendship with the Angiulos, I figured I might never see the North End again. It didn't matter. I knew I wanted to be a tough guy like the men on the street and on the screen."

For Anthony Fiato, the Hanover Street dream would become more real, and more dangerous, than anything he might have imagined.

CHAPTER 1

In the late 1950s, the Fiato family's modest Hollywood flat was a tiny slice of Boston's North End nestled a block off Highland Avenue. On Sunday afternoons, the apartment at 1326 North Citrus Street was filled with the intoxicating scent of old-world cooking. The smell of peppers and onions and fresh-baked bread, of bubbling pans of lasagna and steaming platters of chicken cacciatore wafted through the complex like a garlic-and-tomato-laced dream.

Between Johnny's affable manner and his wife's cooking, it's no wonder friends from all over Los Angeles were drawn to the Fiato's table for Sunday supper. After all, you couldn't get good sauce just any place in California. They weren't the usual assortment of guests. The men, most of whom prided themselves on their toughness, always had a weakness for food, like the gnocci, the pasta e piselli, and the spaghetti with white gravy that reminded them of their East Coast homes. It was one reason they also frequented the Villa Capri, where Johnny Fiato worked as a swing shift bartender. Patsy D'Amore and Frank Sinatra owned the place, and everyone who was anyone in Hollywood wound up there most nights to mix with the dangerous regulars.

"It was like bringing stray dogs to the house," Anthony Fiato recalled. "You gotta understand something: None of these guys were from California. They came from Brooklyn and Harlem, Federal Hill in Providence and the North End of Boston. Even one or two from the old country. But they all loved my mother's cooking, and they were all street guys."

There was "Dago Louie" Piscopo, with his dark suits and broken English, who loansharked and strong-armed bookmakers from Hollywood to Watts on behalf of his boss, Los Angeles godfather Jack Dragna. "Dago Louie" was a fixture at the Villa Capri.

There was "Pat the Priest" LaPrieda, a polite fellow at the dinner table who got his nickname by wearing a priest's collar when he went on contract murders. He also was a Villa Capri regular, and in years to come, would be seen hanging out with big-league pitchers Dean Chance and Bo Belinsky.

There was Nicky Bianco, always homesick for Federal Hill, who was a capodecina in Raymond Patriarca's family. When he wasn't remembering the old neighborhood, he kept himself busy shaking down bookmakers and shopkeepers.

And there were the guys on the rise, Mike Rizzitello and Lefty Castiglione. Rizzitello, who went by the name Mike Rizzi, was already gaining a reputation as an efficient killer on behalf of New York mob bosses. Castiglione was his sidekick. Rizzi was a bartender and Lefty was a waiter at the Villa when they weren't doing odd jobs like robbing restaurants, smashing the kneecaps of late-paying shylock customers, or trying to get their hands on LA bookmaking legend Mickey Cohen.

Then there was Maury Wolf and Jimmy Van Heusen, who wrote and arranged music for Sinatra. And who could forget "General Hospital" heartthrob Johnny Beradino, who had played second base for the St. Louis Browns before stealing the hearts of housewives across America as Dr. Hardy.

Young Anthony Fiato received his first lessons in the mob's friendly relationship with Hollywood across his own dinner table. Years later, he would participate in organized crime's feeding frenzy of the movie business. In the 1950s, organized crime families thrived on Hollywood's dream machine. There were big-budget production companies and recording studios to intimidate, labor unions to infiltrate, plus a lucrative underground pornography industry to extort. Reliable millions were generated through bookmaking and loansharking. In years to come, Fiato would grab pieces of all of it.

Like the rest of Hollywood, the neighborhood surrounding the Citrus Street apartment was home to ambitious dreamers of every station. Budding actress Mary Tyler Moore lived in the complex, and young Anthony never missed an opportunity to focus his adolescent lust her way. He was a constant companion of Mary's brother, John. Fiato went to grade school with future television star Shelley Fabares.

It was common to spot Ricky Nelson and the Everly brothers at Music City, a sprawling record store on Sunset and Vine, where Fiato's cousin, Mario, worked behind the counter. Mario was an aspiring actor who controlled access to the listening booths. Thanks to his cousin, Fiato and his Irish pal, Danny Hutton, could go straight to the front of the line.

"We saw every musician and rock 'n' roll star," Fiato recalled. "We were in an ideal position to get a look at everybody up close."

Around the corner from Music City, a small recording studio captivated Fiato and Hutton. It was there they heard a little-known singer, Donnie Brooks, belt out an early rendition of "Deeper than a Wishing Well," which became a Number One hit single. The song inspired Fiato and Hutton to visions of fame, replete with limitless riches and an ocean of willing, starry-eyed chicks.

Then there were the stars. From Dean Martin and Frank Sinatra to Marilyn Monroe; the legends found their way to the Villa Capri. Anthony parked cars and hung out behind the bar, where his father mixed cocktails for the biggest names in Hollywood. It was there that young Anthony met Robert Mitchum.

But the best star-watching was found on Sunday mornings at Blessed Sacrament Catholic Church on Sunset Boulevard, where Kim Novak, Loretta Young, Douglas Fairbanks Jr., Sal Mineo, and John Wayne were regulars. Anthony Fiato observed that a few of his father's mob friends found their way to mass, too.

It didn't take long for Fiato to trade in his cassock for the uniform of all '50s tough kids. When his mother wasn't looking, Anthony wore pegged pants, a black leather jacket, with a dangling cigarette and greasy hair. He was a reformed altar boy looking hard and full of the same anxiety and indecision that courses through the veins of all 16-year-olds. In a town full of movie tough guys, he was a punk of no distinction who hung out with his friends at Scrivner's Drive-In on Sunset in the heart of Hollywood.

"We were also-rans in a James Dean look-alike contest," Fiato said. "We were rebels without a clue. We took turns talking tough and telling each other how we'd kick the ass of this guy and that guy, how we'd make out with this girl and that girl. It was all bullshit. I mean, I had to sneak downstairs and change my clothes like Superman so my mother wouldn't see that I was wearing a black leather jacket. I lived in constant fear that she'd catch me around town and tell me I was acting like one of the hoodlums on the street corner. I mean, we were cowards. We were boys.

"Here I am, a kid born in Boston and being raised in Hollywood, right in the middle of everything. I swear in those years I looked the spitting image of Sal Mineo and even got mistaken for him a couple times, which I loved. Everywhere I went there was somebody famous. There was Ricky Nelson at the music store. There was Fabian and Frankie Avalon hanging out. All the girls used to go into the stores and gawk at them. Patty McCormack, who played the wicked chick in *The Bad Seed*, was in my class. And everybody had a hard-on for Shelley Fabares. There was Tommy Kirk, the guy from the Mouseketeers, and Jimmy Hawkins, the freckle-faced kid from the Elvis films and all those drive-in movies.

"I befriended an Irish kid, Danny Hutton. We figured we had something in common, both being from Boston. Danny was a year older and star-struck as hell. We'd spend hours talking about the movie stars we wanted to meet. He had real talent. I think he liked me because I was a showoff, a real ham. Like the time we saw Liz Taylor and Eddie Fisher on the street. I rushed over and threw kisses at Liz. She laughed and Danny cracked up. Danny was the kind of guy who could do anything. The first time I played tennis with him I beat him. The next time we played he won and he never lost after that. He played varsity tennis. I was a big strong kid, but he had a real knack for everything. Like when we started singing together. Back then it seemed like everyone was forming a group, a band or a street-corner quartet.

"Do-wop was still alive, but rock 'n' roll was the thing. We'd practice harmonizing at Danny's house. His father was living in Ireland and his mother was not home most of the time. We'd tape record ourselves. It was pretty awful to start with, but like everything else Danny had talent in the singing department, too. I knew my limitations, but pretty soon Danny had two other guys he was singing with and they started a group. It went through a few changes and was eventually named "Three Dog Night."

"'Where the hell did you come up with a name like that?' I asked him years later after deciding my talents were more suited for management. 'In Alaska, a real cold night is called a Three Dog Night,' he said. 'Whatever,' I told him. Hell, at the time I never dreamed anybody would ever buy an album from a band named Three Dog Night. I should have known better, considering it was Danny."

If Anthony Fiato lacked vocal or athletic talent, he possessed ample bravado and brute strength. At 16, he was a muscular six-feet, 180 pounds. He took up weightlifting and added 20 pounds of muscle in a year. Now he had the arms of the bodybuilders advertised in the back covers of comic books. His strength would come in handy in the months and years to come.

On Hollywood Boulevard, high school kids and street urchins mingled freely. When Fiato wasn't looking for girls, he was looking for trouble. He found it in the form of a group of prep school football jocks.

"Danny and I were just hanging out on the street with our pal, Butch King. This was long before the Black and Mexican street gangs took over the place. It was like a carnival, what with all the kids and the sailors and fags," Fiato recalled. "One night we got into it with a bunch of football players. One of them pops off about something. One thing leads to another and Butch tears the side-view mirror off Danny's car and goes after them. There was enough of them that there shouldn't have been any complaints if they got their asses whipped, but Butch just about cut a guy's ear off with the mirror, so there was a lot of blood. He went running down the street, and Danny and I scattered. Danny got into his car and took off. And I figured that was it.

"Three days later, two plainclothes detectives show up and haul me down to the station. I was arrested on assault and battery charges. I'm saying nothing. I've seen the movies. I grew up in Boston and around guys like 'Pat the Priest' and 'Dago Louie.' I'm saying nothing, less than nothing. You see, I'm a real tough guy at this point."

"You cut a young man's ear off," one of the detectives said.

"I denied everything. There was no way they were going to get me to say a word."

"We've got your friend Danny Hutton in the other room," one detective said. "You're a good liar, you know that? But your friend says you're the guy who cut half the other kid's ear off. So now what do you have to say for yourself?"

"My best friend ratted me out in a heartbeat when they threatened to take away his driver's license, and I didn't even do the crime," Anthony Fiato said, laughing. "It was my first experience with a snitch and I didn't like it much. Of course, he was the only guy I knew who owned a car, so I couldn't be too cold to him. Nothing came of the pinch, but I learned a lesson about friendship. It only goes so far."

In the movies, as in the mob, rats were disposed of with an unceremonious bullet to the brain. In reality, a teen-ager with his own car was a valuable commodity. And so Fiato managed to forgive his talented friend. Soon enough, Johnny Fiato was letting his eldest son, Anthony, drive him to his bartending job at the

Villa Capri with its cool shadows, plush booths and star-studded clientele.

"I used to drop my father off and take the car cruising, then come back to the Villa Capri and take in the scene," Anthony Fiato said. "Every night was like watching the Academy Awards. You're talking about the greatest names in Hollywood, the biggest names in entertainment, and the heaviest guys in the mob, all under one roof. Every athlete in the area went to the Villa Capri.

"Three years after I'd been hanging out there, Bo Belinsky and his buddy Dean Chance made it their regular stomping ground after Bo pitched his no-hitter for the Los Angeles Angels. Bo was the talk of the town and sometimes had that old broken-down valise of a gossip columnist, Walter Winchell, tagging along.

"It was a Who's Who and I was a member of the Who's He? I'd work with Eddie in valet, and pick up a few bucks, then back up my father and watch how he worked behind the bar. He was smooth. Didn't make a difference to him whether a guy was Sinatra or Sal the Plumber; he treated everybody the same. Maybe that's why Robert Mitchum liked him so much. After a few belts, near the end of the night my father would buy him a drink and take time to drink one, too.

"Mitchum used to say, 'Johnny, my friend, we were never lovelier.' My father worked parties for Sinatra and even met John Kennedy at the Villa before he became president, but Robert Mitchum was his main man.

"Mitchum used to come in and sit at the corner of the bar with his back to the crowd. He didn't come there to be seen; he came there to drink. And man, he could knock 'em down. He loved my dad. That's how I got to know him.

"I'd sit at the back of the bar and Mitchum would come in and we'd talk the fight game. Who was hot and who was a tomato can. Don Jordan was a big name in Los Angeles in those days. he was a Black welterweight who was in the news because there was a mob fight over his contract between Blinky Palermo and Frankie Carbo against Mickey Cohen. He was Mickey Cohen's fighter, and a good one. But the late '50s and early '60s, you're talking about a great era in boxing history.

"My favorite, of course, was Marciano, an Italian. The fights were always on television, and the Olympic Auditorium featured a lot of the big names. I fancied myself a kid who was good with his hands, and Mitchum used to reminisce about his time in the ring.

"'The fight game, that's too much like work,' Mitchum would say. 'Acting beats working, although you mix with a better class of criminal on a chain gang than you do in the movie business.'"

Taciturn with strangers, Mitchum talked at length to Johnny Fiato's son. Mitchum made women swoon, but even as a teenager Fiato was impressed by the tough guy actor's effect on men. Within a few minutes of being in his presence, they began to imitate his mannerisms.

"He was a man's man and every guy wanted to be like him," Fiato said. "He was like a template for the way real men were supposed to be. The way they were supposed to drink, smoke, speak to other people, the whole bit. Don't think the mob guys at the Villa Capri didn't notice, either. Actors were all over the joint every night, but Robert Mitchum was something special.

"When I wasn't on Hollywood Boulevard or hanging out at the Villa Capri with my dad, I ran around with Danny Hutton. When we were together we would scheme nonstop. We'd talk about this movie star we wanted to meet. And every kid in town wanted to go to bed with Carol Lynley and Tuesday Weld. But how were a couple of punk kids ever going to meet their dream girls? You couldn't exactly walk into Universal Studios or Warner Brothers and set up an appointment."

Not without the proper identification, anyway.

For that, they enlisted Hutton's brother, a printer, to manufacture press credentials from a make believe Teen World magazine.

"We started making calls and found out how it worked, how we'd need the right passes and a letter from our editor," Fiato said. "Of course we didn't have an editor, so we made one up and printed official looking stationery. We had a letter typed up from someone named Elaine Moss to an Eileen Wilcox. All official-looking, of course. And they went for it. Suddenly we were teen correspondents for a magazine that didn't exist. Hey, I could barely read and write and wasn't exactly near the top of my graduating class. But it worked. Even as a teen-ager I was a great idea man."

Pausing at a water cooler, Fiato was approached by Gregory Peck, who acknowledged him and smiled.

"Hi, Sal," Peck said.

For one of the only times in his brash young life, Anthony Fiato was speechless.

"The guy thought I was Sal Mineo," Fiato said. "The rest of the day I thought I was Sal Mineo, too."

That is, until Robert Mitchum saw him in the hallway.

"Hey, tough guy, the kid from Boston. You're Johnny Fiato's kid, right? Haven't seen you in the daylight," an amused Mitchum said. "Boy, this shit's got to cease. What are you doing here?"

"I'm looking for Tuesday Weld."

"You and a million other guys," Mitchum said.

The night the Animal came to Hollywood, Anthony Fiato was a boy barely old enough to drive. George from Philadelphia, however, was a man. Six-four, two-hundred twenty pounds, George was in his early 20s but still hung out around Scrivner's Drive-In. And why not? The wanna-be tough guys there were easy pickings for a bully his size. George made quick work of Anthony and his friends, stealing their money and their pride day after day.

"When he was gone, we'd all whisper how we'd like to kick his ass, but we knew we'd never do it," Fiato said. "It was all bullshit. We were just kidding ourselves."

Until the day George caught Anthony and his girlfriend, Gina, on the way to the theater.

"Give it up," George said. "I know you got some money."

"No, I don't," Anthony said.

George was not going to take no for an answer. Away from his friends and in the company of a female, Fiato was faced with a timeless dilemma: fight or flee?

Frozen by fear, he did neither. George pressed him up against the plate-glass window of a jewelry store, slapped him across the face and exacted his petty street tax. It wasn't Fiato's face that hurt most. He was a coward, again, and this time in front of a girl. His eyes went wet with rage as he watched George walk away.

"We walked down the street and I was so humiliated," Fiato says. "She was saying, 'Are you all right? Are you all right?' I couldn't speak. It was the lowest day of my life."

The movie date was over. He couldn't face the girl knowing he had shown himself a coward. He walked home alone, locked himself in his room, wouldn't eat, and couldn't speak. He hated the fear inside him. The feeling festered until he decided to seek revenge.

The next time he saw him at Scrivner's, instead of avoiding George he approached the bully with a proposition.

"I'll give you fifty bucks if you lay off me," he said. "I'll give you the money, but you have to promise to leave me alone."

"Sure, kid," George said, grinning. "For fifty, I'll leave you alone." He laughed, then added, "But this don't mean I'll stop nailing your sister."

The meeting was arranged for later that night on a side street next to a malt shop near Hollywood High. Fiato knew the malt shop closed early. There, no one would see Anthony Fiato when he made his payoff.

Except, he had no plans to pay off.

"I was reading Socrates for school, his story about the Golden Mean. Socrates talked about extremism, deficiency, and sufficiency. An extremely cautious person is a coward, and I was a coward. A deficiently cautious person was a fool. The sufficiently cautious person was effective. I felt myself applying this philosophy. He was deficiently cautious. After all, I was a coward in his eyes.

"I swiped a hunting knife from one of those stores on Hollywood Boulevard. It was the kind of knife used to gut fish. I go up to the malt shop to meet the guy and sure enough he shows up, gloating, and pleased as hell because I'm giving him fifty dollars. I remind him that he promised never to bother me again and he said, 'Yeah, yeah.' I'm shaking like a leaf, looking at him and afraid to look, afraid of him and of the knife in my pocket."

When George turned away, Anthony Fiato reached into his jacket and pulled out the knife. For a moment, the world moved in slow motion. The first thrust put the bully on his hands and knees. He howled like a dog. Fiato reached around, stabbed him in the forehead and watched blood stream onto the sidewalk. Then he stabbed him again and in his excitement dropped the knife. He picked it out of the gutter, stabbed him again, and felt a world open up before him.

In a moment, it was over.

Seething rage tinted the scene like Technicolor. He felt the face slap and all the humiliations before. But he wasn't afraid. He was dominant, in control. His hands became drenched with blood as he slashed away. George from Philadelphia wasn't such a big man anymore. In fact, George was barely alive. But the man who would become known as Tony the Animal had come to life.

"I felt another part of me I never knew existed," he said. "I felt whole for the first time. For that minute, I felt another half of me that I never knew, but I knew belonged there. It was like the first time I had an orgasm. I never knew that feeling could exist. A peace and calm came over me. I had self-esteem for the first time in my life.

"When you do the thing you're afraid of, it charges you up. I thought I might get killed or go to the electric chair, but I did it anyway. Even with my knees knocking, I did it. Once I stabbed him, I could do anything I wanted. I could suck the fucking blood out of his neck."

At home, he put his hands to his face, smelled the blood of another man, tasted it, scrubbed it away. Then he went to bed.

"All night I thought I heard the cops coming to my door, but they never came," he said. "When I woke up the next day and didn't get arrested, I left the house, skipped school and got a cherry coke at Scrivner's. I knew I needed to keep my mouth shut because the cops were going to come looking for who did it. Sure enough, some detectives show up and ask a few questions. In one day everybody heard about the stabbing. Stabbings weren't common in those days."

Fiato's friends chewed on the news.

"Somebody finally got that guy," one said.

"Betcha some nigger did it," said another.

"I couldn't hold it in," Fiato says. "I couldn't wait to tell them that it was me. At first they didn't believe it, but then I gave them details. Their eyes lit up. Suddenly, I was a big man to them. From that point on, those guys saw me as their leader. I had my first crew, such as it was. They saw that I had a different way about me."

George was in the hospital for three months. He never identified his assailant, never returned to the drive-in, never bothered the young punks again.

"But I was learning that nobody keeps a secret, not even your best friends," Fiato said. "One of the kids who hung out at the drive-in, Jerry Castiglione, Lefty's son, told his old man what I'd done. These people were friends of my family. One afternoon after eating dinner at their house, Lefty gave me a ride back over to my house. While he drove, he told me, 'I want you to stay the fuck away from my kid.' Lefty was a big, muscular guy who'd been a longshoreman and was tight with Mike Rizzitello. I thought a tough guy like Lefty would like what I did, but instead he turned on me and made me feel small. He scared me and made me really angry, so angry I wanted to kill him.

"But there's something I'll never forget about George: The stupid guy didn't even know my name. He couldn't tell the cops anything more than the guy who stabbed him was one of the guys who hangs out at the malt shop. He had humiliated me and I'd almost killed him, and he didn't even know my name."

There would come a time Anthony Fiato would crave such anonymity, but for the moment he reveled in the blood and experienced something akin to a rebirth. He no longer was just another face on the street. He was a predator, to be respected and feared.

Anthony Fiato built his reputation on Hollywood Boulevard, easy pickings in those days for a kid who wasn't afraid to spill a little blood. Just as Villa Capri regulars "Dago Louie" and "Pat the Priest" shook down bookmakers throughout the city, as a teenager Fiato extracted his street tax from the freelance pimps and posturing bullies who inhabited the avenue. It was part of his apprenticeship.

"Of all the guys I knew at that time, there weren't two of them who weren't working some angle, some scam," Fiato said. "They either had a criminal past, even Bob Mitchum admitted he'd been on a chain gang, or they were actively ripping and tearing apart the street on behalf of the Dragnas, Mickey Cohen or some lesser street crew. They were constantly in the headlines. Only my father stayed clear of all that stuff. He was the only honest man in my life, and, like a lot of punk kids, I couldn't hear him when he spoke. Not even when he yelled and grabbed me by the collar. I was listening to everybody else.

"It didn't take much to figure that I wasn't going to be joining Danny in any singing groups. I hadn't seen the inside of a classroom in months. Like most teen-agers I was allergic to real work, so I started dreaming and scheming about being a tough guy. I already had the physique for it, and I'd been in a couple of scraps where I had nearly killed guys. But, you know, it's not like there's some manual you can go out and buy to learn to be a gangster. Hollywood only teaches you so much, and the real tough guys don't talk about what they do. They just do it.

"When Billy McLaughlin showed up in the neighborhood from Boston with a stolen rental car, I figured I was in business. He was a young punk on the make, a friend of my cousin Mario's, and I was impressed by the way he used an alias, 'Francis Meany.'

"Francis Meany thought he was safe driving a stolen car 3,000 miles from its owners, but it wasn't long before I learned other-

wise. One day a couple of squares in gray suits stop me on the
street and ask me if I know Billy. They were FBI agents investigating him for a Dyer Act violation, which means they figured
he'd transported the stolen car across a state line.

"I didn't know much geography, but I figured he'd violated the
law a dozen times crossing all those state lines from Boston to
California. To me, the agents were a couple of oddballs. Real
squares. Dark suits, brown shoes. The whole bit. But they knew
all about Billy McLaughlin, AKA Francis Meany, and that was
impressive.

"But it didn't stop me from hanging around Billy. He had the
vehicle and the motivation.

"So one day we were sitting around doing nothing; we decided
to take off a liquor store not far from the Villa. Mike Rizzi had
been robbing restaurants and liquor stores, so Billy and I would,
too. Billy would do the driving, and I'd do the rest. I managed to
get hold of a pistol and off we went like a couple of comic strip
Dillingers. He pulls up in the alley behind the liquor store and I go
in. I don't even wear a mask. After all, the owner couldn't possibly know me. I was still just a kid. I'd never even held a gun
before. I stick the gun in his face and, sure enough, he pops the
register and is nearly taking a heart attack as he opens the cash
drawer and lets me grab as much as I want. He backs away, and I
run for the back door that leads to the alley. I jump in the car,
breathless and excited enough to pee my pants."

The liquor store owner is a few feet behind me yelling, "I've
been robbed, I've been robbed!"

"About the time I've decided this armed robbery business is
pretty sweet, the alley is blocked by a police car with its sirens
roaring and lights flashing. I look at Billy and we decided against
shooting it out Dillinger-style. He's got tears in his eyes and suddenly I'm hearing my old man's voice. I throw down the gun
quickly to keep them from getting any ideas that we want trouble,
and I'm off to the county jail."

In a matter of hours, Anthony Fiato's acquaintances at the

Villa Capri heard of his predicament and came to his aid. Dago Louie immediately called Mickey Cohen, who contacted Harry Diamond and his lawyer, Eddie Gritz. Within hours, the boys were sprung. Within days, the armed robbery charges were dropped. The official story: a lack of evidence. The truth: through Cohen's well-oiled channels, $100 bills were slipped to each of the detectives working the case. They misplaced the gun and lost the case file.

The liquor store owner's money was returned, and when he heard who was in the car he was officially grateful the fun-loving young men were not charged with anything that would cause them problems as adults. That quickly the mob could make trouble disappear.

Well, almost that quickly.

Neither Mickey Cohen nor Lefty Castiglione could control the temper of Johnny Fiato. The case was fixed, and the arrest was kept quiet, but when Anthony's father discovered the details he was livid. The next time Anthony Fiato bopped into the Villa Capri his father collared him, escorted him to the men's room. Then he slammed his well-groomed young head into the tiled wall.

"Don't you realize what this will do to your mother if she finds out?" he yelled. "You think you're some kind of tough guy, do you? Well, tough guy, you're going to wind up in the penitentiary with all the other tough guys if you don't wise up."

Then he started to laugh.

"Who the hell do you think you are, John Dillinger?"

"I didn't say another word," Anthony Fiato recalled.

That's because, as a matter of fact, he did think he was John Dillinger, or at least Lawrence Tierney.

Lawrence Atillio Fiato was 13 years younger than his brother, but even as a small boy Larry recalled his father's anger over the robbery.

"Anthony was out all the time when I was young," Larry said. "I'll never forget the time he got arrested for armed robbery. My father was talking to him, pointing his finger at him. My father could be pretty intimidating when he wanted to be."

At the Villa Capri, Robert Mitchum held up the far end of the bar. For two weeks he had been asking the whereabouts of the kid with the Boxing Encyclopedia for a brain.

"How'd you make out, kid?"

When Fiato relayed the good news, Mitchum bellylaughed.

"Who do you think you are, me?" he asked. "Kid, you're all right. If I pulled that stunt, I'd have been busting rocks some-where. You land on your feet without a mark on you. You sure this guy you robbed didn't ask you to become his partner? This calls for a drink."

To receive Robert Mitchum's tough guy seal of approval was heady stuff for Anthony Fiato, who was barely old enough to drive.

The lines between cinema life and reality had become hope-lessly blurred. The toughest guy in Tinseltown considered him a tough kid worthy of buying whiskey and slapping on the back. On the street, Fiato lacked direction. He shook down small-time pimps and pushers, but he was just passing the time waiting for someone to discover his talents.

Dago Louie Piscopo, who had heard of the stabbing incident, noticed Fiato first. A soldier in the Dragna family, Piscopo's English was coated with a thick Sicilian accent. His sponsor in Los Angeles was John Rosselli, the dapper criminal born Felippo Sacco and raised in Boston. Rosselli's territory included Las Vegas as well as Hollywood. Fiato's propensity for violence impressed Piscopo almost as much as his staunch refusal to cooperate with law enforcement.

"'Dago Louie' was at my house many times for Sunday din-ner," Fiato said. "He watched me grow up. He knew my parents, especially my father, from the Villa Capri. That's where Dago Louie hangs out every night and pays for nothing. I mean, the guy would literally steal bread from the kitchen. And he's not like some of the guys who come in and tip everybody in sight. He's an old-timer who squeezes every nickel till the buffalo shits. But he's genuine Mafia, a made guy with the Dragnas. If I'm going to get into the life, I figure he's a guy who can do me some good.

"One day 'Dago Louie' approached me in the parking lot outside the Villa Capri. He told me what he had heard about what I'd been up to. 'You nevah letta nobody nevah disarespec' you,' he said. 'You gooda boy.' Other than small talk—and guys like Louie never talked much—it was the first time he'd ever addressed me directly. It was different this time. He said, 'You wanna makea some money for Christmas?' I jumped at the chance. Before he told me what he needed, he said, 'Whata you do with me you tell nobody.'

"I agreed.

"He said a man owed him some money and showed him great disrespect by failing to pay. The man had been warned several times. My job was not to collect the money. I was to deliver a message. At the time, I thought Louie was taking me into his great confidence, but later I figured out he was just using me like the punk I was. He demanded secrecy probably more out of fear of my father's wrath than any Mafia code, but I basked in the moment. A made guy was looking to me for help. I wouldn't let him down.

"'Take a ride with me,' he says, and I get into his new Cadillac. We drove into the black section of Los Angeles, by Crenshaw and Adams, and pulled up outside a furniture store. He pointed out a black guy behind the counter, then handed me his car keys and told me to open the trunk and take out the baseball bat that was in there. He told me to go in and tell, 'This is from Mr. Fox' and whack him.

"So I did. I went inside with the bat under my jacket. I wasn't nervous. The voices in the room faded and I said, 'This is from Mr. Fox' and swung down hard, clipping the guy in the head. Blood spurted three feet and the guy went down in a heap. Nobody tried to stop me. I got in the car and Louie drove me back across town. All the time he was swearing in Italian. What I could understand was, 'That sumabitch. These eggaplants, they no wanna pay nobody. You goodaboy.' He handed me two-hundred dollars. I was seventeen years old and Edward G. Robinson had nothing on me. Louie told me to be on the corner of Hollywood and Highland the next day."

From that point, Louie Piscopo regularly tapped his young apprentice to collect weekly envelopes from bookmakers and loan-shark customers. Fiato began hanging out with Louie's crew, for the most part a bunch of broken-down transplants from New York or the Old Country. He visited Lee's Drug Store on a daily basis to await instructions or deliver the cash-stuffed street mail. That was where he met a collection of characters who would have made Damon Runyon envious. There was Specs, the bookie and collector who sold the daily racing tout sheets to gamblers from every walk of life. "Dago Louie" would leave envelopes with Specs, and the newsy would see they reached their rightful owner. There was John Gavin, who at the time was an unemployed actor. Mae West's musclebound boyfriends and racetrack pickpockets; they all met at Lee's.

"He brought me up to Specs, a little Jewish guy with a baseball cap," Fiato said. "Louie told Specs, 'thisa my friend. If I'm not here, you give envelope to him. Treat him like you treat me.'"

Of all the characters young Anthony Fiato encountered, he gravitated most quickly toward Ernest "Blackie" Gallo, a lifelong thief who dressed like George Raft and bragged of being able to steal anything.

"He used to say, 'I'm the cousin of Ernest and Julio Gallo,'" Fiato recalled. "But he wasn't, of course. He was a booster, maybe the biggest booster in California at the time. He had a crew of guys working Hollywood Boulevard called the Halifax Gang. They worked out of the Halifax Hotel on Yucca Street. 'Dago Louie' introduced me to Blackie Gallo. 'You likea nice clothes. Come take a ride with me,' he said. And we went to Blackie's apartment at the Halifax. It was like a goddamn department store. He had hundreds of suits, all styles and sizes, and all the ties and cuff links you could want. These weren't Sears & Roebuck specials. We're talking about expensive suits, the kind that came from the finest shops in Beverly Hills. Because, as a matter of fact, they did come from the finest shops in Beverly Hills.

"Blackie's crew procured them and sold them to street guys like

'Dago Louie' and the Hollywood set. Mickey Cohen bought from Blackie. So did Jimmy Fratianno and Louie Dragna and the whole L.A. mob. Directors and producers bought from Blackie. Everybody bought from Blackie. Even the cops who weren't working him. In no time I was decked out like a million bucks.

"Blackie from Providence was twenty-three years older than me. He had thinning hair, muscular forearms and he used to lift weights. He used to give 'Dago Louie' Oxford suits and anything else he wanted as a tribute for letting him operate. One thing about wiseguys, they don't pay for nothing.

"I loved Blackie Gallo from the first minute I laid eyes on the guy. Who wouldn't? He was an absolute caricature of a gangster. He stuck out like a sore thumb and didn't give a damn. The cops followed him everywhere he went. They camped outside the Halifax. As if Blackie was hard to spot in his pinstriped suit from the '20s and a big cigar jammed in his mouth. Even when I had nothing to collect on that corner I hung out with Blackie. He was one-part comedian, one-part teacher and one hundred percent thief.

"We'd go eat at Nate & Al's, the Beverly Hills deli and Blackie'd order corned beef, then complain about something. 'Look at all this rich food. This place killed more Jews than Hitler.' And we'd eat at Musso & Frank, the legendary restaurant on Hollywood Boulevard where every star in the town ate. Blackie took me there for the first time and told me to order anything on the menu. We had steak and shrimp cocktail and as much as we could eat. We ordered wine and dessert and ordered the waiter around like a Chinaman. The bill was astronomical, and at the end of the meal Blackie told me to go and wait outside.

"A few minutes later he comes out behind me laughing and we walk down the boulevard. He had waited for the waiters to change shifts and palmed the check. The waiter getting off shift assumed the new waiter would handle the bill. The new waiter thought the previous waiter had taken care of it. Blackie put the check in his pocket and beat 'em. Which was something considering he probably had a thousand dollars in his pocket. But he was a thief through and through.

"I would eat with him almost every night and we never paid as long as we were together. He had to steal. He'd steal a pack of gum. He just couldn't pay for anything. 'I can't do it,' he'd say. 'Why should I pay when I can get everything for nothing? We're crime, my boy, and crime doesn't pay.'"

Gallo had spent a good part of his adult life in prison. As a result, he suffered from claustrophobia. It was rarely noticeable, except when Gallo and Anthony would take in a movie. Blackie would pace the floor in the back of the theater, checking the doors and talk nonstop while fretting the entire time.

Such a proud thief was Blackie Gallo that he bragged of working a straight job only one day in his life. He spent a shift working for the railroad in 1932 and earned thirty-five cents, then decided he would rather steal and take his chances than be a working stiff.

Thanks to Blackie Gallo, young Anthony Fiato's image as a tough enforcer for "Dago Louie" soon took on epic proportions. Gallo whispered the inside dope about Fiato's prowess with a Louisville Slugger, and Specs managed to inform the rest of the free world.

"Soon enough, everyone knew who I was and they showed me a lot of respect," Fiato said. "'This kid is deadly,' they'd whisper. Little did they suspect I'd been an altar boy not three years earlier."

"Dago Louie" used Fiato on increasingly aggressive collections. Then came a far more dangerous assignment.

The Los Angeles mob extorted a percentage of profits from bookmakers all over the city and had a lock on the action in Watts and other black neighborhoods.

"The Jews would be 50-percent partners with a lot of Black bookmakers," he said. "The Jews would be in partners with the Blacks, and we'd take a piece of whatever they generated."

The Dragna family was, in turn, partners with a lot of the Jewish bookmakers. "Dago Louie" dispatched Fiato to Hollywood and Highland to meet "Fat Arnie," a Jewish bookmaker with a problem. "Help him out," 'Dago Louie' had said. "Do what's needed."

"By this time, I was working regularly as a collector for 'Dago Louie'," Fiato said. "He knew I was a crazy kid, and I figured he was my ticket to the big time. I didn't realize then how much I was being used. 'Dago Louie' hands me a .32-caliber pistol. I'd held a gun once before and wound up in jail. The truth was I didn't even know how to shoot it. 'Just pointa and pulla trigger,' Louie said. 'And make sure you no drop it.'

"He tells me to go to the corner in front of Lee's Drugstore and see a guy named Fat Arnie, and help this Fat Arnie with a problem, I think nothing of it."

Once he got there, the rotund bookmaker explained the problem. One of his Watts bookmaking partners, Black Dot Williams, had been robbed of $10,000 by a pair of local gamblers, who hadn't had the good sense to leave the neighborhood. Dot had plenty of sources in Watts, for he booked the action to half the population, but he didn't have the muscle to get his money back. Which is where Fiato came in.

Dot had spotted the thieves in a backroom poker game on Washington Street and had arranged for a pale-faced pigeon to join them for a little friendly Friday night of cards. The sucker was Fiato, who was joined by one of Dot's runners acting as a late-arriving player. In reality, he was there to collect the cash owed the bookie.

Using the introduction to get the front door open, Fiato did the rest.

"I pulled the .32 automatic 'Dago Louie' had given me and yelled, 'Get the money on the fucking table.' And it worked, until another fucking guy appeared from the backroom with a shotgun. I didn't think, just reacted. I shot him two times, turned and ran out the fucking door.

"Another guy chased me down the street. I stopped and shot his direction until he fell down. I'd shot two guys I didn't know, just like that."

Fiato's accomplice collected more than $11,000 from the game, which was ringed with pimps, thieves, and neighborhood dope dealers. Speeding away from the scene, he felt the exhilaration of the chase and laughed when he remembered the fear on the faces of the players. He never found out whether the gunshot victims lived or died.

At the Villa Capri, Anthony Fiato still wasn't old enough to take his place at a crowded dinner table with some of the hoodlums he was now working for. He preferred conversations with Robert Mitchum, Rod Steiger and Lawrence Tierney to small talk with "Dago Louie," who never ran out of reasons to send Fiato on an errand or into increasingly dangerous situations.

The Betty Martin job came along just that simply. Dean Martin's ex-wife was locked in the throes of alcoholism. Her generous alimony checks made her a tempting target for Hollywood's myriad hustlers, and her drinking made her an absolute mark. So when "Dago Louie" noticed "Pat the Priest" and his angle-shooting associates regularly drinking with her at the Villa Capri, he knew it was only a matter of time before she came calling in nonexistent markers and crying for help. Piscopo's senior partner, John Rosselli, was tight with Dean Martin, and Betty regularly exploited that relationship.

Like clockwork Betty Martin approached her ex-husband weeping about the $15,000 she had invested with Pat's loansharking operation, only to be informed that the money was gone and wouldn't be returning anytime soon. Martin called his friend Rosselli, who in turn sent a message to "Dago Louie," who was stuck with the unenviable task of informing a sociopathic hitman that his antics with the lady were not appreciated and that the money must be returned immediately. Compounding the problem was the fact that Prieda was a business associate of Mickey Cohen and the Sica brothers, rivals of Piscopo's Dragna family.

A misunderstanding could mean death.

The Villa Capri was hopping the night the message was delivered. Fiato was sitting with Piscopo and immediately volunteered to deliver the warning to Prieda. He was sitting at the opposite end of the restaurant with baseball pitchers Bo Belinsky and Dean Chance. It wouldn't take long.

"I told 'Dago Louie', 'Hey, I know that guy pretty good. He comes over our house for Sunday dinner,'" Fiato said. "So I got up and marched over to the table. Simple as that. I didn't know what the hell I was doing. I was just winging it."

At the table, Fiato explained Betty Martin's problem.

"You got a problem here," Fiato told his father's friend. "It's got to be solved one way or another."

"It's not true," Prieda snorted. "She's a fucking lush."

"Maybe so, but she knows people," Fiato said. "And she's called them and there you are. Pat, there's no time for story-telling here. They don't want to hear a story."

"All right," Prieda said. "Let me speak to my partner."

"Pat the Priest" repaid the $15,000 a few hundred at a time. "Dago Louie" said nothing of Fiato's diplomacy.

A few weeks later, silver-haired Rosselli appeared in the doorway of the Villa Capri. He was accompanied by Dago Louie and Dean Martin. The three men received the best table in the house and were visited by singer Tony Martin and his wife Cyd Charisse.

"I was sitting at the back of the bar waiting for Robert Mitchum to come in so we could talk boxing, when 'Dago Louie' waved me over to the table," Fiato said. "That's when I met John Rosselli and Dean Martin. Now there was a dapper guy. For me, it was every bit as exciting as meeting a movie star. In my eyes, there wasn't much difference. That night it dawned on me that Dean Martin had contacted John Rosselli, and Rosselli had reached out for 'Dago Louie'."

In broken English, "Dago Louie" introduced Anthony Fiato to John Rosselli.

"Thisa kid I was telling you about," Piscopo said. "Johnny Fiato's boy."

"So you're the kid from Boston," Rosselli said. "Luigi speaks fondly of you. You did a nice thing for me the other day."

Martin interrupted, "No, young man, you did a nice thing for me. It's deeply appreciated."

"You stay close to Luigi Piscopo," Rosselli said. "Can I buy you a drink?"

Fiato almost blushed. He had shot two men, nearly beaten two others to death. He had delivered a small fortune in mob payoffs, had robbed a liquor store and dealt with cold-blooded triggermen.

But he was only 17. He couldn't drink alcohol at the Villa Capri without putting the owners' licenses in jeopardy, and the LAPD's mobster squad seldom was without a representative in the room.

"I'm not old enough," Fiato told the mobster. "But thank you anyway, Mr. Rosselli."

With that, Rosselli laughed out loud.

"You call me Johnny, kid," Rosselli said.

"Yes, sir," Fiato replied.

Life at the Villa was never dull. In those days, Fiato watched the room fill up with the likes of Kirk Douglas, David Jansen, Robert Vaughan, and Steve McQueen. He had seen their movies and watched their action-adventure TV shows. He studied the way they entered a room, the way they treated their women, lit their cigarettes and ordered their drinks. In their way, they taught him first-hand a sense of stylish cool.

But Hollywood and the underworld didn't live on nightlife alone. During the day, there was plenty of action at Southern California's racetracks. Depending on the season, Fiato chauffeured "Dago Louie" and his crew to Santa Anita, Hollywood Park, Del Mar, and the State Fair at Pomona.

"We knew people there, and they treated us like we owned the place," Fiato said. 'Dago Louie' never went anywhere he wasn't taken care of, and I would sometimes bet for him. Other times I'd hang out, blow my bankroll on the horses, or find some of Louie's absent-minded loanshark customers. Once they saw me, half the time I didn't even have to say a word. They just shrugged and started reaching for what was left of their bankroll. If they had a line, I'd grab them by the shirt and say, 'I'm not the guy you make

After helping to put in prison more than 60 men, Anthony Fiato lives under an assumed name somewhere in the United States.

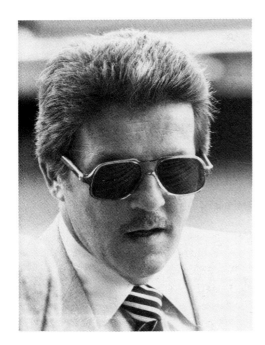

Fiato met in Las Vegas with Anthony Pilotro, the feared hitman who was the city's toughest enforcer.

Willie Fopiano was a rough kid, but he couldn't kill a man unless he was angry.

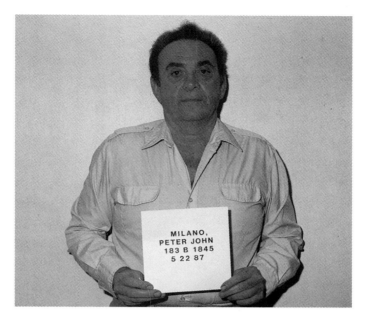

Los Angeles mob boss Pete Milano was elusive, but Fiato managed to capture him on tape and later helped send him to jail.

Reputed Los Angeles mob underboss Carmen Milano is a disbarred attorney.

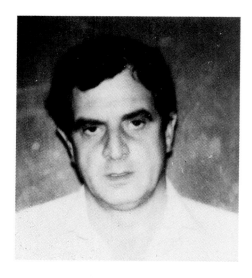

John DiMattia had plenty of book-making contacts in Beverly Hills

Stephen Munichiello was one of Fiato's loyal soldiers.

Vincent "Vinnie Nip" Ferrara is a college-educated man and a respected member of the New England mob.

Robert "Puggy" Zeichick was Anthony Fiato's big-money partner. Together they loaned more than $1 million on the street.

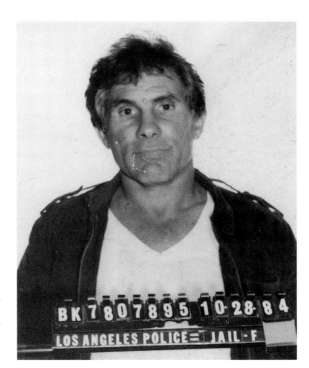

Fiato grew up around some of the biggest legends in organized crime, including Los Angeles racketeer Mickey Cohen.

Dino D'Agostino was another mob associate Fiato put behind bars.

Old-schooler Jimmy Caci is one of the most respected mobsters on the West Coast.

Robert Mitchum was a tough guy actor who taught a generation of wiseguys how to walk the walk and talk the talk.

Art imitating life? Jimmy Caan in one of his most memorable roles as Sonny Corleone in *The Godfather.*

In September 1995 Denise Brown was one of the most sought-after woman in America. But it was she who sought the company of Anthony Fiato.

Frank Christi played a tough guy on the screen, but his acting days ended when he was shot to death in July 1982. Fiato helped solve the murder.

excuses to. You didn't borrow no money from me.' By that time, I weighed nearly 220 pounds and all of it was muscle.

"The best part of those days was meeting with George Raft. He often came to the track and he loved hanging out with 'Dago Louie' and his boys. Everybody believed George Raft knew every gangster in the country. They idolized him and I think he wanted to be one of them. He was a good guy, used to laugh about me being his bodyguard. Like he needed one. Everybody loved him, I swear.

"But, man, was he an awful gambler. He bet on everything and he never won a bet. I don't mean lose a little, or a lot. I mean never won. Never ever. But he talked better than any gangster I've ever met."

"Crazy" Joey Gallo gave Raft a run for his money in the rhetoric department, but there was something different about the New York hitman, who in the early '60s plotted to take over the Profaci family. Gallo came out to Los Angeles to recruit Villa Capri employees Mike Rizzitello and Lefty Castiglione. Raft was just an actor; Gallo was a psychopath.

"I knew who Joey Gallo was before I met him. He was the John Gotti of his day; dangerous and greedy," Fiato said. "His hair was greased back straight and he had black sideburns, a dark blue suit, blue shirt and a white tie. He could have been an extra in one of George Raft's movies. Real old looking. He reminded me of a greaseball from the old country.

"'Dago Louie' introduced me to him, and I played tour guide on one of his trips out West. The show '77 Sunset Strip' was popular at the time, and he wanted me to drive him down the Sunset Strip. He ridiculed everybody on the street. A real odd character, he was. But he had style. He stood out like a real gangster from every gangster movie I'd ever watched, but unlike the actors, he wasn't just talking. The way he spoke to people, you could see he was ready for anything. People were uneasy around him. 'Dago Louie,' Rizzi. Everybody. He didn't give a fuck for anybody. He was like a lone wolf. You could see it in his eyes.

And you never knew what he'd say. We'd pass a big musclebound fella on the street and he'd say, 'That guy'd suck a prick in the can.'

"One night I was driving him and he said, 'We need to do some work tonight. We got to go kill somebody. You know what that means?'

"'Of course I know what that means,' I said. 'Give me the directions. Where do we go?'

"Then Gallo laughed like a madman. 'What I heard about you is true, kid. Do you know how many guys I know, grown men mind you, would have come up with a bad back? Let me tell you something. You ever want to move to a real city, you come back to New York. I'll put you to work, show you some real streets.'

"But I didn't, of course. It was right after that I started getting stopped regularly by the gangster squad, the cops who worked the mob in Los Angeles. Right after Joey Gallo returned home, Lefty Castiglione got nervous about the three guys who started frequenting the Villa Capri. He thought they were sent out West by Profaci to keep an eye on Gallo, so one night he couldn't take it anymore and started brawling with them. He beat the shit out of them before they knew what hit them. He thought they had come to the restaurant to kill him, but they were intelligence cops. He was so paranoid he was ready to punch out his own shadow.

"As for me, I was ready to take on the world. My family moved back to Boston and settled three miles from the North End in Somerville. I stayed behind.

"Joey Gallo's visit put a ton of heat on us, and it wasn't long before he wound up in jail again. The Los Angeles police gangster squad was all over 'Dago Louie,' and he started playing everything close to the vest. That meant I had to pick up the slack elsewhere and move away from our regular spots.

"I was thinking about going back to Boston, but in the meantime I was hanging around at Joe Mar's coffee shop on Highland Avenue near Franklin. This was right up the street from Lee's Drugstore. Joe Mar's was a popular meeting place for Joe and Freddy Sicca and their gang of bookmakers and thieves. The

Siccas were with Mickey Cohen, while I was with 'Dago Louie' on the side of the Dragna family. One day while I was there drinking a cup of coffee, I overheard two brothers, the Russos, talking to Joe Mar, who was into hot swag as we called it. They were talking about the stolen stuff that they didn't want Mike to know about. They talked freely in front of me because they didn't know me.

"I kept it in my mind in a couple days, and I thought it was something I needed to tell Mike Rizzitello about. But how could I tell him without being a snitch? I called my father up in Somerville and asked him what I should do. My father told me, 'The same way you're telling me, tell Mike. Mike will understand.' So I did. A few days later, I told Mike about the guys who were ripping him off. 'Those dirty motherfuckers,' he said. He ruffled my hair and said, 'You've got good instincts. I won't forget this.'"

CHAPTER 2

When it came to La Cosa Nostra traditions, moving from Hollywood to Boston was like leaving the bush leagues and arriving at Fenway Park. Sun-washed Hollywood reinvented itself each season, but the North End never seemed to change. The same butcher shops, sidewalk produce markets and delicatessens that had been in Italian families for generations lined the boulevards. Slaughtered lambs hung in the shop windows near great rolls of supresat and prosciutto. Church bells tolled on Sunday morning, and families gathered for supper. All roads led to the North End and Hanover Street, which makes up in history what it lacks in length.

At 383 Hanover is Langone's Funeral Home, where Nicola Sacco and Bartolomeo Vanzetti were laid on display before thousands of mourners. From the statue of Paul Revere and Christ Church, where Revolutionary lanterns hung in the belfry "One, if by land, and two, if by sea" to warn of the invading British, Hanover holds a special place in American lore.

"In Hollywood with 'Dago Louie,' I was considered a prospect. I'd met Johnny Rosselli, a hundred movie stars, pulled enough felonies to be considered worthy of surveillance by the LAPD's gangster squad," Fiato recalled. "On the North End, I was just another dago. There, the mob was as structured as any place in America. It was a closed society. People in the neighborhood whispered when a local gambler behind on his shylock payments disappeared. They spoke with pride of exchanging pleasantries with men like Raymond Patriarca and Danny Angiulo. There was Ilario Zannino, the head of Boston's Murder Incorporated. He went by the name Larry Baioni. On the North End in the mid-60s, no one was more dapper and respected than an up-and-coming guy named J.R. Russo. He wore the best suits, the most expensive shoes, was better groomed than most of the movie actors I'd met. He was a role model for me."

Hanover Street was the center of the North End. North of Hanover was Prince Street, where the Angiulos had their office and home to Baioni, Steve "The Rifleman" Flemmi, Frankie Salemme, Skinny Carbonas, and Sonny Mercurio. Joe Russo's headquarters was in East Boston, but he and his partner, Vincent "Vinny Jackson" Deciccio spent long hours at the Angiulo's office. On the north corner of Hanover and Commercial was Giro's Restaurant, where Joe Lombardo once held court. Paulie Intiso inherited Lombardo's territory. Nicola "Nicky" Giso acted as Intiso's lieutenant. In Somerville, there was the Winter Hill Gang, led by James "Whitey" Bulger, a South Boston powerhouse who made millions for the Irish mob. But as tough as the Irishman was, he still deferred to murderous Larry Baioni, whose men collected a fortune in protection from Bulger's operation. Baioni used Stevie Flemmi as a buffer between the Italians and the Irish.

When Anthony Fiato hit the street, he was greeted with stares and whispers. In the neighborhood, he was the new guy on the block. Coming from Hollywood made him even more mysterious. Then there was his groomed beard and sideburns. Wiseguys rarely wore facial hair, and Fiato looked more like a biker than a mobster.

But one attribute has always separated the wanna-be wiseguys from the real thing, and Fiato possessed that trait in abundance. He was capable of violence in a finger snap. It was inevitable, then, that he would encounter Willie Fopiano, the toughest street kid on the North End in the early 1960s. With his long sideburns and dark hair combed straight back, Fopiano was a muscular

Elvis look-alike who took pride in keeping the dope pushers and hippies off Hanover Street through the use of brute force. Either with his fists or a sawed-off Louisville Slugger, Fopiano was a one-man gang. Men like J.R. Russo and Larry Baioni kept their eyes on him. They knew the kid had talent. Fopiano was an amateur boxer, but his real fighting talent was demonstrated on the street, where his thumping exploits echoed through the neighborhood.

Fiato liked him immediately.

"Coming back to the North End, I was just another young guy on the make," he said. "Without a sponsor, you're just another punk on your own. That's one reason I liked Willie. He swaggered when he walked and had already been approached by those people, especially Larry Baioni. Larry loved Willie like a son. And even the wiseguys were afraid of Willie. Larry Baioni could always use an effective debt collector.

"'Skinny Al' Silverio introduced us, and I thought I might have to fight Willie just to prove myself, but it never happened. When Willie found out where I was coming from, he about went crazy. He couldn't believe that I'd been around Frank Sinatra, Robert Mitchum, even Marilyn Monroe.

"I run into him a few nights later at the Florentine. I send him a drink and he invites me to sit down. I think he's going to ask me what I've done, jobs I've pulled, who I've worked with and all that. The usual stuff. After all, he's a tough guy, right? But he sits down and gets all wide-eyed and asks me, 'Is it true you met Frank Sinatra in California?'

"I wanted to laugh my head off, but didn't. I told him about the stars, about meeting Joey Gallo when he was out west recruiting for the Profaci War. I said the things he wanted to hear, because I saw Willie as my ticket to the inside. I even put up with him giving me a nickname: Tony Rome(a Sinatra character in the movie of the same name). Through him, I could meet somebody who I could do something with. Willie already drove a brand-new Cadillac. He had it all together, and he was just a kid really. We all were kids. The weird part is, Willie immediately started including me on his scores. He'd take off a bookmaker or grab some guy and shake him down, and he'd cut me in for a part. Basically, he wants my friendship. Shows you something about the power of celebrity. Frank Sinatra and Robert Mitchum were sending me spending money and didn't even know it.

"So we go for rides at night, and I'm so itching to get into the action I can barely stand it. And Willie starts telling me his goals. This guy knocks out a half-dozen people a week and he says he really wants to be a disk jockey. Spin the platters, have his own radio show. The works. Either that or be the heavyweight champion of the world. Some choice, huh?

"As time goes on, I tell him I'll take him to California some day, show him around, maybe even get him started in the fight game. Half the wiseguys in Hollywood had a piece of one fighter or another. But Willie didn't look like he'd ever leave the neighborhood. He had status there. He was somebody there. And he'd already started borrowing from every bookmaker on the North End. He'd have to hit a lottery to pay his markers.

"It didn't take long before I started looking at Willie differently. He was a tough guy with his hands, all right, don't misunderstand. This guy could break ribs with one punch, knock a bigger man out with one hand. And he was loyal as hell. But he didn't have the killer instinct. You could see it in his eyes when he asked about Sinatra.

"When he wouldn't stop going on and on about it, I told him, 'Hey, I just met the guy. I'm not his agent.' Willie and I were destined to become the best of friends and the worst of enemies. He saw me as his right arm, but he didn't like it when that right arm slapped him. And I did, when the time was right. The guy was tough, but he wasn't Machiavellian. All good wiseguys are Machiavellian, that much I picked up from watching the way Johnny Rosselli manipulated 'Dago Louie,' and the way 'Dago Louie' made me do his bidding. And I used Willie and some of his boys every chance I could.

"For instance, I never wanted to be known as a guy who robbed bookmakers. I wanted to own bookmakers. 'Dago Louie' owned them. J.R. Russo owned them. So I suggested to Willie that he send two or three of his guys to do the small jobs. We'd whack up the money. We'd go out, eat dinner, go to the Florentine for a drink and scheme all night long around the North End."

On a night like any other, their friendship was sealed. As they cruised late on Salem Street, they came up on a car parked in the middle of the road. A guy was kissing his girl goodnight. The car blocked their way, but they thought little enough of it. After all, surely Romeo saw their headlights. They waited, waited and waited some more. Then Fopiano lost his patience, rapped the horn in his Cadillac. Then came the finger.

"The guy was just trying to impress his girl. That was enough to set Willie off. I figure it's going to be one, two, three, Willie hits the guy, the guy hits the pavement, right? Well, Willie calls the guy a motherfucker, hops out of the Cadillac and strides up to the car. Before the guy can say a word Willie's pulling him out through the open window. And they start going at it. I'll tell you this, the guy could take a punch because Willie started pounding on him.

"For ten minutes they went at it. I was like a pitbull ready to pounce, and when he hit Willie with a couple lucky shots I couldn't stand it. I took over the pummeling and whacked him in the ribs and busted my fucking hand. Then I was hot as hell. And still the guy wouldn't stop motherfucking us, wouldn't go down and stay down. I kick him in the stomach and finally get him in a headlock. I remember seeing our reflections in a butcher shop window. Meanwhile, Willie marches back to his Cadillac, opens the trunk and pulls out a ball bat. I look over at him, see what he's doing and retrieve a tire iron from the trunk. We beat him and beat him and that was that.

"All that time we never even heard his girlfriend scream."

Through Willie Fopiano, the street began to open up to Anthony Fiato. He met bookmakers and moneylenders, small-time scammers and, in time, the older, more experienced men who hovered on the periphery of the Angiulo and Patriarca crime families.

After the restaurants and bars closed for the night, the sporting crowd gravitated toward the Coliseum, an after-hours club operated by Nicky Giso. Greeting visitors at the door was Joe Penn, who had a pig face. After being goaded into action by Vito Popolo, Vinny Nip Ferrara would later whack out Joe Penn over a perceived slight. At the Coliseum, there was a story at every table.

Nicky ran the Coliseum for Paulie Intiso and Sammy Granito. One-part Don Rickles, one-part stone killer, Giso was a homely little man with greased-back hair, long sideburns and dark circles under his eyes. Although he rarely left the North End, he had logged thousands of miles flying around the country carrying out contract hits for the Patriarca crime family and other groups.

In the North End hierarchy, Nicky Giso reported to big earner Paulie Intiso, who in turn kicked up to family capo Sammy Granito. He was a made guy who loved playing the boss in his own nightclub. He drank constantly, cheated strangers who found their way into his domain, and hit on anything that moved.

"Nicky was a piece of work. He was like a kid. All he ever thought about was booze and sex and eventually got in trouble with his people for bringing around a teen-age girl," Fiato said. "We hit it off immediately because I was a young guy, and somewhat handsome if I do say so myself, with a groomed beard and mustache. Nicky knew my father and accepted me as one of the kids from the neighborhood, but more than that he liked me for my ability to pick up hippie chics, which he of course took a shot at. The rings around his eyes were so bad we used to say, 'Hey, Nicky, why don't you take your sunglasses off?' He'd laugh, but let me tell you, his eyes told you deep down he was nobody to fool with. He wasn't exactly the easiest guy in the world to find a date for.

"I'd meet a girl, turn on the charm and take her out for the night. We'd screw around awhile, but eventually I'd give her a line about being in debt to this mean old Mafia loanshark. The guy is going to break my legs if I don't help him with his problem.

'What problem?' the chick would ask. 'He's apparently got one of these permanent hard-ons, the kind the doctors implant. Hurts him like hell. If I don't get him some relief the guy's gonna go crazy and whack me out.' And it always worked. They were so dazzled by the romance or the booze or the mystery of the Mafia kid story that they always did their part for the cause. Nicky would grin, pat back his greasy hair and take the chicks to a shabby little studio apartment he called his pad on St. Charles Street. It had a mattress and an orange crate and a bottle of whiskey. He'd bang the girls, and they'd invariably come back with a line, 'I thought you said he had a permanent hard-on. I think he must have lied to you.'

"After the chicks had gone we'd mimic them and embarrass the hell out of Nicky, who usually took it like a good sport. I played the pimp for him I don't know how many times. As you might imagine, it endeared me to him. He was a nut and a killer, but, don't get me wrong, I loved the guy.

"He employed a group of guys who could have tested for a Cagney movie. They were so full of malaprops they barely spoke English. One of them was Pegleg, the bartender. He spent his nights running drinks for Nicky, charming theater-goers who'd arrived at the Coliseum after the final curtain, and thinning the booze and short-changing the merchant marine sailors who came in late. To Pegleg, 'swag' was stolen goods and a 'muzzler' was a cheap bastard. A guy who used other guys to pull scores was a 'Fagin,' like right out of Dickens, and a 'bloke' was another word for a drunk who wasn't from the neighborhood."

Bankrolled by the Angiulos, the Coliseum had no difficulty staying open and ahead of the law. Nicola Giso minimized the bureaucratic red tape by paying area police officers regularly, and giving them generous gifts at Christmas.

Despite his reputation as Raymond Patriarca's most aggressive killer, Joseph Barboza was not the most feared man in Boston. He wasn't a made guy, nor was he a particularly well-mannered one. Police buzzed around the big, square-headed bruiser like seagulls, and anyone seen with Joe was sure to become the subject of intense surveillance and harassment. Barboza had a habit of shooting people and neglecting to dispose of the bodies, which not only made trouble for the mob but also work for the cops as well.

"Like everybody in those days, he loved to come to up the Coliseum," Fiato said. "He always had a couple of his henchmen with him, and he loved to throw his weight around. But since he wasn't made, he wound up taking orders from everybody who was, and some nights half the guys in the Coliseum were connected better than Joe Barboza, who wasn't Italian but Portuguese. One night he comes swaggering in like he owns the joint. His victims are still on the front-page of the newspaper. The cops are everywhere. To give you an example of how the business works, by this time Joe Barboza probably has half of his kills, and he wound up whacking out 30 guys before Joe Russo blew him away in San Francisco a few years later. Barboza's a big, strong ape, capable of choking a guy to death with one hand. A real sweetheart of a guy, you know? But he's not made and when he comes up the stairs to enter the Coliseum with his boys, Sammy Granito, who's half Joe's size, greets him with, 'What the fuck you think you're doing coming in here bringing heat on my place? What are you, stupid? Get the fuck out of here before you get us all in trouble.'

"And just like that, Joe shrugs like a dog and turns away. Sammy was only a part-owner of the club, and Joe could have tried to beef it, but he knew the score. If you're not made, you're not much in that world. It's something I knew I'd never forget.

"On the street, there was a pecking order that everyone had to respect, or there would be trouble. The hard part was, in a closed society you couldn't always tell how strong a guy was. That's how a loser like 'Fat Vinny' Teresa, who wound up a government snitch, could get away with calling himself the Number Three man in Boston. He was the Number Three man like I was Al Capone. If you believe the book he wrote [*My Life in the Mafia*, 1973], his grandfather was a Sicilian duke. Number Three man in

Boston? Put it this way, we used to spit on "Fat Vinny" Teresa on the street. He couldn't do any work. He wasn't a tough guy, he was a tub of shit. I think people kept him around because he was a go-fer. People ribbed him unmercifully about his weight. Nicky Giso used to call Vinny Fatty Arbuckle. That's how little respect "Fat Vinny" Teresa got.

"The day people found out he was cooperating with the government, his whole family had to feel like dying. And they would have died if he hadn't taken them with him into witness protection. Larry Baioni and Jerry Angiulo were ready to kill him, his wife and family, his dog, anyone who'd ever said a good word about him."

Giso soon realized that Anthony Fiato's understanding of youth culture extended beyond his ability to get the older man laid. Giso might not have comprehended the psychedelic fashion of the day, but he knew there was money in it. So he bankrolled Fiato in a clothing and accessories store at various times called the Mod Shop, the Thread Shed and the Tobacco Hut. To ensure the investment risk matched the financial reward, Giso and Fiato set up a high-stakes poker game in the back room amid the bell-bottom pants and long-collared shirts. Some fashions never went out of style.

"And of course we were there with a quick thousand at street interest whenever one of the players busted out," Fiato said. "It was a sweet deal."

The shop also introduced Larry Fiato to his brother's friends. Larry began working in the front of the store. He took orders for sandwiches and snacks from the card players in the back. He booked numbers from neighborhood customers. He roped players for the card games. He helped with the bookmaking. He sometimes even sold magazines and tobacco.

"The front half was legitimate," Larry said. "The back half was illegal. My dad was sick but still alive. He hung out there, too. It wasn't that I was a hustler or street guy like my brother. All that came afterwards.

"I was just helping out, making a few dollars. All my exploits stayed within the store, but that's where I met half the Mafia guys in Boston. My brother was up-and-coming, a guy with a future on the North End, and I lived off his reputation. My peers feared me because of my brother. They liked me because of my brother, and at times hated me because of my brother. Everything that went on in the North End as far as how people treated me, was through my brother. I was still a kid. I took it all for granted. Watching all the Mafia guys come and go on the street, I believed that's how it always was and always would be."

In the late 1960s, there were a million ways for wiseguys to make money. Fiato soon recruited North End men with no apparent link to each other for a sore-neck auto accident scam which netted himself, his friend Sonny Polosi, Giso and their personal claims agent, "Easy Al," hundreds of thousands of dollars. In a no-fault insurance state, the setup was simple: A carload of passengers are rear-ended by a single, heavily insured driver. Every passenger claimed a medical malady, and the claims were backed up by a physician, who was in on the setup. The insurance settlements were substantial. The players received $500 apiece, the doctor double that, and the mob guys split the rest.

"They'd go to a quack doctor three or four times and get five hundred, which was worth a lot more than it is today," Anthony Fiato said. "Al had claims adjusters in his pocket. I took care of the recruiting, which was easy since everybody knew everybody in our neighborhood. And Nicky sat back and made a score. We'd clear thirty thousand per car. We bankrupted the whole fucking system. And it was so easy. The system was set up to give honest people a hard time. But, hey, we weren't honest people."

With Giso behind him, and Joe Russo beginning to take notice, Fiato stretched his range of criminal expertise. With Fopiano, he borrowed thousands from bookmakers with no intention of repayment. He robbed restaurants when they were fat with cash, nightclubs when they were fatter. He loansharked some of the money, blew the rest on hippie chicks and at Suffolk Downs Race Track.

And every night was the same: The Bella Napoli or Giro's on Hanover for dinner, meet with the boys, drinks, then after midnight to the Coliseum.

Mob activity was the same in every major city, but no wiseguy ever referred to himself as a member of Organized Crime. Such labels were for the FBI and the local mob squad. Although thuggish Genovese soldier Joe Valachi brought La Cosa Nostra into the lexicon of mob watchers when he turned snitch on New York's crime families, no one on the North End called their thing by that name. So secret was New York's criminal subculture that not even veteran wiseguys used the term. Instead, they used an intricate series of working relationships. For instance, Valachi was "with" Vito Genovese, a made member of his family. In Chicago, there is no talk of family. Organized criminal activity is run by the Outfit.

On the North End, there was the Office. Until his deportation to Sicily, the head of the Office was Philip Buccola. Buccola's trusted underlings included Raymond Patriarca, Sammy Granito, Joseph Lombardo, and Leo Santanelo. With Buccola gone, those four men divided New England's bookmaking, loansharking, policy and extortion rackets. To be sure there were other mobs in other enclaves of Boston and Providence, most notably Whitey Bulger's Winter Hill Gang. Boston's Irish mob was powerful and led by Bernard McLaughlin, whose murder sparked one of the bloodiest gang wars in the history of American organized crime. But in New England, the Office dictated policy on the street.

By the late 1960s, Patriarca had emerged as the head of the family. Granito's back was guarded by Joseph "J.R." Russo and Vincent "Vinny Jackson" DeCiccio, young toughs who collectively were referred to as the Gold Dust Twins. Santanelo's crew handled much of the dirty work for the family, and none in his crew was more ruthless and efficient than Ilario "Larry Baioni" Zannino. Baioni and J.R. Russo most impressed Fiato, not only for their capacities for violence but also for their sense of personal style.

"In my eyes, these were classy guys," he said. "Larry Baioni was a conservative dresser, a quiet man who was always respectful of women. Russo was a dapper guy who wore the finest suits, silk shirts, the most expensive shoes. He was prematurely gray, like me, and I identified with him closely. I wanted to be like them, and I knew I would be if I ever got the chance."

Although Giso never would rise to the level of Russo and Baioni, it was through Giso that Fiato gained entree into the world he had been dreaming of. Although it was common for the associates, soldiers and street lieutenants to drink, dine, and do business together, no one forgot to whom he owed allegiance. And although those alliances shifted—Baioni and Russo eventually would become partners in crime—forgetting where you came from was a good way to get killed. And so Willie Fopiano, who as a young tough teen-ager had impressed Baioni, become the hitman's protege.

Fiato remained with Giso. "Fat Johnny" Cincotti was with Ralphie Chong. And on it went.

"But Larry Baioni was a fucking man's man," Fiato said. "He was not someone a young kid like me could just walk up to. He was with Leo Santanelo, who was an insider with Batista in Cuba and owned casinos there before Castro came in. Leo had great political contacts, and he had plenty of insiders on the police department. But his strength came from being known as a man who could take care of business, and for business he had guys like Larry around.

"Larry was a purist, in the sense that he was pure gangster, a very capable man who could get work done in a finger snap. Of course, when he went to work someone disappeared. Like Joe Porter, a shylock in Revere who was connected. I saw Porter come into the Bella Napoli plenty of times. He was friendly with everybody, and everybody knew he was with Larry. One night I'm standing there and Joe brushes past me, with eyes like a deer in headlights, really scared. He rushes over to Larry's table and gets down on one knee and literally starts begging for his life. The guy is crying and you can hear him throughout the place. To hear a guy talk like that really hits you, but it didn't have an affect on Larry Baioni. All he said was, 'Get the fuck out of here. You're a dead man.'

"Less than twenty-four hours later, he was."

Part of Larry Baioni's job was providing protection for the Angiulos, a family of bookmakers who started out independent of the Office, but wound up paying tribute and eventually became leaders of the family business. Gerardo "Jerry" Angiulo would become as notorious in Boston as Patriarca himself was on Federal Hill in Providence.

Fopiano adored Larry Baioni, but Fiato knew the young tough's secret: He wasn't a killer. He might beat someone to death in a fit of rage, but Willie Fopiano lacked the capacity to murder on orders, not even on an order from his hero, Larry Baioni.

When Baioni asked Fopiano to join the family, to become a made member, Willie knew he couldn't agree to a key part of the code of honor and was tormented by it.

"I remember how torn up Willie was," Fiato said. "You have to remember something. This was back at a time when the Mafia was all-powerful. In my neighborhood, everyone wanted to play for the Red Sox, become a cop, or be a gangster. A few guys wanted to become priests, but they didn't count. So Willie's life's dream was to become a boxer and a gangster, and he couldn't do it.

"But he couldn't just say no to Larry Baioni, either. I mean, no one just said no to him. It was like saying no to the President, if the President might shoot you in the head for showing disrespect.

"I think Willie handled it as well as anyone could under the circumstances. When Larry asked him, Willie said, 'I have to be mad at somebody to do that.' Larry liked the answer. He didn't lose respect for Willie, but Willie lost all his confidence around the wiseguys. There was no question about Fopiano's nerve. He just couldn't go out cold and whack somebody.

That might work for a while on the West Coast, where the mob is more liberal and lacks anything resembling a real strong structure like it has in New York and Boston. But it wouldn't work for long on the East Coast. The incident with Larry is one reason Willie started bugging me again about going out to California and turning pro in the fight game. He was always good with his hands."

Willie Fopiano's relationship with Larry Baioni is perhaps best illustrated by the time he saved the life of Ronnie Rome.

"When he was younger Ronnie had been the doorman at a Boston nightclub called the Sugar Shack," Fiato recalled. "His boss was a crippled guy named 'Hippo,' real name Rudy Guarino. Hippo had words with Stevie Flemmi and Frankie Salemme, two of Baioni's toughest soldiers. Ronnie jumped in to defend his boss and wound up giving a beating to the two of them. He didn't know who they were. They went to get guns to kill Ronnie, but someone told him that they were with Larry Baioni and he ran. Ronnie got in touch with Willie Fopiano, and Larry made a meet. Ronnie Rome showed up and told Larry he didn't know that Stevie and Frankie were with him. 'They were giving Hippo shit and I jumped in,' Ronnie said. Larry Baioni said, 'You're lucky you're a friend of Willie's. You want to be a tough guy? All the tough guys are dead. We do away with them all.' Ronnie walked away from that meeting with his knees knocking."

"Thanks to Nicky, I was earning a living," Fiato said. "I helped Nicky with his card games. I did everything from driving his car to getting his veal cutlet sandwiches. I'd collect the rake from the poker games, pick up envelopes from bookmakers and listen to Nicky's stories. I was accepted. I didn't have a history. I was like a new experience to these guys. They didn't know enough about me to treat me like one of the neighborhood stooges, and I already had proved I could play their game.

"Nicky guided me through the streets and I got him girls. One day at the Coliseum I said, off the cuff, that I'd probably make a good pimp. Nicky got mad. 'If you were, kid, I wouldn't sit down with you. You wouldn't be welcome here. We can't sit down with no pimps. We can own them, take money off them, but we can't sit down with them. It shows disrespect.' Strange as that sounds, that's the logic of the Mafia.

"They can take a pimp's money, but that doesn't make them pimps. It was the same thing with drugs. Nobody ever admitted dealing drugs. To admit it would get you hurt. But that didn't stop people from robbing drug dealers, taking their money and their dope and selling the junk to other dealers out of town. It was lucrative as hell. But as long as you didn't sit down with one and didn't deal directly with a peddler, you weren't a pusher yourself. I just accepted it as the way things were and never thought to ask questions."

There were plenty of jobs for a person willing to do the work, and Fiato knew that he'd spend the next twenty years trying to climb a rung in the organization if he remained merely a strong-arm collector for Nicky Giso and Paulie Intiso.

But with Anthony Fiato's exuberance and Nicky Giso's bankroll, the Mod Shop thrived. It also gave terminally ill Johnny Fiato a place to hang out and swap stories with the backroom card players.

"By then we knew he had cancer and he was very depressed. It was the best thing for him. He loved to talk football and bet the ponies. All his old friends came around. It was hilarious. You had hippie-type kids and early disco kings dropping by the store, and these old-timers and all the wiseguys would pass them on the way to the back room. For him it was like being a kid again.

"You have to understand something, my father was a good, decent man, but everyone in the old neighborhood were knockaround guys. They drank, they bet, they made book. It wasn't any big deal, just part of the times. My father was no wiseguy, he was a working stiff who worked his ass off his whole life. But bookmaking and lending money wasn't foreign to him. Until he got real sick, it was like a big party atmosphere. And it made a bundle."

The Mod Shop made more money in the back office than the

showroom, and it was there Fiato noticed that a lucrative segment of street business was slipping past him and Giso. Many of the young people who came in to buy his shirts and pants and play his pinball games rarely failed to hint around about the availability of drugs. Fiato was raised with the traditional American mob edict that dealing drugs was a capital offense, and those caught selling would be put to death. He had no interest in getting involved. But he also saw the tempting potential.

Selling only a few bags of grass and a small quantity of pills would be worth hundreds of dollars. Getting the stuff was never difficult; in those days, most of the pushers were hippies who didn't carry weapons and were easy to victimize. He didn't need Mexican marijuana contacts; all he needed were his fists. Was any amount of money worth the ultimate downside that accompanied getting caught? That's what Fiato wondered in those early days.

"I'm getting work through Nicky and Paulie Intiso. It's not much, collecting and so forth, but between that and the Mod Shop I'm making out all right. In Hollywood, there was plenty of money, plenty of action. Back East, wiseguys were constantly fighting over scraps. There were so many guys trying to make a name for themselves, you had to take advantage of any situation.

"One afternoon I received a call from Nicky at the Mod Shop. He told me to come up to the Coliseum right away. Then he hung the phone down. I could sense the urgency in his voice. I drove there and when I reached the top stairs I entered the dining room and saw Nicky and Joe Russo sitting in a booth. I walked over to them and I could see Joe Russo looked troubled. As I approached, Nicky got out of the booth and said, 'Joe would like to talk to you.' When Nicky left the table, I knew it was something serious. That's when Joe Russo told me about his problem.

"In the booth, I sit next to him and he says, 'I got some work to do and I need your help. There's a guy who comes into a certain bar at night. I want you to go there and wait for him. When he comes in, I want you to go to a pay phone and call this number.

Then you get up and leave. I'll do the rest.' As he says that, he opens his coat and I can see the pistol. He takes it out and places it on the table.

""That's it? You want me to finger a guy and leave?"' I asked him.

"'I'll take care of the rest.'

"And he would have. But before he put the gun back in his coat I picked it up. He looked at me, didn't say anything. I said, 'I'll handle this.' He pushed the gun toward me with confidence. I could see a new respect for me in his eyes. As I was leaving, Nicky came up to me and put his arm around me. He walked me to the door and displayed an affection I'd never seen from him. Before I descended the stairs, he whispered to me: 'Your friend Willie was asked to help and he refused.'

"As I walked down the stairs, I knew my life would never be the same again. I knew all my relationships with these men would be different. There would be money and opportunities. I knew being taken into their confidence was my ticket to the top. I'd shown myself capable of doing the work."

CHAPTER 3

After he picked up the gun, Anthony Fiato's status rose overnight. He travelled with Nicky Giso throughout the North End from one club to another, where he met with bar owners and bookmakers, made pickups and occasionally wound up busted at the track. Fiato dined regularly with J.R. Russo, whose influence was substantial. Fiato shaved his beard and stopped rinsing his prematurely gray hair. He began dressing like Russo, all the while learning the way the criminal element operated, how it remained on friendly terms with local judges, and how it managed to keep beat cops happy and to elude the hard-nosed mob busters.

"In those days, I never worried about the heat," Fiato said. "Cops were easy to spot and no one gave a thought to the FBI. Every once in a while they'd show up with, 'You're Tony Rome. You're making a name for yourself, Tony Rome. We're watching you, Tony Rome.' But it was nothing. I didn't care how many pictures they took for their photo albums. They could take a picture of my ass for all I cared. I was with Nicky, and through him with Joe Russo and Larry Baioni. I believed we owned the town.

"One day I'm bopping down Hanover Street passing the Cafe Pompeii and Joe Russo spots me and waves me inside. You got to understand something, being invited into the Cafe Pompeii in those days was like visiting the White House. You could run into the President, if you know what I mean. And from the look of things the Cabinet is in session. There's Joe Russo and Larry

Baioni and Leo Santanelo. I sit down and listen to Leo talk about the time he owned a piece of the action in the casinos in Havana. And everyone who walks into the fucking place is seeing me with them, these men who are twice my age.

"Suddenly I was in the inner circle. From then on, whenever I was at the Coliseum, or Giro's, or the Night Life or any of a dozen other places I never sat alone but was invited to the head table. I'd babysit Jerry Angiulo while Nicky Giso ran the Coliseum. I saw my life changing.

"And so did the FBI. I'd come out of a cafe and they'd bump into me on the street and say, 'Hey, Tony Rome. You're really going places.' But I had no fear of them or anybody else. I was bulletproof in those days."

Giso loved Russo and Baioni, but he saw the stars in Fiato's eyes.

"Let me tell you something, kid," he said in a quiet moment. "You don't want to hang out with Larry and Joe Russo. You want to hang out with them, you'll go to the can with them, too. Better you keep a low profile. That goes for Jerry Angiulo, too. Cops are all over them. You don't want to get a reputation before you deserve one."

But Fiato enjoyed hanging out with the men who were his heroes, especially now that they had accepted him as one of their own. It was during that time he began working with Ronnie Rome, who operated the Angiulo's vending machine business. Rome, whose real name was Romanowski, placed cigarette and pinball machines in neighborhood bars and restaurants and all the Italian-American clubs.

When Johnny Fiato died in 1974, Ronnie Rome was one of dozens of local wiseguys who attended the funeral and gave envelopes filled with cash to Anthony's mother.

"We became very good friends," Fiato recalled. "I got to know Ronnie well, and I learned his capabilities. He was a good operator, but a terrible gambler. And not being a tough guy eventually would get him in trouble.

"Ronnie Rome was related through marriage to a made guy named Ronnie "The Pig" Cassesso, who was in prison for murder at Walpole courtesy of the snitch Joe Barboza. The Pig had a pock-marked face and a deep tan. Cassesso had the run of Walpole in those days. Here's how strong Cassesso was: He had Ronnie deliver a pinball machine to the warden as a gift. One day Ronnie gets a call and has to go to Walpole, and this time I go with him. When we get there, I expect to be frisked by the guards, but it's not that way. Then I see that Cassesso really has the run of the place. He's in for murder and not only is he not behind bars, he's not even on the inside of the prison. He's lying on the grass working on his tan outside the front gate. He acted like he was the warden's brother-in-law more than a prisoner. We greet each other and it was then I learned how strong he was. Cassesso was really happy to see Ronnie Rome. Ronnie told him that I was with Nicky Giso, but Cassesso had already heard. He had better news reports than the Boston Globe. I didn't know whether that was bad or good, but he said, 'It's good' and smiled. He asked us if we wanted something to drink. For a guy in prison, he was a gracious host.

"We asked him about a couple of the local guys like Ricky Costa and Jimmy 'The Bear' Flemmi. Ricky was in for chopping a guy's fingers off, and Jimmy the Bear was in Joe Barboza's crew. The guy had patted his wife's ass. Cassesso was taking good care of Ricky. 'You just missed the Bear,' Cassesso said. 'We were laying out here getting a tan. We're eating good tonight: Chinese food. We don't eat it here. We go down the street and eat it. It's a good little restaurant.' I couldn't believe it. He was living better than most guys on the street. He got anything he wanted. He stayed overnight at a motel, laid women and dropped in on the warden anytime he wanted. He was more free than the guards. Everyone was afraid of him because he was Raymond Patriarca's buttonman. He'd killed plenty of guys, and everybody knew it. Before we left Cassesso warned us that the guys I was hanging out with were a bunch of users. He told us to be careful."

Money never stayed in Anthony Fiato's pocket long. There were women to impress, and ponies and ball games to bet. For a working wiseguy, the main thing is to keep building scores, sharing the wealth and impressing the boss. Next to having a reputation for violence, it's the best way to increase in importance.

So when Willie Fopiano worked his way into a deal to take off the Thunderbird Casino in Las Vegas, Anthony Fiato jumped at the chance to share the wealth. In the wake of his humiliation in front of Larry Baioni, Willie had moved to Las Vegas, where he collected for loansharks and worked his way into the casino culture through Patriarca family representative Elliot Paul Price.

Junket scams were common in Las Vegas casinos in the early 1970s. The setup was simple enough: Find a willing casino operator or high-ranking official to approve undeserved credit for players from out of town. When a 200-passenger planeload of players arrives, issue them casino chips, say, $2,500 apiece. They gamble a few bucks, turn the rest in to the take-off guys staying at the hotel. The players get a weekend in Las Vegas with all expenses paid. The wiseguys get between $250,000 and $500,000 in casino chips, which they run through the casino cage all weekend. By the end of the trip, the casino is missing a bundle of money, which is later split up with the inside and outside schemers.

The junket operator, who had to put up at least a partial guarantee in the form of a bond on each flight, wasn't always in on the scam. And one weekend could ruin his business and his reputation.

"But who was he going to go to? He lived in our town. He wasn't going to go anywhere. He could complain, but as long as we were kicking money up the line, nobody would do a thing to stop us. We were careful to work with an inside guy at the casino. And contrary to popular belief, every casino had guys who were with connected people.

"Boston was well-represented in those days in Las Vegas. Wherever Elliot Paul Price was welcome, our people could work a deal. He represented the Patriarcas for years in Vegas. Made a fortune and moved money for a couple of decades, at least. He knew everybody from 'Fat Tony' Salerno and Vincent 'Jimmy Blue Eyes' Alo of the Genovese family, to Sam Giancana and Tony Spilotro, out of Chicago.

"Well, when I worked with Willie to fill up the plane for the charter to Vegas, we took everybody from the neighborhood. Not just the working stiffs with a few bucks in their pockets, but everybody. It didn't matter. They all knew the score and, since they were from the neighborhood, they weren't going to say shit about it. Besides, they got to eat steak and lobster all weekend and get out of the cold for a few hours. You couldn't beat the deal.

"Our best trip was a $10,000 credit line charter, where everybody on the junket received a $10,000 credit line. Talk about sweet. We didn't have as many people on the junket, but with fewer people it was a lot easier to handle. We took bookmakers and the butcher, a gas station attendant and a few guys we had to buy a suit of clothes for so they wouldn't blow the play. We put the chump who posted the bond out of business that trip. I mean, we had a couple million in credit working. I oversaw the whole thing and Fopiano made sure the group didn't forget who they were working for.

"One guy took a heart attack on the ride over. People were playing cards and drinking and having a helluva time, but we were a little nervous. After all, you add it all up and you're talking about a major score. A fortune in credit that nobody has any intention of paying back.

"I stayed over at the Stardust that time. Willie gave everyone my room number. They were instructed to take $2,000 in credit at a time. They gambled a few bucks of the money and left the casino. Some were better at it than others, but nobody saw the guys going over to the cashier's cage. They played different games, tipped the dealers to make it look legitimate. Pretty soon, everyone's streaming in to drop their chips on the bed. Then they headed back across the street. Willie and I took the chips over to his house off the Strip. We put a big blanket on the floor and we just kept tossing all the fucking chips, black and green, into bags. It was fucking unbelievable."

Back home, Fiato returned to work on smaller deals. One presented itself in the form of a Boston-area factory that stored platinum wire in large spools. The spools were each worth tens of thousands of dollars, and, thanks to a little help on the inside, pulling off the job was easy.

"Sonny Polosi had a bar in Beverly not far from the factory. One of the foremen would come in every night and shoot the breeze. Well, before long the foreman learns that Sonny is connected, and that gets him bragging about how much he knows, what he has access to, and so forth. Some people are like that. The Mafia mystique gets in their eyes.

"Sonny was my friend, but he wasn't a mob boss. He was just another wiseguy. Over time, the foreman fell in with Sonny and began playing cards with his crew. Which led to him losing at cards and going into debt. Well, Sonny didn't want to lose a good customer, and the guy needed a way to get even. So this foreman, basically an honest man, is turned into a thief just like that. He outlines the plant, tells us how to get in and out without being spotted by the guard, and even gives us the guard's nightly routine. He sets it up like he's been pulling scores his whole life. He was stuck $5,000 and he wasn't going to get hurt if he could help it.

"So we took the score. He even helped us with the right people to move the material. There were spools of platinum wire and something called saccaro, which is gold and silver mixed. We didn't know what it was used for, we only knew that if we melted it down or got it into the right hands we'd make a quick killing. When we got inside, it was even better than we expected. There was some cash, bottles of expensive chemicals and all kinds of stuff. We loaded it in sacks like Santa Claus. The fact we might be helping to bankrupt a whole fucking company never entered our minds. We took some of the material to a jeweler on the North End we knew through Nicky Giso who moved stolen merchandise for us. He wanted to buy all the platinum and he promised to find somebody who would take the rest of the stuff. We moved the entire load for $75,000. If we'd known what to do with it, it might have been worth half-a-million.

"We'd steal anything that wasn't nailed down. We stole paintings from art galleries, antiques, all kinds of big-name merchandise. And we moved it through Nicky, who knew everybody in the city. I mean he had connections everywhere. I was called his eyes and ears. And he would set up the meetings with people I never heard of. Looking back, his fingerprints were rarely on anything, which was pretty slick on his part."

"Not everybody who talks the talk is the genuine article," Anthony Fiato said. "Just like with any line of work you have your contenders and your pretenders. Joe Nap, whose real last name was Napolitano, was one of the pretenders. Me and Ronnie Rome were hanging out at the Playboy Club in Boston, checking out the action and taking in the shows. In those days the Playboy Club had a lot of singing acts and comedians.

"We got to know those people. Guys like Bert Convy and Bill Dana. At the time, Bill was a famous comedian who everyone knew for the line, 'My name Jose Jimenez.' Bert Convy was a pretty boy who was part of a nightclub act and later became a musical comedy star and gameshow host. They loved us. They always were attracted to the wiseguys, and Ronnie Rome was with Jerry and Danny Angiulo. He represented them in Rome Vending.

"Well, we're hanging out at the Playboy Club and we begin running into Joe Nap, who was talking-the-talk and walking-the-walk and acting like he's a fingersnap from becoming the Godfather himself. Well, Joe Nap's daddy was with Raymond Patriarca, who was the fucking godfather. But that don't make Joe Nap anything but a pain in the ass and a monkey with a big mouth. The street is full of these guys. Every time we see Joe Nap, he starts in with 'fuck the Angiulos' this and 'fuck the Angiulos' that, and he knows full well that Ronnie is with those people. With Joe Nap, it's 'Ray this' and 'Ray that.' To hear him speak, him and Ray are thick as thieves, which anyone with half a brain knows is pure bullshit.

"I interrupted him one night in the middle of one of his speeches and said I'd had enough. I told Ronnie, 'You want to sit here and listen to this asshole, it's up to you. But I'm telling you he's out of his fucking mind talking like that. I think he wants to make a name for himself in the obituaries.'

"Ronnie knew I was right, but Joe Nap was giving him names of joints where he could install his vending machines. In no time, word gets back to the Angiulos that Joe Nap is bad-mouthing them in public and Ronnie Rome is listening to it. They call Ronnie in for a meet and ask him, 'What are you doing with this Joe Nap? If anybody hurts you, what would we do for you? If anybody was looking to hurt me, what would you do for me?' Ronnie says, 'I'd hurt them, Danny.' And Angiulo says, 'Well, somebody's hurting us.' By laying out the situation that way, they were basically asking him to take out Joe Nap, but Ronnie Rome was no killer and he was sick about the whole thing. He was in large debt to the Angiulos, was making late payments and having a helluva time keeping his head above water. It would have been the perfect way to square himself with them. But he couldn't do the work, and that presented a problem. If he couldn't do it, someone else would, and he would be shamed. Even though I offered to do the job for him, he might be killed for disobeying an order.

"It was then I knew I had to help him out or watch him get hurt. I had to think of something quick. By running out on a hit, Ronnie Rome was digging himself a grave in Boston big enough for him and Joe Nap to both fit in, so I decided to take him to California. He knew too much about the plan to murder Joe Nap, and he owed the Angiulos thousands. A few weeks after Ronnie disappeared with me, Joe Nap was shot in the stomach. I later learned that a friend of ours, Dennis LePore, was the shooter. On orders from who else? Danny Angiulo, who of course had ears in the place and was told what Joe Nap was saying. Thing is, Joe Nap didn't die. Got shot in the stomach and didn't die because the gun jammed after one shot.

"He was the luckiest man in Massachusetts, right? Wrong. He was a loud-mouthed punk who thought he was connected. He didn't rat Dennis LePore out. But it didn't matter. Unfortunately for Joe Nap, Dennis didn't shoot him in the mouth. He kept on talking about who he was and how many friends he had.

"Then one day he disappeared. And that was that. A couple of weeks later he turned up in the trunk of his own car in the Bronx, which is a long way from the North End. His head was cut off. I can only presume he had finally shut the fuck up.

"That was fine with me. He was a rat bastard to begin with, but it all put Ronnie Rome in a helluva spot. Whoever had to do Ronnie's killing for him was likely to be pretty upset. That's why I took him to California. I figured we'd see the sights, drop by the Villa Capri just like in the old days, get a tan, nail a few California broads, and maybe save Ronnie's life."

CHAPTER 4

Patsy was gone by then, but the D'Amore family still ran the Villa Capri. Fiato and Ronnie Rome drove across the country in a Lincoln Towncar and took a small apartment in Hollywood not far from the restaurant.

In short order he renewed his acquaintance with Dean Martin, who was highly intoxicated and had to be reminded that the gray-haired Fiato had been the dark-haired teen-ager who had straightened out the extortion attempt on Betty Martin. The two shared a drink.

"It had been more than 16 years since I had seen Dean Martin," Fiato recalled. "It looked like he had aged forty years. He asked me if I had seen Johnny Rosselli, and I told him that he wasn't around much anymore. It was only a few months after that Johnny wound up in the drum off the Florida coast. I think Dean Martin was just happy to have someone different to talk about old times with. He liked to talk about mob guys, people he knew from the old days and he'd talk about how the new breed wasn't like the old breed. He was really smashed. I told him what I'd been up to and he mentioned different wiseguys' names.

"A few weeks later I saw him at Carmine's restaurant, and that night he was so drunk he passed out in his pasta fagole. I gave the maitre' d a forty-dollar tip and told him to take care of the guy. I mean, he was Dean Martin. How could these people let him sit like that? I made sure he got home in a taxi."

For a short time, life at the Villa Capri was sweet. When Fiato saw Mike Rizzitello come through the door, he was sure it was just like old times. The two men hugged, and Rizzi told Anthony how sorry he was to hear about the death of Johnny Fiato. Rizzi had been in and out of prison twice since they had last seen each other, but he was still big as a bear. And he still had the respect of every Mafia general from New York to Chicago. Most of the years Fiato had spent in Boston, Rizzitello had spent in prison. The mob soldier, who had provided substantial firepower for Joey Gallo during his temporary takeover of the Profaci/Colombo crime family, had big plans for Los Angeles.

Acting under the protection of Gambino crime family underboss Aniello "Mr. Neil" Dellacroce, Rizzitello was out to re-establish the family's foothold in Southern California. There were bookmakers to organize, loansharks and fences to shake down, and Rizzi had his hands full. He also had a crew whose strength ranged from fair to only marginal, and was in the middle of negotiating territory not only with Aladena "Jimmy the Weasel" Fratianno, but with Cleveland transplant Peter John Milano as well.

"When I first got back to Hollywood, it was a nonstop party," Fiato said. "Rizzi was back, but I was more concerned about getting to know Phyllis D'Amore, Rose's daughter, and hanging around the Villa than I was in doing some work. Willie Fopiano moved to Southern California to try to turn pro as a fighter, and Ronnie Rome was caught between a rock and a hard place. He was supposed to open a vending machine business, but he was looking over his shoulder constantly. The word was out on him. It was just a matter of time before someone tried to clip him or bust him up and take over his action for the Angiulos.

"With Fopiano, the toughest part was reminding him what weight class he was supposed to be fighting at. I knew some people connected to the fight game, and we had several guys who were willing to sponsor Willie and manage him. He was a smooth talker, and they knew his reputation with his hands, so it was easy for them to figure they had a real contender on their hands. And, to coin a phrase, he could have been a contender.

"They set him up in an apartment, gave him walking around money and started working to line up some fights. But Willie wasn't a boxer; he was a tough guy. The difference is, boxers train and run and work their asses off. Tough guys show up, take off their jackets and try to knock your head off.

"Willie wouldn't train. The guy was a natural middleweight, that's 160 pounds, and he trained his way up to heavyweight. The more he trained, the more he ate. I'd run him in the morning, seven, eight miles a day, watch him like a hawk, go with him to the gym and work out with him. But at the end of a few weeks I was in better shape than he was! The guy kept working out and eating, and he wasn't satisfied with the blue plate special. No, this guy had to have steak. He ate himself out of one or two sponsors, and pretty soon we were at the point we were stealing meat from the supermarket. Keeping this guy fed was like keeping a lion fed. He ate nothing but steak—along with anything else we'd let him get his hands on.

"I took Willie to the Villa Capri, introduced him to "Dago Louie," who wanted to give him money to get a piece of his contract. Louie knew everybody in the local fight racket and could make money with a good-looking white kid who could box a little. Fopiano was taking money from everybody, probably had 200 percent of his contract sold within a few months of hitting town. If he boxed as well as he talked, he'd have been a millionaire.

"But I could spot bullshit when it was served, and Willie's routine started getting a little thick. I finally got tired of him trying to order people around like he was Rocky Marciano, so I cut out. We parted company with a handshake.

"It wasn't long after that I heard that Willie had been shot in the face at point-blank range by a junkie named Guy De Prizio. He was shot right on Prince Street near Hanover. And Willie didn't die. I knew the guy could take a punch, but this De Prizio used a .38. It took a while, but in July 1976 De Prizio's corpse was found floating in Boston Harbor. Some people had beaten him to death, and I was surprised to find out who was behind it."

"I started working at the Villa Capri and was the manager for a while," Fiato said. "Patsy's son, Joey, ran the place, and I loved being there."

At the Villa, Fiato used his contacts to fill the piano bar and sharpen the profile of the once-hot restaurant. He arranged for a little-known singer, Adele Blue, to headline and used his contacts to fill the place with celebrities. Blue was the girlfriend of an up-and-coming comedian, Jay Leno. For her opening night, Freddy Prinz, Bill Dana, Louie Nye and astronaut Scott Carpenter were in the audience.

"Those were interesting days," Fiato said. "Bill Dana helped bring in other comedians. I'd met him at the Playboy Club in Boston, and he never forgot me. Unlike Bert Convy, who I helped out of a jackpot in Boston and later turned his back on me when Ronnie Rome and I came out to Los Angeles. I was working at the Villa one night when who should come in but Bert Convy. I spot him and I start to steam. I walked up to him and asked to speak to him. We went into the men's room and I exploded. 'You fucking scumbag. You weren't ducking guys like us when you needed help.' He was scared to death. I told him I needed to borrow five-thousand, and damned if he didn't deliver it. I told him I'd pay him back when my hunchback aunt straightens out.

"I actually thought for a while that I'd found a home at the Villa Capri. I fell in love with Rose's daughter, Phyllis, and started managing and working at the restaurant. In my mind, I really had a good thing going. It was probably the closest thing to a straight life I'd had since I was a kid, and I was getting used to it. But I guess it was too good to be true.

"It wasn't long before the LAPD figured out who was managing the joint. They started putting heat on Rose and Joey, asking them what kind of place they were running letting guys like me on the payroll. Pretty soon the whole thing blew up. It was about as close to a normal life as I'd had in years, and it lasted a couple months."

When Rose D'Amore informed Fiato that he could no longer work at the Villa, he reacted by tipping over a table and storming out of the restaurant. He knew his days with Phyllis were numbered, too. As a gesture of his friendship, Joey D'Amore gave Fiato $1,000 in $1 stock in a company called Weeks, which had advanced drill bit technology. Fiato sold the stock soon after receiving it and years later found that the shares soon rose to $30 each.

"By then I knew where my life was headed," Anthony Fiato said. "I was working with Rizzitello."

About two weeks after his return Fiato introduced Rizzitello to Ronnie Rome.

"I explained what was happening to Ronnie, said he had been asked to do a thing he couldn't do and now was in danger. Remember, this is a guy who came to my father's wake, gave my mother an envelope. These fucking guys in Boston just wanted to use him, you know how it is. I know Mike is the guy anyone inquiring about Ronnie is going to contact, and I don't want there to be any confusion. In these matters, confusion can get you killed.

"Mike said to Ronnie, 'Anybody looking for you, as far as I'm concerned I haven't seen you.' And finishes the conversation with Ronnie. Then he gets up and starts to leave, says to me away from Ronnie, 'Call me tomorrow without this guy.' It was obvious to me that the business with Ronnie Rome wasn't news to Mike.

"The next day, I met him and he says, 'If you want to do anything here with me, you're going to have to straighten this thing out. The only way to do that is to go back and straighten it out. They like you and that might play for the other kid. You know I'll never give you up to any of these guys, but business is business.' And that day I decided I'd fly back, arrange a meeting and straighten it out. I told Ronnie where I was going, that I had to square it away if I was going to do anything in California with

Mike. In reality, I was going back to ask the Angiulos to spare his life.

"When I got back to the North End, I was too anxious to enjoy myself. I made a few quick contacts, talked to Nicky and set up a meeting with Danny Angiulo. I was nervous as hell, but I couldn't let it show or it would ruin the whole thing. At the same time, if Danny decided to take it out on me, I'd be in more hot water than I could handle. I'd disappear the way Joe Nap did and that would be that.

"I met Angiulo in the cellar of a house. He's got his guys all over the place, and I get to the point. 'I know Ronnie's got a problem, but he's a good kid,' I said. 'He made a mistake. He's sorry as hell, but he's embarrassed and doesn't feel like a man around you guys.'

"'And you do, is that it?' Angiulo said.

"'I was born a man. I'll die a man, Danny. If I can't be destined to be like you, then I'm as good as dead anyway. This kid, he came to my father's wake, gave my mother an envelope. He was a friend, and I'm trying to help him out.'

"'Kid,' Angiulo said, 'it took a lot of balls to come here. If this friend of yours put me in that position, I know what I'd do to him, but you're welcome to stay here.'

"Yeah, like I was going to hang around and bullshit with guys who were an inch from changing their minds and killing me as a lesson to Ronnie Rome. I took the next plane back to Los Angeles.

"It wasn't until I got back to Southern California that I realized what had actually happened. Mike Rizzitello had saved my life. What I didn't know, and he couldn't tell me, is that he'd already been given a call about Ronnie Rome. He knew the wheels were in motion. Mike also knew I might not be needing my return ticket from Boston, so he made a call to Frankie Scibelli, the man nicknamed "Frankie Skyball," and explained the problem. "Frankie Skyball" is with the Genovese family, and Joe Nap wound up in their territory and brought them a lot of heat.

"Skyball" called Larry Baioni and Joe Russo, who reached the Angiulos and explained the story.

"When I saw Mike again, he came up to me like a big, laughing bear and hugged me and kissed me on the cheeks. He said, 'Kid you gotta lotta balls. You didn't know I made any phone call. You realize how close to dead you were? You're a hardhead, I'll tell you that. I hope this pal of yours is worth it. But let me tell you something: before we're through we're going to do a lot of things in this town. And before we're done we might just own the whole damn place.'"

Over the next few weeks, Fiato and Rizzitello were seldom out of each other's sight. They travelled to Las Vegas together, met on several occasions with that city's street boss, Anthony Spilotro. At Spilotro's side was his constant companion, Herbert "Fat Herbie" Blitzstein. Talk ranged from the odd doings in Los Angeles to the rumors circulating about Frank Bompensiero, Jimmy Fratianno and LA Family acting boss Louie Tom Dragna. Snitch rumors. It was dangerous talk, and Fiato listened closely but refrained from adding to the conversation.

Rizzitello's world was complex. He had been a player in the world of organized crime most of his adult life. He had fought in the Gallo war in New York, had done time off and on since the 1960s. For all his love of tradition, he wasn't much interested in carrying on in the Dragna family and had no patience for the soft hands of the Peter John Milano crew. Rizzitello dreamed of bigger things, of a family of his own just as Joey Gallo had years earlier, and he planned to take Anthony Fiato with him. And Rizzi had the credentials to do the job. He was known in every social club on Manhattan's Mulberry Street and had the respect of bosses from New England to Chicago, Cleveland to Kansas City.

In the mid 1970s, California's traditional mob families were undergoing a dramatic transition. As the ranking underboss acting on behalf of an aging and incarcerated Dominic Brooklier, Jimmy Fratianno ran LA's street operations and worked closely with Rizzitello, who had long since distinguished himself as a capable killer in the Gallo insurrection and had designs on Southern California's lucrative rackets.

Fratianno and Rizzitello were traditionalists, men who had risen in organized crime through violence. As such, both had spent portions of their adult lives in prison. Neither had much respect for the acting boss of the family, Louis Tom Dragna, whose business interests were in part legitimate. Dragna owned the Roberta clothing company in LA's garment district.

Although they would have strong disagreements, Rizzitello and Fiato were fated to work together one day independently of Southern California's sleepy Mafia clans.

One night while Fiato was sitting at the bar at the Villa Capri, Rizzi came through the door in a rush. He needed a place to meet, and Fiato set him up away from the main section of the restaurant in the Jimmy Durante Room, where publicity-shy movie stars often met for dinner. But Rizzitello wasn't there for the pasta. He had important business.

"When Rizzi told me who was coming in, I knew something was up," Fiato said. "A few minutes after we met, in comes Jimmy Fratianno. After him there was Louis Tom Dragna and then Happy Meltzer. There's a ton of fucking heat on them, so I placed them in the back. Little did I know at the time I was pissing off some FBI agents who were positioned to take in their meeting. One of them turned out to be Mike Wacks, a guy I'd one day know well. Of course, I didn't spot him that night."

Fratianno and Rizzitello had worked overtime to force the region's bookmakers to pay tribute to the family. They also extorted pornography distributorships from West Hollywood to the San Fernando Valley. The strong-arming of an upstart porno operation called Forex led to the fracturing of the Los Angeles Family.

It also nearly landed Anthony Fiato in prison.

Acting on a tip from Family consigliere Frank Bompensiero, Fratianno instructed Rizzitello to send part of his crew to the offices of Forex, where two unknown brothers were rumored to be making a killing distributing pornography. Forex was actually a sting operation set up by the local FBI.

Rizzitello sent Jack LoCicero, a stocky soldier with hair dyed as black as India ink and a bowery boy's taste in clothes. LoCicero was the sort of man who, no matter what time of day it was, looked as if he had slept in his clothes. With LoCicero was Dominic "The Pig" Raffone, another portly wiseguy who was looking to make a name for himself with Rizzi. Fiato joined Rizzitello at Page's Coffee Shop in the San Fernando Valley. The normally taciturn Rizzi was in an especially upbeat mood, and over coffee Fiato learned why: Thanks to Fratianno, Rizzi was now a made member of La Cosa Nostra.

"I remember he was wearing a pair of tennis shorts and a tennis shirt like he'd just come in off the court," Fiato said. "It was early in the morning and he was going to play tennis. He didn't tell me all the circumstances; I later learned that the heat was all over them and Rizzi got made in the back seat of a car. Fratianno was there along with Bompensiero and Louie Dragna. He tells me they're going to bring the whole family together, really strengthen it, and I'm psyched up about it.

"Then he says, 'I'm a capo and I'm bringing you into this thing. Nobody will be higher with me than you. But, remember, it's for good. There's no getting out. You come in alive and the only way out is dead. I want you to take a couple, three days to think it over.' But I told him I didn't need time to think about it. After all, it's what I've wanted to hear most of my life. It's what I've been waiting for. When the time was right, I'd be made into the family

"Rizzi said he's already talked to people and they liked my attitude, the way I conducted myself. He says, 'We're going to do this the right way, a way it's never been done out here.' He's as happy as can be. Before he leaves for his tennis match, we arrange to meet again and talk the next morning. He tells me to wear a suit. The rest of the day I'm on a cloud. I figure I'm on my way. You know, this is something you work for and strive for. It's like getting called up to the Big Leagues, getting made. I've got visions of grandeur running through my head. I'm like a kid at Christmas.

"The next morning I'm up early, a little anxious. I put on my best suit and I'm looking sharp if I do say so myself. I've got a pocket watch and a pair of $200 Italian shoes. I'm ready to take on the town.

"We meet at Dupar's Restaurant in Studio City at 10:30 for coffee. It's a business meeting and I'm all business. When I get there, Rizzi is there with Jack LoCicero. Rizzi doesn't look me straight in the eyes and he's got a lot more authority in his voice in front of Jack. I was this cocky guy, ready to take whatever they dished out. Rizzi was acting like a boss, and I had to get used to it. He was no longer just the guy who came over our house for Sunday dinner, bartended with my dad, or who watched me grow up. He was boss of the crew and he was showing that he was bigger than I was.

"He laid it out: We were going to shake down two pornographers, put ourselves on their payroll. Rizzi had checked and they weren't with Terry Zappi's people in the Gambino crew, the people who were with Robert "DeBe" DeBernardo and associated with Dellacroce, John Gotti, Natale Richichi and the like. They weren't connected, and that meant they were going to be with us. They were supposed to be selling pornos through Mexico with an office here. Jack LoCicero was with Rizzi and with Nick Licata, who had taken over the family after Jack Dragna died. I'd seen Nick Licata plenty of times at the Villa Capri with "Dago Louie."

"When I get a look at this Jack LoCicero, I almost fell down. He was an old man. Here is one shabby fucking gangster, let me tell you. I felt like loaning him a few bucks for a cup of coffee and a meal, I swear to God. It was like he was wearing a Superman toupee or something. And he spoke with a broken accent like a guy just off the boat. He was with Dominic "The Pig," Raffone and let met tell you something, they didn't call him "The Pig" because he ate a lot of pork. He stunk the fucking car up he smelled so bad. And LoCicero had a pacemaker that would set off alarms all over town. I looked at Mike as if to say, 'You gotta be kidding me,' but he wasn't joking. Well, I couldn't help it. I busted out laughing. 'Hey, this thing of ours don't pay as well as I thought,' I said, and at first they didn't understand what I was saying. LoCicero says, 'Mike tolla me lotta 'bout you.' But already I could tell good help was hard to find.

"Mike says to me, 'I don't want you to do anything but walk up a flight of stairs to that office. Tell them you want 50 percent of their business if they want to stay in business in this town.' He waits behind. We drive over and park the car. On the way I notice we're being followed. The tail was easy to spot. When we get to this two-story office that looks like it used to be a motel, there's nobody around. So we wait and wait.

"All the while, half-a-block away there's a buzz of activity. It's the cops and probably the FBI with a long lens taking pictures of us. We're supposed to be lamping out the place and instead we're on Candid fucking Camera.

"We go across the street and stand around on display for the menagerie of law enforcement. I'm angry as hell by now and flipping them off. They come by us slow, like a matador teasing the fucking bull. We're waiting and waiting, looking like the Three Stooges, then one of the brothers shows up. I start laughing I'm so angry. I'm in my best clothes and these two motherfuckers are dripping oil. I was ready to kill somebody. Was Mike crazy or what? Putting me with a fucking old greaseball and a fucking gas station attendant.

"When one brother finally shows up, that's enough for me. I tell the other two I'm going to take care of business, and LoCicero says, 'You knowa Mike say no go no place till they're botha together.' And I say, 'Yeah, by then they ought to have those fucking photographs they've been taking blown up to some pretty eight-by-tens.'

"Jack follows me. He doesn't want to look bad in front of Raffone. Raffone follows because he'd follow Jack anywhere. I knock on the door, then open it and walk into this little office. I smash my fists on the desk and say, 'I represent the people who run this fucking town. Who the fuck do you think you are trying to operate without us?' I scare the guy to death. We wait around another ten minutes for his brother to show up, but he never does.

"We delivered the message, and it was clear we weren't going to get any trouble out of these Forex guys. But Jack couldn't let a young kid like me do all the talking. So he starts in with 'You gotta no right ado these kinda tings in thisa town.' I told him, 'Yeah, Jack, he knows already.' I mean, just in case the guy couldn't speak English and only spoke broken English I had Jack there to translate into broken English. Perfect. Oh, this was such a lame move. We're up in this little shitty office scaring this guy to death and outside half the organized crime squad is poised like the papparazzi to take our pictures.

"I'm fuming all the way back to Dupar's, saying what kind of a fucking operation is this? We're standing out like three fucking cartoon characters, and Jack's going on about the protocol and how Mike say this and Mike say that. And I said something I'd regret for many years, 'Fuck Mike. Mike isn't here to see this situation, to see this fucking cartoon.' Well, you can imagine how long it took those two guys to mention that line in passing to Mike Rizzitello."

Word that he had disobeyed the boss's orders traveled fast. Fiato received a call and was told to meet Rizzitello at Rubio's on Ventura Boulevard. So much for Omerta, the Mafia's battered code of silence. Rubio's was a regular hangout for bookmakers and wiseguys, and Rizzitello felt comfortable there.

At the restaurant, Rizzitello waved Fiato over to the back table.

"Why don't you tell me what happened," Rizzitello said.

"How the fuck could you put me in such a fucking situation? The cops were crawling all over the place and I'm supposed to work with two fucking fireplugs who can't get out of their own way? So I got tired of having my picture taken and delivered the message myself."

Suddenly, Rizzitello wasn't avoiding Anthony Fiato's eyes.

"I explained to him that every cop in California was down the street watching us standing like three chumps waiting for a bus.

Jack LoCicero and Dominic Raffone had no imagination. We should have forgot the whole situation and made it for another day. But he didn't like that answer, either."

Rizzitello said, "You always got this habit of doing your own thing, not listening. You're a cocky guy, you know that. You know what I am and what I'm trying to do, and you better have respect for that."

Fiato replied, "Of course I respect you, but those are my honest feelings. I wouldn't have any self-respect if I didn't say how I felt. If you want to get me wrong, that's fine, but you weren't there."

Rizzitello said, "If you want to do your own thing, you go ahead and do it. You just do anything you want to. The rules don't apply to you. You just go your own way."

"Well, I read the whole fucking play. I'm supposed to go along and apologize for my disobedient behavior and all this bullshit. I had spoken my mind. The only thing I was in trouble for is, I told the fucking truth. So I shrugged and wished him well and walked away. Mike and I would always be related, but from then on I became known as an uncontrollable hothead.

"It was obvious the cops were onto them in a big way, but I didn't think much more about it at the time. I was sick of the city and decided to go to Hawaii for a few weeks. When I got there, I began to relax, but after a few days the police let it be known they knew I was in their town. I wasn't doing anything, though, and so I didn't give a fuck. It told me plenty about how close a watch they were keeping on Los Angeles, though. And I decided that when I got back to the mainland I would return to Boston to check in."

Before Anthony Fiato returned to his hometown, he learned why there was so much heat on him, LoCicero and Raffone because of that day outside the nondescript offices of the Forex Corporation. Forex was an FBI sting. A federal grand jury had been convened in the matter, and in November 1976 Fratianno, Rizzitello, Tommy Ricciardi, Jack LoCicero and several lesser players had been subpoenaed.

The LA family was clearly the target of a major federal push, and Fiato smelled a rat. Rizzi never would have set him up, but how did Mike Rizzitello learn about the Forex case? Through Jimmy Fratianno. And Fratianno, Fiato later learned, had first heard about Forex from none other than Frank "The Bomp" Bompensiero, the family's cagy capo. Bomp had designs on setting up a family in San Diego and inserting himself as the boss of the city's rackets with men like Chris Petti assisting him.

In a battle within his own family, Fratianno was headed for the other side as a cooperating witness. With little to tie Fiato to the case and less to connect him to Los Angeles, he built a travelling stake by pulling a series of high-class shoplifting schemes with Blackie Gallo, whom he had met so many years earlier on a street corner. Blackie was still stripping the Garment District in downtown Los Angeles down to its socks, and Fiato assisted him in relieving one men's store of more than $250,000 in merchandise, which Gallo sold for twenty-five percent of retail.

With a bankroll, Fiato returned to Boston and listened as the North End capos whispered about what they were hearing from California. In a society in which secrets are supposed to be kept, Anthony Fiato was learning that almost no one ever kept one. By Christmas, there were strong rumors a ranking member of the LA family was to die violently and soon.

The speculation ended on February 10, 1977, when Frank Bompensiero stepped in a pay phone near his San Diego home and was confronted by a stocky, dark-haired man, who proceeded to fire away at close range. Bompensiero fell but continued to struggle. The bullets kept coming until he no longer moved. The long hand of family boss Dominic Brooklier was being felt from behind bars through his minion, Tommy Ricciardi. Like Fratianno, Brooklier also had traced his knowledge of Forex to Bompensiero's mouth. For his act of violence, Ricciardi would be rewarded with membership in the Los Angeles family. For Bompensiero's treachery in acting as a setup man for the FBI, the penalty was death.

The killing of Bompensiero didn't dissuade a grand jury from returning a RICO indictment against Brooklier, Sam Sciortino, Louie Tom Dragna, Mike Rizzitello, Jack LoCicero and Tommy Ricciardi in what the government called the Pornex case. LoCicero was accused of driving the getaway car for the Bompensiero hit. The press continued to refer to the case by the name of the front company. One of the predicate offenses in the racketeering case: conspiring to murder Frank Bompensiero.

By having his argument and falling out with Mike Rizzitello when he did, and going to Hawaii on a whim, Anthony Fiato saved himself what promised to be a substantial stretch in the penitentiary. But by then, the street guys knew that more than one person was cooperating with the government: Fratianno, who crime experts believed had been directly involved in at least sixteen homicides, had joined the government after learning that he, too, was on a hit list and that his long-time buddy, Mike Rizzitello, was setting him up.

"It put Rizzitello in a whole other light," Fiato said. "I knew the guy was ruthless, but I didn't appreciate how crafty he was. It's something I'll never forget."

Fiato returned to his usual routine on the North End. There were people to meet, restaurants to frequent, bets to make and take. At night, there was the Coliseum or one of the other after-hours joints where the people he knew converged.

Hobbling around behind the bar was Pegleg, who looked like Igor and the sailors who wandered in there for a late-night drink.

There was Seven-Up, the village idiot, who believed everything he was told. If Nicky said, "I'm sweating my ass off in this place. Somebody turn down the heat," it could be fifty degrees and Seven-Up would break out in a sweat and start repeating what he'd heard. He loved Nicky, who looked like Dracula or Gomez from "The Addams Family" and was unmerciful to Seven-Up, and everybody else.

The neighborhood teemed with oddball characters. Among the dimmest bulbs was Mikey B., whose reading comprehension skills left something to be desired. While reading the *Boston Herald* one morning, Mikey announced to Fiato, "Did you read this about the millionaire who went nuts and killed 67 people?"

No, Fiato hadn't. But obviously neither had Mikey. The headline read, "Typhoon Kills 67."

And there was Joey D., a burglar whose lengthy arrest record belied his best efforts. He once cased a furniture store six straight days in order to be certain when it closed for the night, and on the seventh day he broke in through the ceiling. It was a Saturday.

As he crashed through an air vent in the ceiling and dropped down into the showroom, Joey learned the hard way that the store remained open late on Saturday.

But the Mafia was changing, and so were its rules. Despite the mob's prohibition on narcotics dealing, half the street guys he met were involved with either marijuana or cocaine. Most weren't selling it in deference to the rule and the threat of being murdered for breaking it. But others were trafficking and getting away with it. The scene ran against everything Anthony Fiato was raised to believe. And yet he couldn't discuss it with Nicky Giso or Joe Russo without ratting out his associates.

Fiato retained little of his idealized image of life in the Mafia. With guys like Jimmy Fratianno and "Fat Vinny" Teresa turning snitch, omerta, the code of silence, was a bad joke. Nor was messing with dope getting anyone killed. It was, in fact, earning Giso and his friends plenty of money through payments of tribute.

Fiato beat up a hundred dope dealers in his life. He couldn't bring himself to sell cocaine in bars, or pot on street corners. But he wasn't about to let all that money end up in other pockets. So he structured a compromise he could live with: He'd rip off cocaine from dealers and transfer it at a tidy profit to sources outside the city. He had the muscle to accomplish the task; a neighborhood guy named Sonny Polosi, who had brokered the platinum and precious metals robbery a few years earlier, had a contact in Las Vegas, former North End resident Jerry Matricia, who could use all the cocaine they could send him. And so they started filling Matricia's requests.

Matricia had outlets at bars throughout Las Vegas, where he was known as Jerry Boston. In Las Vegas, Anthony Spilotro was in the process of organizing traditional street racket activities on behalf of the Chicago Outfit, and his crew of burglars, thugs, bookmakers and killers was tearing up the town. They had already drawn the attention of local police and the FBI, which was investigating Spilotro and the Chicago's association with Allen Glick's Stardust, Fremont and Hacienda casinos. As the head of Argent Corp., Glick, a San Diego real estate developer with no background in the gaming industry, had obtained more than $100 million in Teamsters Central States Pension Fund loans to purchase the casinos. Glick's portfolio was clean enough to pass Nevada's Gaming Control Board scrutiny, but law enforcement was cynical about his relationship with Stardust entertainment director Frank Rosenthal, a notorious bookmaker and sports fixer who had been affiliated with the Chicago mob most of his life. Rosenthal had his own television show, was a generous political contributor and was regularly spotted at the Las Vegas Country Club mixing with the city's most respected businessmen. He also maintained regular contact with his old pal, Spilotro.

In the late 1970s on the streets of Las Vegas, Spilotro's activities were the focus of heavy law enforcement scrutiny. With help from police department insiders, Spilotro managed to stay several steps ahead of the law. Matricia, on the run from Boston, wisely maintained a respectful acquaintance with Spilotro. If he was going to move cocaine in Las Vegas, he had to stay on friendly terms with "Tough Tony."

In Boston, Fiato and Polosi quickly sidled up to their cocaine contact, a cocky young Irishman who was plenty impressed with his new Mafia friends. Joe Mack fancied himself as a guy capable of muscling his way out of trouble, but it was clear to Fiato that the redheaded punk didn't know what trouble was.

"He was easy," Fiato said. "There was a lot of bravado, but he had soft hands. By that I mean it was obvious he was more talk than action. That was fine with me. The easier the score, the better. Taking him off was a breeze. He had the contact with some

Colombians in Florida. I didn't care how he got them, only that they could supply him with large amounts of material. I didn't like cocaine, was afraid of it and all it meant to what I was all about, but it was like an auction on the street. Everybody was bidding for it and selling it. So Sonny and I convinced Joe that we could move his stuff, big time stuff, and were on the up-and-up.

"We took him in and showed him around. He hung out with the boys, you know? He loved that kind of stuff. Sonny had a coffee shop and we brought Joe around there. We took him around the North End, over to meet 'Ralphie Chiong' Lamattina and over to the Bella Napoli to meet Joe Russo. We never talked about drugs with them; Joe would have had a fit. But we were out to impress Joe on the way to stripping him naked as the day he was born.

"He was really impressed that he met Ralphie Chong. And he opened up to us about his connection. At the time cocaine was going for $60,000 a kilo, but we had tons of connections on the street as Joe could tell.

"We told him we weren't going to up front any money, but we'd move the first kilo so fast it would make his head spin. By then big Bobby Luisi was with us. Like Sonny, he was a guy from the neighborhood who you'd never want to meet in a dark alley. He thrived on violence. So with all the muscle around us, Joe was persuaded into fronting us a kilo of cocaine. He believed I could move it with a phone call.

"Trouble is, I can't sell it the normal way because I'm a wiseguy. A wiseguy who openly goes into the drug business in those years was a dead man. Joe doesn't know that, of course, the stupid mick. 'Now you're with me,' I tell him, and he's ready to walk through walls for me. You see, everyone wants to be a gangster. Once you empower them, touch that place in their ego that wants to be an animal, they're yours. I mean, this Irishman was ready to change his name to Al Capone. I tell him, 'When you're with me, you don't have any enemies,' and that kept him calm. Because, frankly, once this guy's cocaine disappeared and he didn't have the cash to pay his debts, his life wasn't worth much.

"While I worked with Joe, Sonny was working on his Las Vegas contact, Jerry Matricia. Jerry had been run out of the North End for too many gambling debts. We were going to give him all the business he could handle.

"We start moving product to him and, of course, Nicky Giso finds out about it. I explained the setup to Nicky, reminded him that I was kicking into him and he was making money on the deal in a roundabout way, and he grinned. 'Just make sure it don't take place around here. You want to rip off a guy and sell his dope out of town, okay, but you know the rules.' You see, all this talk about dealing dope in the mob always comes with an escape clause—as long as you're kicking money up the ladder."

Once the Matricia connection was established, the transfer was as easy as booking a flight to Las Vegas and coming west for a weekend in the sun. Between Polosi's Brookline and Las Vegas contacts, they moved six kilos in a short order.

"Once we get out to Las Vegas, Matricia introduces me to his contact, a guy named Jerry Costanza, who's cutting the cocaine with novocain and doubling our profits. I didn't like Matricia from the moment I met him. He was a cocaine user who lived in an apartment off the Vegas Strip, but he was my contact to Costanza, the man who really did the work. I ask whether Jerry's related to Nicky Costanza, who I'd met on previous trips to Las Vegas, and he said he was. I told him to have his old man call me, and when Nicky called I had him relay a message to the Little Guy, Spilotro.

"We got together at the Flame, and I introduced Spilotro to Sonny Polosi and explained the deal. I wanted the Little Guy to eat. That way he not only wouldn't give us any trouble, but he'd keep quiet about the fact we were ripping off dealers and reselling their cocaine. 'If things go well,' I told Spilotro, 'you'll be hearing from me again.' For six weeks the shipments went like clockwork. We made some serious money, most of which we gambled and partied away.

"While the system was working, Matricia and Nicky Costanza Jr. talked constantly about how tight they were with Spilotro.

They were real chatterboxes, especially Nicky. The kid was nervous, wired to the gills on cocaine. He talked nonstop and got on my nerves. But the money was so good, I tried to be patient. We soon had enough cash to play on the Strip like high rollers."

"At the Dunes, Johnny George and guys connected to Chicago and Detroit were all over the place. The Aladdin was full of mob guys. Angelo Urgitano was there. He was with the Lucchese crew. They called him the Jet and Cheesecake. The Jet because he moved money across the country by the suitcase for his people. Cheesecake, I guess, because he liked cheesecake. Rizzi had been trying to work a protection deal with Benny Binion, the owner of the Horseshoe, and with Moe Dalitz, who'd built half the joints on the Strip, and was very guarded about sharing information on it. In those days the Jet was out on bail on the Forex beef. But I was in Las Vegas independent of him and had to be careful not to mix this business with his business. It was a good way to get killed.

"In Las Vegas, Matricia steered clear of Spilotro, and he was nervous when he found out that I already knew him. Matricia believed that if his enemies in Boston were going to get him, they would go through Spilotro to get the job done. In those days, Spilotro's name carried serious weight in Las Vegas. He was feared, which is kind of funny, really, because, in our world, he was nothing special. He had this reputation for ruthlessness, had put a guy's head in a vice and twisted it until the eyes popped out, had shotgunned a few people along the way, but to me he was just another guy. A capable man, but nothing like a monster. In the mob, a lot of guys are monsters. I had my own reputation as a doer.

"When we met with Spilotro at the Flame, he was surprised I was being seen with the Costanzas. Obviously, there were some things about this big-mouthed kid, Nicky Constanza, that I didn't know. So I called around and found out he wasn't well thought of because of the dope and, as if I had to guess, his big mouth.

"The Costanzas were a joke to the Ant man, but I knew Tony Spilotro wasn't much for jokes. I decided I wouldn't be seen any more with them. Within a few weeks, I heard people talking about him being seen with some police detectives. And that's how it starts. I knew what was going to happen next and there was nothing I could do about it. Not that I really cared. I had other outlets in Vegas for the dope Joe Mack was bringing in.

"In Las Vegas, we ran into Jack Strauss, the man they called "Treetop" because he was so tall. He was involved in dope and moved money for some people. We were at Jerry Matricia's place and there were always broads around. It was a good time, and with the pipeline working there was plenty of money. When you have access to cocaine, you never had a shortage of girlfriends. Some broads love the stuff.

"Back home, Joe Mack is getting by with what we send him. And I'm thinking everybody's happy. I was gambling like a fool, and these Costanzas are talking like a radio. I know this isn't going to last, but I'm reluctant to quit. I wasn't the greatest gambler in the world and was blowing most of what I earned on the tables. We'd get $2,500 one day and I'd spend it. We'd get $8,000 another day and I'd spend that, too. Blackjack, dice, baccarat. It didn't matter. I liked to play, liked being treated like a king at these joints, and they didn't mind my money. I made sure Spilotro got a regular present. By the end of the trip, we'd blown most of the money. In two weeks I'm sure we threw away $100,000. It didn't matter. With our contacts, we figured we'd always have a way to get more. With a little luck we scraped up about $50,000 to take back home, distribute to Joe Mack and kick up to Nicky Giso.

"Not long after we returned to the North End we heard about Nicky Costanza Jr. Like Joe Nap and a lot of other guys, someone had got tired of hearing him pop off about what a gangster he was. They found him in his car with a couple bullets in the head. Of course, everybody suspected Spilotro of ordering the hit. But it could have been any of a number of other guys.

"Once the Boston supply stopped, Matricia still owed me $30,000. He figured out a helluva way to keep from paying. He told his old North End pal Fat Johnny Cincotti that I was dealing drugs, and Cincotti let the word out, where Ralphie Chiong got hold of it. I was moving the stuff we'd stolen from Joe Mack, and taking care of Nicky in Boston and the Little Guy in Vegas, but that didn't mean I couldn't be killed."

Word that Fiato was sending kilos of cocaine to Las Vegas was bound to circulate the North End. When it did, he heard about it from "Ralphie Chiong," a man whose virtues were few. Lamattina's vocal opposition to narcotics belied the fact he was willing to rob old neighborhood women of their life savings. But as a made guy, Ralphie operated on a higher level than Anthony Fiato, and that meant trouble.

Lamattina dressed as though he had stepped out of a George Raft movie. He wore the most expensive suits, an overcoat and a hat pulled down over one eye. He never smiled and was known as a loyal soldier.

When Ralphie walked into Stella's Restaurant one night and saw the whole room catering to Anthony Fiato, he couldn't stand it. He held his tongue that evening, but a few days later exploded before the crowded room.

"I was at the restaurant with my pal Socks Gravalisi, and Ralph Lamattina comes in," Fiato recalled. "I'd loaned money to half the staff in the place, and I was banging the young bartender's girlfriend. All of a sudden Ralphie starts yelling at me from across the room. Understand, he was a big boss at this time, not just a soldier, but the guy who took over a ton of turf after Joe Burns died. He probably ran half of Boston.

"He's calling me a fucking drug dealer, saying that I'm no good. And you understand, you can't just go up and slap him, and he knows it. He's trying to get me to make a play, because then I'm dead. So I ask him where he got his information, from that fence-jumper Jerry Matricia, who ran away from his neighborhood and the debts he owes his friends.

"Everybody's staring, and I know that I'm on the line with this guy. I go overboard and I'm dead. I admit I have anything to do with drugs—even though my own boss Nicky knows what I'm doing—and I'm dead. Finally Ralphie tells me to meet him the next day at noon on the corner outside the Bella Napoli Restaurant, where Larry Baioni eats and does his business. So I go there, but first I call Paulie and Nicky and tell them what's going on. When I get to the corner, I have a .32 automatic in my pocket and I'm careful as I can be in that situation. The way Ralphie is talking, it sounds like somebody wants me dead, and there's no way I'm going quietly.

"He doesn't show up. Paulie and Nicky send him a message that they are offended that he doesn't eat in their place, where the food is much superior to the Stella brothers, who are mutts and not connected. Nicky knew what I was doing and convinced him and Paulie to go to J.R. Russo to straighten it out and put Ralphie Chiong in his place. J.R. sat down with Ralphie and reminded him of what I had done for the family. He told Ralphie I was no drug dealer and reminded him that it was Jerry Matricia who was the fucking fence-jumper hiding out in Vegas.

"I went back into Stella's a few nights later and Ralphie Chiong was there. I could have killed him I hated him so bad, but instead I sent over a drink. True to his nature, he ordered a bottle of expensive champagne just to rub it in."

"In the mob, it's not the honest thing that counts. It's the smart thing," Anthony Fiato said. "You have to know how to speak in such a way that your lie is acceptable to your superior. Like the prohibition on narcotics. In the old days, most of the guys took that very seriously, but I discovered over time that a lot of the people I knew didn't. They'd never admit it, of course. When he found out we were ripping off coke dealers and selling the stuff in Vegas, Nicky naturally wanted his share. And he said, 'Keep dealing until you get caught.' But we both knew that if I got caught I'd be shot in the head. It's that kind of world."

Once the Joe Mack connection dried up, and the Costanzas were in no shape to cut any more product, Fiato shifted his focus elsewhere. With a little creativity, there was easy money in white-collar crime. Fiato put together a check-kiting scheme that earned him plenty of walking-around money. As with the insurance scam setup, he fronted young guys from the neighborhood and explained the deal: Open a checking account with a small deposit. With a half dozen check-writers, the scam took on the makings of a pyramid scheme. Checks were sent back and forth between accounts. The more checks were written, the more money temporarily made its way into the accounts.

Many of the checks were rejected for insufficient funds, but others made it through. With calls to find the status of their checking account balances, the kiters soon discovered that some accounts had several thousand dollars in them. Once an account showed funds present, the customer rushed down and took out cash. With the help of an insider at two banks, the accounting delays were easy to obtain.

"We wrote checks for as high as $10,000 and the banks would cover them for a short time. We would add up the checks and keep writing them to each others' accounts. Bang, bang, bang. The banks would get wise with one, but they didn't spot the pattern. And we had a little help. Somewhere, those checks would clear in one account. It was like hitting a Vegas jackpot. Nothing, nothing, nothing and then, cash.

"At the time they had a thing called Telecredit, it was like a short-term loan you could get put into your account over the phone. The interest rates were high and the loans were for suckers only. But only if you planned to repay them. We got loans put into our accounts and created enough confusion with the paperwork to keep the banks busy. Before all the accounts were closed we took out $300,000 in cash.

"And not one of the bank executives knew our real identities. My brother Larry was in the middle of all of it. He was a lot younger than me, but he was a smooth-talker. Today, the banks have safeguards for that kind of stuff. Bells and whistles go off left and right. But then, hey, they wanted our business and were only too happy to make a loan that would bury the average square. But we weren't squares. We didn't play by their rules, and we didn't feel bound to repay any money. In fact, most of it was spent shortly after it was collected. We would stay at the Hyatt Regency Hotel. It was a move Nicky would have been proud of: clean, non-violent, profitable. The bill was more than eight thousand after we finished partying. Larry went downstairs and paid by check."

"The Hyatt Regency was the first real score that we made together," Larry Fiato said. "I was proud to put it over on them. We partied and charged everything to our room, then paid with a worthless check. It was a great feeling. I was proud to be with my brother."

CHAPTER 5

Making money illegally was never difficult for Anthony Fiato. Keeping it was his problem. About the time bank examiners and local fraud investigators recognized the problem with their system, Fiato, his brother Larry, and Ralph "Socks" Gravalisi were headed West again. Las Vegas was still too hot for Fiato in the wake of the cocaine trafficking, so they figured Reno was the next best thing. They flew out and checked into the MGM Grand.

"If I go to Vegas, I'm going to have a ton of fucking heat on me," he said. "In Reno, I figure I'm not known. The organized crime squad isn't going to hassle me. My end of the check-kiting scam was about $70,000, and I figured I'd break the bank in Reno. I was wrong, of course. Nobody breaks a casino's bank unless they're skimming off the top. I bet on everything that moved. Baseball, especially. By the time we left that place every employee in the joint knew us. The manager comped our rooms. Of course, he could afford to. It took two weeks to lose most of the money. Larry, Socks and I lived like kings for that time, and Socks got to like the town. When we were running low enough to start thinking about moving on, I decided to take Larry to visit our cousin Mario in Hollywood. Socks decided to stay in Reno, where he became a blackjack dealer and, as far as I know, stopped stealing.

"I was down to $1,700, but that was more than enough to get us to California. We flew to LAX and contacted our cousin

Mario, who had acted in a ton of movies. You might have seen him in some episodes of *The Untouchables* and in *The Young Savages*. Once I got to his house and we started talking about what was going on in our lives, it dawned on me how much times had changed. All the mob guys I knew in Hollywood were either in prison or heading there.

"The old bosses were in jail, and Mike should have been in line for a shot at the head of the family. But he was on the outs with the family because he had been so loyal to Jimmy Fratianno and had gone to bat for Jimmy even after he'd been suspected of being a rat, which he indeed turned out to be. Mike was an outcast and was shunned by Dominic Brooklier. That put Pete Milano in line to assume the role of boss of the family. Milano was a capo who wasn't known as much of a tough guy, but he was handed the mantle to become acting boss of the Los Angeles family. In response, Mike went to New York and got sanctioned by Neil Dellacroce of the Gambino family. While Pete was collecting soldiers and making new members, Mike was doing the same.

"Mike Rizzi and his guys represented Neil Dellacroce and the Gambino crew. Rizzi didn't think much of Pete Milano, but Mike was in no shape to go pulling anything. He was in trouble on the Forex beef that nearly nailed me, and everyone knew he was going back inside. When I met up with him again he was glad to see me and we talked a little about his troubles. He was drinking heavily and not watching what he said too much. It wasn't like him to be loose-lipped, so I knew he knew he was going away. The guy had spent a large part of his life behind bars, and I don't care what anybody says. It can't ever be easy to lose your freedom. I don't care how tough you think you are."

With the Milanos apparently disinterested in doing any real work, and Rizzitello laying low as he prepared to return to the penitentiary, Fiato decided he had returned to Hollywood for good. Through his cousin, he was introduced to a small-time actor and bookmaker Norman Freedberg, whose stage name was Norman Cole. Freedberg was a heavy cocaine user and small-time bookmaker.

"'What happened with Mike and all that stuff you had going?'" Mario asked Fiato. "I told him those guys got arrested and he said, 'You're lucky you got out when you did.' I laid it out to my cousin. He knew what kind of guy I was. I wasn't about to go taking a straight job. Not after I'd had all that money in my life.

"I asked him if he knew of any scores I might go after, and he just laughed. He was a straight arrow. An actor is all he's ever been. But he knew about Norman Cole, who lived out in the Valley, and said he'd give him a call. Coles's real name was Norman Freedberg. At least Norman and I would have one friend in common, Tommy Ricciardi, who died in prison. But Tommy went out a made man and that meant something to him. It meant something to Bomp, too, I'll tell you. The funny thing is, Rizzi and Tommy were good friends, but it was Rizzi who had put a bullet in Tommy and wounded him during the Profaci problems back East. My cousin Mario told me Freedberg wanted to meet me, and it was arranged."

When he first met Freedberg, Fiato was none too impressed. He was a typical paranoid drug user who booked heavy action but gambled almost as much as he booked. On his first trip to Norman's house in the Valley, he met Frank Christi, a Brooklyn-born character actor who shared Freedberg's affinity for sex, drugs and sports betting. Christi was also in love with the mob. Although he had played roles in numerous movies and television shows, he was most fond of his bit appearance in *The Godfather*. For all his tough talk, and a burglary, grand theft, counterfeiting and drug trafficking arrest record as far back as the 1950s, Christi was a TV tough guy with who made a living cracking wise on *Beretta*, *Mannix*, and *The Rockford Files*, and in forgettable movies such as *The Don is Dead* and *Terminal Island*.

Through Freedberg, Fiato also met Las Vegas comedian Joey Villa and his gorgeous wife, Kathy.

"Kathy Villa was a beautiful girl, a striking five-foot-ten blonde," Fiato said. "She drove a canary yellow Mercedes convertible. I first met her at Norman's house when Joey Villa dropped by on a

Sunday. Joey was a nightclub comedian who had come to pick up some tapes. Norman introduces me to them. Frankie Christi was also there. When she walked out the door, Christi said 'What the fuck does that gorgeous broad see in that fat little prick. I can't believe it.' Joey owed Norman money and that's how I got to know Joey. I'd go over to his house to collect, and he'd soft soap me by inviting me to a big pasta dinner. He was a great chef.

"Later, I moved to an apartment in Beverly Hills down the street from Joey's place. he began inviting me over regularly for dinner, and he liked introducing me to his celebrity friends, guys like Mickey Rourke and Jerry Vale. Joey loved to entertain, but I was beginning to fall for Kathy. Norman put me wise to the situation between Joey and Kathy, who weren't getting along. In time, I'd get to know her a lot better.

I wanted to stay away from her because I liked Joey, but my heart won out over my head with Kathy. "Joey went away a lot," Fiato continued. "He entertained on cruise ships and his friends would take Kathy out to dinner in his absense. I took her out a few times too, and after a few dates we started having an affair. We fell in love; she moved out of his place and in with me.

"Kathy was a midwestern girl, born and raised in Lincoln, Nebraska. Her father was an army major in the second World War and an elder in his church. Real square people. I'm sure her father couldn't understand how she ever got involved with me, but at the time I didn't care. Kathy educated me about Beverly Hills society. She started shopping for me, buying the best clothes. I started wearing thousand dollar cashmere sweaters and fifteen hundred dollar sports jackets. She had great taste, and I could afford it." Joey was a jealous man and began bad-mouthing me to some of his connected friends. One of them was Anthony Beratto, who was with the Tony Ducks Corrallo crew out of Harlem.

"Joey complained to Beratto, who sent the word to his capo, Angelo 'Cheesecake' Urgitano, who'd made many trips to Las Vegas and Los Angeles to move money for the family. Angelo was a respected man, whom I'd met before. Problem with Joey Villa was, he was in way over his head. Angelo flew out to meet with me to make sure I wasn't offended by this Beratto. Cheesecake was showing me respect, and I knew he was concerned for his man. He didn't want any confusion to lead to the disappearance of anyone in his crew. I kept seeing Kathy, and we eventually got married. Anthony Beratto came to the wedding."

Norman Freedberg's love life was substantially less successful. He was, in fact, having trouble holding onto his girlfriend, a blonde as big as a power forward who should have been just his type.

"I met Norman at the Hamburger Hamlet and we drove out to the Valley," Fiato recalled. "I knew from my cousin that he was a friend of Tommy Ricciardi, who had died in prison. I knew Tommy had pulled the trigger on Bompensiero. It's a small world. Norman was friendly as hell, said he'd wanted to meet me, that he heard about me through Tommy.

"He drove like a sonofabitch, crazy as hell, and it dawned on me that half the people I knew were on junk of one kind or another. This Jewish guy loved talking to Italians like me. He said he could use my help on some matters, that he would get me an apartment and take care of me because of who I was friends with.

"It was easy to like Norman. His door was always open, and you never knew who you'd meet there. The women, all good-looking, streamed through his place day and night looking for cocaine, and it was about as easy to score with them as falling off a log. Having a different girl every night was no big deal. I'd like to think it was my animal magnetism, but I know it was the power of those goddamn drugs. Norman told me he had stashed the .22 pistol that had whacked Frankie Bompensiero, and that he had handed the gun to Rizzitello.

"The first time I'd seen the gun was when Rizzi gave it to me to hold for him. 'If you get caught with this gun, you might as well turn it on yourself. It's killed so many guys, there aren't enough life sentences in a hundred courts to take care of them all.' I brought that gun back to my apartment and I was testing it out. I shot it into the telephone book. When my brother got popped on a small beef, I took the gun out of my place and took it over to Norman's. Two days later, Jack Motto and his boys in L.A.P.D. Administrative Vice raided my place looking for bookmaking information. If they'd found that gun, I'd have gone away for a million years.

"When I handed the gun to Norman, he told me that it was the pistol Tommy Ricciardi had given him, the one that killed Bomp. Norman had the arsenal for most of the LA mob stored at his house and a few other places."

Norman's house in Panorama City was a weed-infested two-bedroom place with a swimming pool in the back. Two mangy dogs roamed the yard and yapped at the steady stream of visitors who came there to score everything from dope to the latest football line.

"He called it low key," Fiato said. "I called it low rent."

Fiato began working out there, hitting a heavy bag he had set up and attempting to stay in physical condition. More than a place to hole up, Norman's house was a supermarket and loan office whose customers dropped in at all hours. He accepted collateral and traded out with his patrons, which is how he wound up in possession of a diamond.

In an effort to have the gem appraised, Norman took Fiato with him to a San Fernando Valley pawnshop run by Steve Diamond, who turned out to be the son of Harry Diamond—the same Harry Diamond who had saved a brash young Fiato from a robbery conviction. Once Fiato made the connection, Steve Diamond called his silent partner, Big Al Martel, out from the back room.

Big Al was a beefy, gregarious fellow who reminded Fiato of John Belushi. He wore blue jeans, pinky rings and enough gold around his neck to bring down a Clydesdale. His hair was black and slicked back. He was partial to cigars, expensive women and vast quantities of cocaine.

"He looked like a guy you'd call Big Al," Fiato said. "He was from New York. We had contacts in common, and he gravitated toward me immediately. I liked him, too, and not just because he gave me jewelry as gifts. I mean, I'd see him at a place, we'd sit down and have a few drinks and the next thing you know he's reaching into the brief case he carried like a businessman and pulling out a chain or a ring or something, a token of his esteem.

"Al was different from most of the guys in the crew. Where the big muscle guys were ready for anything and were willing to follow orders, they were absolutely devoid of an original thought. They were there to do the work I assigned them. They'd never come up with a score on their own. That's where Big Al Martel was different. He lived different than most other people, and he robbed different. He lived with a doctor in a mansion in Hidden Hills and threw parties a few times a week. He trafficked in cocaine, a lot of it, and had the contacts Norman lacked. He moved gold and diamonds, and stole, stole, stole. I don't know when he slept.

"A typical night out with Big Al went like this. He'd show up at Le Hot Club on Ventura Boulevard, around nine o'clock, with Hy and Joe, a couple of Israeli guys as big as trees. They partied constantly, Hy and Joe did. First he'd meet with a few people, trying to put together some money. Long before midnight, he was surrounded by people. Big Israelis, all the girls, real estate people, business owners. They swarmed him like he really was John Belushi. All the while he's tipping the waitresses, buying drinks and shoving half of Colombia under peoples' noses. I see Al and think of Joe Russo, Nicky Giso and Larry Baioni and what they would think of wiseguys acting like this. The dope alone would scare them to death. Big Al would be a dead man inside of ten minutes on the North End. But out in Hollywood, his style played well with everybody. Then it's off to the doctor's mansion, where the girls start stripping and hanging around the pool and more people show up. I'm telling you Al was like this every night. The mansion had ten bedrooms and I'd find my way to one with some broad. I'm in there fucking her brains out and who comes in but Big Al, the life of the party, just to watch and laugh at us. He's wired as hell, and I'm beginning to think he's a complete nutcase.

"The next morning, I'm at my house drinking a cup of coffee when the phone rings. It's Big Al. He needs some help with something. I remind him what fucking time it is, and he says he knows but it will be worth my while. He comes by and picks me up at my apartment and says, 'Let's take a ride.' I'm thinking we're going to go out for a few minutes, and I can't fault the guy, he so damn friendly. He drives over toward Beverly Hills. I know this sounds funny, but I thought he was still in the jewelry and drug business. By the time I ask him, 'Where are we going?' I've noticed that he's packed a shotgun and pistol in the backseat. I figure we're not going shopping on Rodeo Drive, but I figured wrong.

"When I tell him just that, he laughs. 'We are going shopping,' he said and in a couple minutes we're cruising slow in his Mercedes on Rodeo. He stops at a light. It's broad daylight and there are people around him. He eyes a tall woman, a real beauty, walking with her son down the street. And he gets out of the car, runs up to her, and from where I'm sitting it looks like they're having a conversation. Then he grabs her arm, struggles with her and returns to the car. She's screaming as he plops down in the seat next to me, panting like hell, and drives off. He's going 80 and swerving all over the road and I slap him across the face. 'What the fuck was that all about?' I asked him. I mean, I thought he saw a girlfriend or something and got in an argument with her."

Big Al laughed off the slap in the face.

"See," he said, revealing the diamond encrusted ring he had stolen from the woman. "You just made yourself fifteen grand."

Fiato slapped him again, this time harder and the car nearly went off the road.

"I just made seven grand and I could have gone away for fifty fucking years," he said. Then he took the ring.

As if on cue, the finale of "Casablanca" entered Fiato's mind.

"You know, Al, this could be the beginning of a beautiful friendship," Fiato said, laughing. He never apologized for the slap in the face.

Al Martel's original name was Arnie Seltzer. He had committed dozens of armed robberies of the wealthy in the Beverly Hills area and would continue his rampage.

"Al had a great eye for diamonds. He didn't need a magnifying glass, either. He could spot them fifty feet away and could tell by who was wearing it whether the stones were going to be any good. And he spent weeks scoping out his victims. He'd sit in the parking lot of a supermarket in Beverly Hills that sold health food and that sort of stuff and wait for the Rolls-Royces and top-end Mercedes to show up. His method of operation was simple, but effective. If the drivers were female and older, he'd follow them into the store, sidle up to them in an aisle and check out their hands. You'd be amazed how many of these old broads used to wear a fortune on their fingers, and Al was there shopping for their diamonds while they were shopping for their groceries.

"Once he found his mark of the day, he'd leave the store, follow her as she got in her car and tail her all the way home. It was that simple. When she exited her car with her groceries, he would come up behind her, grab her by the arm and start yanking. It was a terrible thing to do to people, but he did it a couple times a week. The result was impressive. Big Al had enough money to play the Big Man at the Hot Club, buy all the coke and women anyone could ever want, and make his way into the most influential circles in Hollywood. This guy was a regular at the Playboy mansion, knew half the actors in Hollywood. They liked him for his sense of humor, I'm sure, but they were more attracted to his cocaine supply. Those fucking actors, directors, producers and the like were always scoring dope. It was a never-ending thing with them.

"A couple weeks after that experience on Rodeo Drive, I get a call from Big Al early in the morning. He says he's got a score and wants me to be a part of it. I know from experience to ask him if it's a drive-by thing and whether I'm going to have to slap him again. He just laughs. The layout is simple enough. An older woman living in Encino waits every morning for her husband to go to work, then goes shopping. Like clockwork. She goes to

Gelson's, a gourmet food store, and shops for nothing in particular, then comes back home. We arrive early enough and watch the husband take off.

"Now I can see why this guy's living like a king. He's always robbing somebody. He's got duplicate plates and a car he only uses on scores. We catch a break in traffic and in a short time we're practically right outside her door, we make the approach. The woman is wearing a diamond the size of a doorknob on her finger. It might have been the biggest ring I'd ever seen. And she's not giving it up. Big Al, who outweighs her by a couple hundred pounds, is struggling with her and losing. He pulls out a pair of snips to cut the band of the ring and winds up clipping most of her finger off, too.

"I'm out of the car, pull out my two-shot Derringer, and press it to her head. She's bleeding all over and finally stops struggling. I'd never robbed a woman before in my life and didn't like the feel of it, but when we get that ring my conscience, such as it is, fades quickly. In two minutes we're on the outskirts of Encino.

"You can do this forever," Big Al says. "Your end for this stone is fifteen grand."

"Not bad for a morning's work," Fiato said.

In the weeks to come, they scored more than $1 million in stolen jewels and sold the stones for a healthy profit to jewelers throughout Southern California. Their finest gem was one three-and-a-half carat emerald-cut diamond worth $120,000. It was flawless.

Larry Fiato's luck with Big Al was not as good.

"I went with Big Al to Pacific Palisades," Larry said. "He was doing me a favor. He said, 'You drive and I'll give you a piece.' We took the Cadillac. We go to the market, and he finds a lady, follows her from the market to her house. He goes in for a couple minutes, comes out with a ring and we drive away normally. We head to Sunset Boulevard. Just then a police cruiser sees us going the other way and locks up his brakes. And the chase is on."

Within minutes, a dozen black-and-whites and a police heli-
copter pursued the Cadillac driven by Larry.

"I drove over islands like a maniac through traffic. Two cop
cars cracked up, just like in the movies, and I couldn't believe how
calm I was. Big Al was sweating like mad and staring at me. It
was like I was taking a Sunday drive in the country or something.
I just wasn't nervous. It was ridiculous. Definitely an out-of-body
experience. We went down the middle of the street, jumped a
huge island on San Vincente Boulevard. It was a TV chase, no
doubt about it. But then a kid got in the way.

"I didn't want to hit the kid, so I swerved and crashed into a
tree. I wasn't going anywhere, but Big Al opens the door and off
he goes. I stayed by the car. The cops caught up with Big Al in
about a minute and he'd shit his pants."

Larry Fiato pleaded guilty to a reduced charge and received six
months in the county jail. Big Al was bailed out by Norman
Freedberg and disappeared into the street before the authorities
learned his true identity, and that he had pulled more than 80 robberies. Larry was back on the street in four months. By then,
much had changed.

"When I went to jail on the armed robbery beef my brother
was still hanging with Norman," Larry said. "When I came out of
jail four months later, he was almost on top and working with
Puggy Zeichick. It happened just that quickly. I mean, he was in
Beverly Hills. He was moving a ton of money on the street. He
had guys who hung on his every word. He was really going
places. And I figured I'd go with him, just like in the old days at
the store on the North End.

"As it all progressed, I found I could do anything I wanted.
Nobody would say shit to me. I could take drugs off drug dealers,
start booking sports, grab a couple guys and go on a collection. It
was easy because I had my brother behind me, and he meant business. It wasn't like Pete Milano and Mike Rizzi. Everyone knows
everyone in L.A. is a stool pigeon. We'd beat the shit out of people and didn't care, and that got everyone's attention."

Anthony Fiato: "After hanging out with Big Al for a month, I got to know him pretty well. It was then he felt comfortable admitting to me that he had borrowed some money from a guy named Joe Santone, who was with Pete Milano.

"Joe hung out at Danny's Apple. He knew the Dragnas from the old days. Big Al figures he's got to pay this guy, but Big Al's got big overhead. His lifestyle was not conducive to savings plans. He said he owed ten-and-a-half large ones at two-and-a-half points. So I told him, 'Duke me into this guy and I'll tell him I need to borrow some fucking money.' So Big Al arranges it.

"When we get to the restaurant a few days later, Big Al points out Joe Santone and we head over and sit down at the table. Once we get there, I have Big Al excuse himself."

Joe Santone knew something was up.

"What the fuck is this?" he asked. "You think I was born yesterday? You think I'm a fucking sucker?"

Fiato reached across the table and slapped the loanshark.

"Who the fuck told you that you could shylock money in this town? You take a dime and call whoever you want to call and that won't change a thing. Al isn't gonna pay you the time of day. What he owes you is even. And if I hear again that you're shylocking in my town without taking care of business, you don't know what I'm going to do. Now go wherever the fuck you want to go."

When Big Al returned to the table, Santone looked as if he had aged twenty years.

"When I slapped him, I scared him, and he realized he was living on false dreams and a false reputation. He knew too that nobody in his life was going to help him. Sure, he was connected to people, but I didn't give a fuck. As I walked out, he must have had a smile on his face because he was determined to get the last laugh.

"After relieving Big Al of his obligation with Joe Santone, Al tells me about a kid named Lonnie whose family owns the Tiffany Club in Encino. It's a nightclub and lounge, a real nice place. He tells me how Lonnie's brother muscled his way into owning half the place and then got in deep with a gangster named Eddie. Eddie took over the restaurant and was ripping off the club every night.

"Well, I checked it out and it was a nice operation. And I checked out Eddie the Gangster and, guess what? Eddie the Gangster wasn't much of a gangster. I made a couple calls, had Norman retrieve my two-shot derringer. I take my brother and Norman and Big Al to the club and it was going to be High Noon for Eddie the Gangster.

"Norman is nervous and he's even packing a gun, which is sort of scary considering he might shoot the wrong person. We get to the door and a bruiser security guard greets us. We tell him we're friends of Lonnie's, but the guy doesn't know us. I reach inside my shirt and pull out the derringer and stick it in his face. I cock the hammer, tell him I'll blow his fucking brains out. Then Big Al takes out a pistol and sticks it under his chin. We get inside all right.

"Now Big Al's got all the courage in the fucking world. The security guard makes a move and Larry is holding him while we disarm him. Then we send for Lonnie, who comes through the door yelling, 'Don't kill him. Don't kill him.' I said to the security guard, 'We're on the same team, you fucking moron,' and that settled him down. Big Al pulls Lonnie aside and tells him to give the security guard $500 for his trouble. The guard was pretty messed up and wanted to call the police, but the cash cooled him down.

"We wait and in a little while who comes bopping into the place but Eddie the Gangster. Well, we get hold of Eddie and give him the beating of his life.

"He was kicked to pieces. I said to him, 'If you don't get out and stay out of this fucking restaurant, you're going to get whacked. If you think I'm messing around, say a fucking word.' He was quiet as a mouse. Of course, his mouth was bleeding and he'd lost a few teeth, so maybe that had something to do with it. Either way, that was the end of Eddie the Gangster."

Larry Fiato said, "At the Tiffany Club that night, we literally threw the other brother out. The nightclub was jammed. I punched him out of the club. All of a sudden, everyone wanted to know who these cowboys were. Everyone knew what we did. The Milanos knew. And Mike Rizzi knew, too. Rizzi had a bad reputation, but he was just about ready to go back to jail on the Forex beef. He wasn't going to do anything that was going to get him more trouble, and that left an opening for my brother and his crew. We'd punch out guys in card clubs, terrorize bookmakers, thump tardy loanshark customers. And every day more money would pour in. Puggy Zeichick was the money man, and my brother was the muscle, but my brother's greatest strength was his ability to read people. Once the money flowed in, they looked for legitimate businesses to buy."

At the Tiffany, the accounting was simple: The Fiatos received 50 percent of the club for throwing the bum out. Lonnie could run it the way he always wanted to run it. And Anthony Fiato's burgeoning crew had a new place to hang out.

"I brought in Mikey Sands to hang around the door. He knew every mob guy in the city and half the guys in New York," Anthony Fiato said. "Mike was a friend of Big Al's dad, Seymour. Ours was a small world. Mike had a cauliflower ear and a mashed nose and looked a boxer, which he was in his youth. He was about 55 years old, but I wouldn't have wanted to tangle with him. We had a lot of black couples coming into the place, and Mikey had everybody convinced that he was a boxing insider. He'd give out tips on the fights, like Ali vs. Holmes. He told half the guys to bet on Ali and the other half to take Holmes. That way, no matter who won he'd have ingratiated himself to half the crowd. And they knew to show their appreciation with a double sawbuck.

"In no time I got more friends than I can deal with. Everybody is coming over to the club, which has a reputation for a good time and, from the look of the undercover cops who start frequenting the place, a mob joint as well. Which had an interesting effect on some people.

"Two of Big Al's friends, Hy and Joe, started bringing in guys they knew from Israel, as recruits for my army. Hy and Joe were both big, strong Israelis who were willing to go to war in a minute. In no time I had enough muscle to strong-arm half the city. The thing is, they'd work for nothing. All they wanted was a drink and a broad and some place to rob. They turned in their money, and it piled up. They'd treat me like I'm Carlo Gambino. All they're looking for is direction. Their friends would come up to me and say, 'Mr. Anthony, I want to be with you. The Israeli people say that I can make money with you.'"

Hy and Joe weren't a couple of brain surgeons, but they knew how to steal. And they could score swag by the truckload. They terrorized the garment district and got their hands on jewelry as well, which disappeared into Fiato's expanding pipeline as fast as they could deliver it.

"One night I'm in Tracton's with Al, and I'm feeling no pain. Al's in better shape yet. He's taken a girl he knows out to his Mercedes for a little spiritual therapy. I'd been to the dentist that day and had some bridge work done, and he'd given me Percodan for the pain. Well, I'd been taking Percodan and I had a couple drinks at the bar, and that was trouble. The first thing I notice is some guy looking at me and whispering something to his partner, and that's enough to get me going. He's playing the big, tough guy and he don't look so tough to me. I have always been able to feel trouble in my bones and my bones were aching at that moment.

"He walks up, sits down at the bar next to me and starts in with, 'I hear you're a tough guy. You, with all that gray hair, a real tough guy. Well, you don't look so tough to me.' I just shrugged, watching him every second. When I turned my head, I heard him say, 'This is from Joe Santone' and my head rocked. He'd hit me with a sap. I dropped to my knees and other guys started kicking me. I could barely see from the blood, but with a sudden rush of adrenaline I got to my feet and rushed out the door. The three motherfuckers followed me. I ran to the car and Al's in there getting a blow job and I interrupt him. The girl screams and runs off and I yelled to Al, 'Get that fucking shotgun.' Al did what I said and greeted the three guys with the shotgun. 'Hold it on them. If they move, shoot them,' I said. And they were stuck. They couldn't run, or they'd be shot. I got into the trunk and dug out a jack handle and started whipping them. It took about a minute before they were crying like babies, one with a broken leg, another with a shattered shoulder, another with a head worse than mine. Oh, what a great feeling that was. I maimed them and loved every minute of it. I'd burn in hell to do it all over again. 'How do you like it now, motherfuckers?' I told them. Big Al said, 'Those guys would have been better off if I'd shot them.'

"Big Al and I left the parking lot ahead of the cops. He took me to his place to meet the doctor. Took 40 stitches from Big Al's friend the doctor to close the wound. We stopped going into Tracton's for a while after that."

"I met Harvey Rosenthal at Norman's house," Fiato said. "He went by the name Harvey Ross. He knew everybody in the porno business in the Valley, and that's the center of the universe for pornography. Harvey had a cocaine habit, and he dropped by Norman's regularly. Christi was a regular, too, and he and Norman were supposed to be writing a script together, but it never seemed to get anywhere. They were too busy with broads and all the rest of it. I remember Christi had done a part on *Beretta*, the cop show with Robert Blake.

"I was introduced to everybody and before long I had enough information to put Norman on the spot. It was obvious he was using me to impress his friends and customers that he was with people, and his bills would have to be paid. You could see it in his eyes. They glowed and it wasn't just from the drugs.

"How did I become his partner? I just moved in and started giving him orders. In no time my brother Larry and I controlled 60 percent of Norman's action, and he couldn't do anything about it.

"Bootleg videotapes of legit movies were one of Norman's rackets. He sold them by the gross. You have to remember that this was in 1980. There weren't all the video stores like they have today, and tapes were expensive as hell.

"Models and actresses would show up, and he'd sell them diet pills. He'd take football bets. He had quite a cottage industry going for himself. Scott Wells, the actor, would drop by along with all the rest, including a bunch of directors, John Derek and so forth. Not just bit players, but big names, too."

"Harvey Ross was one of Norman's customers. He also was a partner in a major pornography operation linked to Southern California organized crime figure Walter Stevens. Ross's partner was Marty Krause, who also had a partner in Stevens and friends throughout LA's underworld. Ross was Norman's friend, and I was Norman's godfather figure, so naturally Ross came to me for help with this Marty Krause. With Norman paying me to hang around and look tough, it was the least I could do.

"All the while I was targeting this guy; he was perfect for me. He introduced me to dozens of people, and the word got out who I was. And I was collecting for Norman, who loved to think he could sic me on some deadbeat. So Norman introduces me to Harvey, who explains the problem he's having with Marty Krause. The real problem, of course, is Walter Stevens, who is one tough sonofabitch who constantly defied the LA mob, largely because he'd mostly dealt with the soft-bellied Milano family. Stevens wouldn't give in, wouldn't pay off. He fancied himself as a tough guy, but the world is full of tough guys. Harvey Ross is saying his partner is robbing him and has Walter for protection.

Accompanied by his Israeli offensive linemen, Fiato met Ross at a Howard Johnson's. In exchange for $1,500, Ross wanted Fiato to force Krause to cough up $15,000—and stop stealing from the adult video business.

"I tell Harvey Ross not to worry, I'll take care of it. I found Marty Krause standing behind the counter. 'Do you know who I am?' I asked him. 'Do you know why I'm here? I understand you've got a friend in Walter Stevens. Well, you better call him because you're going to need every friend you got.' I reached over the counter and grabbed him by the collar, yanked him over the top. He was shaking something awful. I thought he was going to take a heart attack right there. I said. 'Harvey Ross is with me. You got a problem. You owe him money.' That means you owe me money, and you don't want to owe me money.' I didn't hit him. I didn't need to. I knew what his next move would be: He'd go to Stevens and we'd wind up banging heads, which was all right with me. Stevens beat Norman out of a $6,000 football bet. He lost and wouldn't pay. Krause owed Harvey $15,000 and wouldn't pay. Well, somebody was gonna pay.

Joe and Hy go through his pockets and grab another grand from him. 'Listen to me carefully, you sniveling little fuck. I want you to go to your rabbi. Tell him to come to the Tiffany Club in Encino and ask for Anthony.' So now we wait. We're expecting Walter Stevens to come into the Tiffany Club.

Early one evening, Anthony Fiato got a call from Mike Sands at the Tiffany Club.

"Mike Rizzi's here with five other guys," Sands said. "They're looking for you. I told them you'd be in later."

With his head mostly healed, and his hands bruised from the beating, Fiato got dressed and prepared for a night at the Tiffany.

"Mikey Sands watches the bar and runs the front door of the Tiffany," Fiato recalled. "He's a real colorful character, an ex-fighter who knows guys like Corky Ferraro and Burt Young. Mikey can spot trouble a mile off, so when he calls and says Rizzitello's in the house asking for me with a bunch of guys, I know to come prepared. I made a few calls and told my crew to get to the Tiffany and bring a friend. Rizzi hasn't seen me in almost three years since the Forex beef, and I didn't think much of our last meeting.

"When I got to the club, I slipped the .357 derringer that I always carried to Mikey Sands. I removed the pistol because I knew what would happen next. Rizzi hadn't aged much since I'd

seen him last. He was still an imposing figure. When Rizzi saw
me, it was like we were long lost brothers. 'When I heard about
this guy Anthony, I figured it was you,' he said, smiling. And he
hugged me, as I knew he would. He made sure to pat me for a
gun, and I returned the favor, just so no one would be confused.
Wearing a gun on another wiseguy is a sign of disrespect and is
enough to start some guys shooting."

With Rizzi bringing his crew around, anything was possible.
The Forex trial had begun, and Rizzitello faced a decade in prison.

Then he brought up the situation with Marty Krause.

"Harvey Ross had Marty Krause figured wrong. He was tight
with Stevens, all right, but he had plenty of friends. He was tight
with Michael Esposito, whose father, Sal Esposito, was with the
Anthony 'Tony Ducks' Corrallo crew out of Harlem. They call in
Marty Taccetta, Bucky Carravaggio and Anthony Tumac
Acceturro, and obviously the phone lines are being lit somewhere.
What I thought was a simple piece of work turns into a meeting
of the United Nations.

"Michael Esposito had his own porno business. But instead of
going to Walter Stevens he goes to none other than Mike Rizzitello.
And that brings Rizzi to the Tiffany Club.

"Mike makes a big deal out of introducing me to his friends,
Mike and Sal Esposito, Johnny Branco, John DiMattia, two of his
sons, who both have the name Mike, Rocky Durosia, and a couple
other guys I didn't know. By the time he's through introducing me
to everyone, I'm supposed to assume a more respectful posture.
But, you know, it's my club and, besides, I've got two tons of fucking protection standing behind me. And my guys dwarf his. So I
snap my fingers and start in with my own introductions as my
guys saunter over like they own the joint. I liked to call them my
Israeli Army. 'Mike, I want you to meet Hy and Joe Graciani, and
this is Ruben. This is Big Al, and this is my brother, Larry. You
already know Norman. He was with Tommy Ricciardi.'

"And I wave for a round of drinks and the tension drops a few
notches."

A few minutes later, Mike Rizzitello said, "I like what you're doing with that guy, Marty Krause."

"I thought the guy was going to Walter," Fiato said. "He owes a friend of mine some money, $15,000, plus what Stevens owes Norman."

"You scared him so much he came to me," Rizzitello said. "He's a friend of Esposito."

"I knew I was going to get a payday out of this," Fiato said, smiling. "I'll create and you alleviate."

And that's how it worked. By going to the mob, Krause was on the hook for a tribute in the form of $5,000. He also had to work out his business with Harvey Ross or face the bloody consequences.

After things settled down, Fiato again reminded Rizzi of Freedberg's relationship with Ricciardi.

"You know, this guy Norman's got the whole arsenal. He's got all the guns Tommy gave him, plus machine guns, grenades, dynamite, enough for World War Three."

Rizzitello said, "I always wondered where Tommy put that shit."

Sal Esposito wasn't giving up easily. After hearing both sides, he said to Fiato, "We heard this guy Harvey's a stool pigeon."

Fiato replied, "So who isn't a stool pigeon in this town? He's been around here long enough. If he's a stool pigeon, why isn't he dead? I'll tell you why, because some of the people in this town are still looking for their balls. Well let me tell you something, he's no stool pigeon with me. Because he knows what day it is. Here's the deal; your friend Marty will stop fucking with him now. Harvey's with good people."

Fiato's end of the Krause tribute was $2,500, which he distributed to his men.

"That money was nothing, but the show of strength was worth a fortune," Fiato said. "To my guys, it meant I wasn't greedy, that I was going to let them eat and not be a glutton. But there was no way Rizzi would be looking at me the same way again.

"I knew a few things about Rizzi and Walter Stevens. They weren't exactly friends. Until he got made in 1975, Rizzi was putting together a hit on Stevens. We had him clocked to the minute and we weren't more than a few days from carrying out the hit. He had it all set to go down outside Vic Werber's, a clothier in the garment district. But Rizzi backed off the hit.

"We'd try to do something and the cops would be following us. Rizzi wanted me to clip him and was taking me around to find him so I could get a good look at him. We're driving downtown and wherever we stop there's an unmarked police car near us with two guys inside, watching us. Rizzi gets tired of this and when we pull into a gas station and they pull up next to us, Rizzi gets out and walks over to them. He leans in the window and scares the hell out of them because, you know, we're not supposed to know who they are. They wind up following us all over downtown. We finally quit and got an espresso at an Italian deli.

"Rizzi was in trouble for other things at the time. Back then, he met with John Rosselli and Jimmy Fratianno, and they had designs on the whole family. That was always Mike's goal, but he kept getting stuck with the law.

"You have to remember something. At this time, Rizzi is on trial in the Forex case with all those guys like Jack LoCicero, Dominic Brooklier and the rest. Rizzi is reaching the conclusion that he's going to go away for a long stretch. When he was convicted, he managed to score an appeal bond, which meant he could stay on the street while his appeal was in the system. He's on the street, but there isn't much left in Mike. He's a warrior. His manhood is not negotiable, but he's in a bind. I mean, here is a guy who grew up in Brooklyn and killed I don't know how many guys, and he was concerned about making a move. He needed me if he was going to become the boss of a family in Los Angeles.

"My plan was to go to San Jose and speak to Angelo Marino, a capo of the Fresno family. Angelo could sanction me to take over Southern California independent of the Milanos, who were nothing but a bunch of bookmakers.

"The night after Mike arrived with his crew, Johnny Branco, John DiMattia and Rocky Durosia come into the club. They want to sit down and have a discussion, and I find it strange because it's obvious these are Mike's guys. I told them my intentions up front and Rocky said he could take me to see the old man, Marino. You have to remember something, I wanted to do this all the right way, the traditional way. I wanted to be the boss in Southern California, and I had no intention of sitting around bullshitting with bookmakers.

"Johnny Branco and John DiMattia started hanging out with me. They are talking about what a piece of shit Pete Milano is and how they hate the way the town is run. They're tired of walking between the raindrops, letting the Jews in the city get away with murder while they take all the heat. 'Mike told us you're a very capable guy,' DiMattia said. They were there to catch on with me. They knew I was putting guys to work and that there was plenty of money. They also knew, through guys like Joe Santone, that I didn't give a shit about the Milanos.

"Rizzi was headed back to prison on the Forex case, and the Milanos were hiding like a bunch of women out in Palm Springs. That left an opening a mile wide.

"The way was clear for me to make the move of my life."

If winning a piece of the Tiffany was a victory, hanging onto it was a challenge. Lonnie soon realized that Fiato and his friends weren't going to leave and that they were as costly to the club's bottom line as Eddie. One night, a tall, muscular man appeared at the Tiffany, took a seat at the bar and told Mike Sands that he wanted to see Anthony. When Fiato showed up, he saw from the size of the guy that he hadn't come to the club to check the plumbing. He sat next to the big man and was introduced to Scott Zooks, who immediately announced that there would be some changes at the club. Scott began dropping names of wiseguys in Las Vegas and even mentioned Rizzitello.

"We're making a clean sweep of this place," he said. "You're going to stop right now."

"And you're going to stop me?" Fiato asked, talking with his hands. "I can't understand something . . . " but before he finished his sentence he drew his right hand in and clipped Zooks on the chin. It wasn't his hardest punch, but it was just enough to knock him from the bar stool and onto the ground, where Fiato kicked him repeatedly. Zooks managed to get to his feet and run into the office, where he locked the door and called the police, then squeezed through a back window.

Fiato, incensed, grabbed Hy and a handgun and got into a car to find the fool who dared to challenge him at his own club.

Half a block away, he saw the tall man standing in a phone booth.

"I was this close to shooting the motherfucker, but we could already hear the sirens," Fiato said.

The next day at John DiMattia's house, Fiato's meeting with Rizzi's underling was interrupted by a knock at the door. It was big John St. John and another cop. Both men worked out of the LAPD's organized crime unit. They were mob cops. (St. John should not be confused with the Los Angeles police officer of the same name whose life experiences were the basis for the television series "Jigsaw John.")

"Unbelievably, DiMattia lets them in," Fiato said. "They didn't have a search warrant. They were just there to roust us. It was then I realized this DiMattia wasn't too bright, or maybe he was too friendly with the police. 'Are you out of your fucking mind?' I told him right in front of them. 'Who do you think these guys are, our buddies?' He was pretty embarrassed.

"They had come to interview me about what had happened at the club the night before. They told me this Scott said I had a gun, but I told them that he had the gun. He made an out of line remark and I slapped him. Apparently the guy had a black eye and a smashed nose."

After hearing Fiato's version of events, St. John said, "Don't give me that line of shit." Then he reached over and took him by the hand, placing it on the breast pocket of his sports coat. "Feel that? That's a gun. We're the only ones who carry guns in this town; are we clear on that?"

But St. John, the department's Gambino crime family specialist, was working the room. He outlined a few of the things he knew about Fiato's operation and dropped the name Guido Penosi, then a Gambino associate who had been involved with an extortion plot involving entertainer Wayne Newton.

"You know," the cop said, "You're almost as active as Guido. I hear he's making quite a move in this town."

The presence of St. John, who would later run afoul of his department and be accused of providing confidential information to organized crime associates, meant that the Tiffany Club had become a hot spot for the mob cops.

As St. John and his partner were leaving Fiato said, "Watch out you don't shoot yourself in the foot with that gun."

CHAPTER 6

"It's hard to express in words you'll understand, but my whole life was consumed with the Mafia," Anthony Fiato said. "It was more important than anything. I loved women, and after Phyllis, as I told you, I hooked up with a great gal, Kathy Villa. But any relationship was secondary to my love for crime.

"Being who I was, I could have all the women I wanted. But I was living that life. I set out to be this. From an early age that's all I did. When other guys went dancing, I hung out with J.R. Russo. In Hollywood, I loved the night life—as long as it led to doing business. That's the way I was. All business.

"I didn't flinch when I heard the news about Big Al. He had gone on the lam after Norman bailed him out and it looked like he was going to get away with all those robberies, but the prostitute he stiffed in Arizona didn't care what his name was. She called her pimp, and he came running with a gun. Big Al died in the street.

"My mind was on the business at hand. When John DiMattia came to me with a proposition, I had to remind him of who he was with. He was with Mike Rizzitello, not me. 'You keep Mike informed of all this. I don't want any confusion,' I told him.

"He squared it away with Mike. The deal was this: There was a guy who knew John. His name was Robert Zeichick, but everyone called him Puggy. He was a Pug, all right. He was five-foot-eleven, two hundred and twenty pounds and looked a lot like Jack

Palance with a rugged face, dark hair and eyes close together. Powerfully built. Puggy was a bookmaker, a gambler, a drug dealer, a loanshark, a bootlegger of films. He made porno movies and he loansharked large sums and had partners but nobody owned him. All these other guys are going to jail and Puggy was on the street for years not getting hassled. No OC jacket, nothing. I drive with DiMattia to a McDonald's in Encino and meet with Puggy, who's eating with his two sons like an honest citizen. We're sitting in the sunshine having a picnic, and Puggy lays out what's going on.

"Two kilos of cocaine disappeared on him and he wants the dope back. He wants to know if he's been ripped off by one of his own people, and he's willing to pay $5,000 to find out.

"The guy he was bankrolling was a Mexican named Mario, who was buying the dope and moving it to another guy, an old man he used to sell the stuff. Well, Mario made the switch with the old-timer, but the old-timer doesn't have the dope. He stopped off at a restaurant with the dope in his trunk, and when he got home and opened the trunk, the stuff was gone. He suspected a parking attendant at the restaurant, and I had a feeling that Mario might have some explaining to do. Puggy just wanted to get to the bottom line.

"When it's time to check out the old man's story, John DiMattia meets me and who's with him in the car but Mike Rizzitello. When we get to the old man's apartment, Mike sends John in and it's easy to see John's not excited about going inside by himself. I tell him I'll join him and when we get to the apartment the door is wide open. The old man is sitting bare-chested on a chair, a long scar running down the front of his chest. He was expecting us."

"You come to see me, here I am," he said. "I've had open-heart surgery. I won't lie to you. You can do with me what you want, but that won't get your stuff back."

Fiato and DiMattia talked to the old man for twenty minutes and came away convinced that he did not have a hand in the disappearance of the cocaine. They reported that to Zeichick, who shrugged and handed over the $5,000, which they split three ways.

"The money was nothing compared to the introduction to Puggy. I made it a habit to run into him again, and we started doing business. DiMattia couldn't help him the way I could and he knew it, and John stayed in the background. Of all the relationships I had with people in those days, none was more important than the one I had with Puggy."

And so Puggy Zeichick began dropping by the Tiffany at night. In a short time Fiato and his girlfriend were double dating with Zeichick and his girlfriend. The couples were joined by DiMattia and Rizzitello and their wives. During conversations Fiato began to realize that Puggy's business was not limited to a few drug deals and some bookmaking. He owned a half dozen apartment buildings and had a large cash flow. What he didn't have was consistent muscle behind him.

"You can move this Jew," Rizzi whispered to Fiato one night. "He really likes you."

Rizzitello, still out on an appeal bond, was in no position to become high profile. He was gradually turning over his action to Fiato. And Zeichick saw that.

"I let Puggy know that if he worked with me, nobody would bother him," Fiato said. "I told him if we loaned money, we'd get our money back and nobody would shake us down. We met with one of Puggy's associates, Gene Holden, and made a proposition to loanshark money on the street. Holden had a Las Vegas contact with a virtually limitless supply of dead money, cash that could not surface legally because it couldn't be explained to the government. I assumed it was skim cash, but it could have been drug money. Either way, when Holden got the go-ahead, there was plenty of money to get started."

The lending operation was simple enough. Morry, Holden's Las Vegas contact, loaned the money to Holden for one percent weekly interest. Holden then loaned the money to Zeichick and Fiato at one-and-a-half points. They loaned the cash on the street at five percent. Shylock loans weren't tough to understand: You receive the money and agree to the terms of the loan. The catch is, you must repay the loan in full, not a bit at a time. In that way, a degenerate gambler who borrowed even $1,000 from a loan-shark at five percent interest owed only $50-a-week juice. But then the gambler faced the far longer odds of being able to repay the $1,000 in a lump sum. At the end of one year, a loanshark will have collected $2,600 on his $1,000 loan, and the borrower will still owe the original sum.

And if he couldn't pay?

"That's where I came in," Fiato said. "I made it clear from the outset that nonpayment was not acceptable. Actually, I told them I'd break their fucking hands and beat them in front of their wives until they begged for forgiveness. Most of the time a warning was all it took."

Once the money arrived, Fiato and Zeichick realized their loan-shark business would not be any run-of-the-mill operation. The money arrived in boxes, nearly $500,000 in cash. They started with gamblers and bookmakers and quickly graduated to small-business owners. The numbers ranged from $500 to $50,000.

A typical morning went this way: Zeichick picked up Fiato, and the pair made their first stop at Nate & Al's deli in Beverly Hills. They took a booth and spent the next three hours eating breakfast and meeting with customers. Between deals they met Tony Curtis, Jack Lemmon and other actors who frequented the deli for its New York atmosphere and its blintzes.

Fiato kept his remarks simple.

"You're giving me your word that you're going to repay this money, and I'm giving you my word that if you don't wherever you go you won't be safe from me.' And the money came in like you wouldn't believe. We had more money than we could spend, and we kept churning the juice back into our bankroll. In a few months we had a million bucks on the street.

"Rizzi would come in every once in a while and introduce us to a guy who needed $35,000 to set up a bustout business. Pizza parlor owners borrowed from us, and when they couldn't come up with the money we became partners in their pizza joints. It was that simple."

But protecting that much money is not as easy as it seems. Put it in a bank, and the Internal Revenue Service is bound to find out. Buy big-ticket items, such as houses or a fleet of automobiles, and again the government will get wise. Located in a Beverly Hills home more suited to his stature, Fiato hid $160,000 under a rock in his backyard. He piled up more cash in the closet, stuffed it into his boots.

When he wasn't working, he shopped like a fiend and favored Mr. Guy's in Beverly Hills. He bought $1,500 sports coats, $1000 cashmere sweaters, the most expensive handmade Italian shoes.

At night, a tab for a dinner party was more than his father had earned in three months tending bar. With Dom Perignon and Kristal champagne flowing, dinner for his crowd could exceed $3,000. The staff hovered around the table as the cash slipped through Fiato's fingers. He tipped bartenders $100 for a round of drinks, handed $20 to restroom attendants for a paper towel.

Soon Fiato was travelling by limousine with his own personal driver, Steve Finkel, whose relationship had gone from loanshark customer to running mate in a short time.

Zeichick and Fiato loaned tens of thousands of dollars to close-out hustlers in the garment district. The scams of the so-called legitimate businessmen were impressive. They'd borrow $50,000 from Fiato, use it to buy a wholesale closeout on, for instance, 100,000 silk scarves. They'd pay a purchasing agent for a big department store a few thousand to buy the scarves for, say $2 apiece. The scarves would wind up on store shelves, $200,000 would wind up in the closeout hustler's pocket, and Fiato and Zeichick would get their money back with interest in a matter of weeks. After the closeout specialists worked their magic a few times, Fiato decided he and his partner would become their partners. Instead of the usual five percent interest, he put up the money for half the profit.

Fiato and his partner bankrolled jewelry heists and took a large slice of the profits. It was during just such a deal that they met Alan Betts and Ronald Coe, criminal associates of Puggy and Harvey Ross. Betts and Coe remained on the periphery of the crew for several months.

In the Valley, they backed an adult video bootlegging operation that turned out thousands of copies of such X-rated classics as *Deep Throat* and *Debbie Does Dallas*. They hired a printer to duplicate the boxes the authentic tapes were sold in, then had dozens of cassettes dubbed at a time. The result was the flooding of the market in video stores throughout Southern California. And it all paid big bucks.

On the street, an odd thing began to happen. The loanshark customers and small-time bookmakers they were shaking down began to find other customers and victims for Fiato. In his macho way, he had empowered them, and they, too, began to act as if they were connected to the Mafia. Which, at least in a monetary sense, they were.

"In early 1980, I started seeing a guy's face pop up in the bars and restaurants I frequented. At first I didn't know who he was, but then I discovered it was a cop named Jack Motto. Motto looked like an actor. His graying hair was always well groomed, and he dressed like a wiseguy. And he was everywhere. He worked for LAPD Administrative Vice, which chases the bookmakers all over California and mostly develops them as snitches.

"We were getting the bookmakers to kick in to us through their agents, and John DiMattia and my brother were taking action. All that was bound to get the attention of somebody, and so Motto started showing up wherever I went.

"He was never rude, and he didn't act like he thought bookmaking was the biggest sin in the world. That's how he developed so many sources. We continued to receive layoff action from some bookmakers but were careful to watch out for Motto. We knew he really wanted to get us and not just some illegal bookies. We had plenty of bookmakers from Marina Del Rey to Hollywood, and one of the Hollywood bookies, Marty the Nose, was taking action from James Caan. I'd always been a big fan of his and wound up being pretty close to the actor. I gave him the nickname Top Cat. He loved that nickname.

"One of the guys who wouldn't pay his debts was Vince Edwards, who you'd remember as television's Dr. Ben Casey. He was a degenerate gambler and a big drinker. And he stiffed everybody. But he saw the light after I gave him a beating. He'd stiffed one of our friends for something like thirty-five thousand. He used to lie and scam and bullshit everybody. He had credit from all these fucking guys. And he was what you'd call snake bit. He couldn't pick his nose. I mean every bet he made was a loser.

"Edwards must have gone through millions and millions gambling. He was a big muscular guy, a weight lifter and a pretty boy, so most of the time if he didn't want to pay, he would puff out his chest and stiff some little bookmaker. People tried to be nice to him. They'd loan him money, thinking they were investing in some movie or another, and he'd gamble it away. His name was coming up left and right with bookmakers.

"I was with my brother when I approached him. I told him, gently, that he owes us money and asked him when we were going to see some of it. He said, 'Fuck you.'

"I said, 'Jesus Christ almighty. What a bad temper for a movie actor. If I knew it was you I wouldn't have talked like that. Geez, I used to watch 'Ben Casey' and I'm awfully sorry about this.' Then I leaned over and whacked him in the face with a pair of brass knuckles. I kneed him in the balls and left him gasping for air. A day or so later he made a gesture. He had a watch and hocked it. I felt sorry for the guy, really. He put me onto this other bookmaker who wasn't with the program and I made money off that guy."

In time, the Fiato brothers and John DiMattia had a piece of numerous bookmaking operations. Their own backroom sports book took up to $10,000 per football bet, large even by Las Vegas standards.

"We're winning every week and we're keeping thirty-five or forty thousand a week in profit," Fiato said. "And we were doing it apart from Rizzi, who had nothing to do with it and wasn't kicking anything our way in those days. But for some reason John can't stand a good thing. He starts talking about it and Rizzi gets wind of it. I fixed it by giving Rizzi a piece. For a few thousand, he cooled down and didn't think anything more of it. I don't think he realized the scope of the operation, which was fine with me. I loved Mike and had known him since I was a kid, but he was a one-way street when it came to scores. He was preoccupied about doing time, and most of the time just left me alone to do my own thing.

"Maybe the best part of having our hands on the bookmaking operations was the access it gave us to gamblers who were always in need of a few thousand. That's where the real money is, in loansharking. Bookmaking just makes the loansharks fat. Anyone who tells you bookmaking is no big deal, that it's not connected to organized crime, is a fucking liar. It is organized crime. It's at the root of most of it.

"Jack Motto is looking to nail me in the worst way. He knows we have this giant bookmaking business. Everyone is talking about it, and he's dying to bust us. They set up a raid at my apartment for a Sunday morning during the height of the football season. Larry was working out of there and we kept records there. But it was like somebody was watching over us because that was the same weekend I moved to a place in Beverly Hills. When Motto and his boys got there, they woke up Larry and his wife. They were in bed and all of a sudden the bedroom is full of cops. 'Where's your brother,' Motto asked him. 'He moved out,' Larry said. When I heard the story I about busted a gut. Always a step ahead, that's Anthony Fiato. In reality, I knew it was blind luck.

"When I called my brother later that morning somebody else answers the phone, and it's nobody I recognize. I called up to find out the amount of play that morning, and now I know my brother's pinched."

Back at police headquarters, Larry sat in an office while the cops rousted him. On the wall was a link chart with the names of more than two dozen of his friends and associates. Rizzitello was circled at the top of the chart. He was out of action. The acting boss came next and Larry Fiato recognized the name: Craig Anthony Fiato.

There were times when it seemed to Anthony Fiato that John DiMattia knew every bookmaker and degenerate gambler in Beverly Hills. Among those inveterate players were a fair number of women.

"There's something most people don't realize when they enter a business agreement with us," Fiato said. "They think it's going to be a one-shot deal. They can't go to a bank or, in this case, the lady couldn't go to her husband, who was a big jeweler. She was losing thousands at backgammon at the Cavandish Club. So she came to us. We were easy to find, and once we found out who she was we kept her in our pocket. In a few weeks, she was hinting around that she could find us scores. Her husband knew every jeweler in the city, and she wasn't shy about sharing information. That's how Harvey's pals Betts and Coe started making some money. They would burglarize a house knowing it was likely to have more than the usual goods inside. And our girl was accurate. We set up B&Es all over the place. She'd say, 'A jeweler just came into town and he has diamonds in his safe.' She'd overhear her husband talking to these guys. Here's the best part. Once she saw we were capable, she started to get greedy. She'd set up a score, even manage to provide us the combination to a safe, and she wanted half the money. This is the power of the Mafia mystique. You could call these people victims, but they're not innocent. We'd sell the diamonds to our contacts for about twenty-five percent of their value in cash.

"One day she came to us and said she'd found out where a guy kept all his really good stones. And Betts and Coe, who had done time and were a couple of Aryan Brotherhood types, real trailer trash, wound up going in on the job. I didn't like them from the start. They were all tattoos and bad-ass looks, the kind of guys who leave behind tools with their finger prints on them. They were used to being in jail. But I was using them, and they were kicking in to me, Puggy and DiMattia. They needed a third man and I put them with Harvey Ross. I didn't have to get my hands on anything, and I was making a big chunk of whatever they made. So they burglarize a place and bring back the diamonds, just like our girl had said. The diamonds were worth $120,000. We moved them to our broker and whacked up the money. John DiMattia got a piece of everything because he is the one who roped the girl.

"Here's how brazen the broad got. While her husband was entertaining a group of jewelers, she opened one of their brief-cases and saw it had thousands in diamonds in it. She called us up from home and had two guys come over and burglarize her own house while her husband and the rest of the jewelers were in the other room. There was a time when absolutely every deal we touched turned into twenty-thousand here, fifty-thousand there. I never left the house with less than ten-thousand in my pocket. I never knew when we were going to do business. Things moved that quickly. My brother Larry was making book and taking care of straightening out other bookmakers. For Puggy and me, our goal was to make five-thousand apiece a day. Some days we made five-thousand before lunch. Some days it was twenty-five-hun-dred. We never made less than a thousand. The funny thing is, the only thing I couldn't do was keep off the weight. We were con-stantly at delis and restaurants. I gained 20 pounds in a couple months and ate more kosher food than most Jews."

John DiMattia, who had grown up around Lucchese crime fam-ily powerhouse Anthony "Tumac" Accuturro, already had faded from the duo's daily operations when he was sentenced to a year in prison in New Jersey on an old extortion charge. Privately, he also was maintaining contact with Luigi Gelfuso and Pete Milano's crew. With Mike Rizzitello's days on the outside numbered, Anthony Fiato was in line to emerge as the acting boss.

Sensing Fiato's increasing power, Rizzitello met with him.

"I'm going on record with you," Rizzi said. "You're going to be made in our family. I'm flying to New York and will meet with Neil. You and that kid Puggy are doing it right. I can make you the Lucky Luciano of this town. That's why I'm going on record with you."

These were the words Fiato longed to hear. He was to become a made member. He was excited, but he also understood Rizzitello was merely covering his bases.

"I was a doer and Mike liked doers in his family," Fiato said. "He knew he was going to go away eventually and turned his family over to me by making me a lieutenant. And he was sanctioned to do it."

Rizzitello flew to New York and met with Aniello "Mr. Neil" Dellacroce, the Gambino underboss whose power in the La Cosa Nostra family was second only to Big Paul Castellano. As a sign of his emerging status, Fiato began receiving instructions from Gambino family messengers speaking on behalf of Dellacroce, who had sanctioned Rizzitello's Los Angeles family.

Larry Fiato hadn't grown up with Mike Rizzitello. His perception of him was different than his brother's.

"Mike Rizzitello was the real deal, a stone-cold killer, but towards the end he absolutely was two-faced with my brother," Larry said. "He was a liar, a manipulator who would put a knife in your back as soon as you turned around. He wouldn't play fair. By that I mean, with my brother he'd call on things out of the past. He'd say, 'I carried you when you were a baby. I knew your family.' Stuff like that. My brother tried to be loyal to him, but Mike was a manipulator."

As the money poured in, Anthony Fiato's circle of acquaintances grew diverse. More than bookmakers and bandits, he often found himself in the company of actors and directors who were drawn to his outlaw image.

Aaron Russo is best known as the producer of *The Rose* and *Trading Places*, huge hits which showcased the talents of their respective stars, Bette Midler and Eddie Murphy. Russo was a free spirit given to wearing long hair and espousing libertarian philosophy. In the early 1980s, he was one of the hottest producers in Hollywood and also managed Midler's career.

The two became lovers for a time, but when they broke up Fiato recalled that Russo took the end of their relationship, both personal and managerial, very hard.

"Norman called me one afternoon and said Aaron Russo wanted to talk to me," Fiato said. "We'd met a few times at Norman's place and I liked the guy. With a name like Russo, you'd expect him to be Italian, but he's a Sephardic Jew. Dark-haired, big-chested, talked with a New York accent. I told Norman I'd meet them over at the Hamburger Hamlet.

"When we sit down, he orders a lobster bisque and we make small talk. I like his movies, but I know I'm not there as a fan. He's got something on his mind and is taking his time getting around to it. In a few minutes he starts motherfucking the guy who stole Bette Midler from him, and how he wants to see that guy hurt.

"He's obviously no tough guy himself. Nor was he acting like his normal self. It's corny to say it, but I think his heart was broken. He blurts out too loud about how he wants to see this guy pay and how Norman says I'd be willing to do the job. I can't believe he's serious. He goes on and on and at one point I suggest we throw acid in Bette Midler's face, change her career from comedies to horror flicks, if you know what I mean. You could see this guy was really hurt.

"But as he's talking he realizes what is being said and starts to cool down, and then I ask him for his phone number and the address of the offending parties. When he saw I was deadly serious, he got scared. His eyes got wide and you could hear the wheels turning in his head. He started to stammer and stutter and could barely finish his lobster bisque.

"As I'm getting ready to leave, he changes his mind. And he begs me not to do anything and he's sweating like hell. He liked to talk that Hollywood gangster talk, the kind of thing half the mopes in the city are into. They'll fuck with this guy and they'll fuck with that guy. You know, it's all phony. When he saw what kind of guy he was dealing with, he got scared. I think he thought it was bad karma or some fucking thing. That's the kind of guy he was. And by the end of the conversation he knew what kind of guy I was, too.

"As we were leaving the parking lot, Aaron pulled out in his sports car. Our eyes met and he flips me a peace sign like an old hippie. Ten minutes earlier he was wanting me to cut some guy's balls off, and now he's flipping me a peace sign. Crazy motherfucker. All I can say is, he must have really loved that broad.

"From then on, whenever we met at Norman's house or somewhere else he was always friendly. We watched the Duran-Leonard fight together and he took my call at Paramount anytime I needed to ask him about someone. He liked having me around and bragged about knowing me. He called me 'The Doberman, a real animal' and part of the name stuck. I had become known as the Animal, and I liked the feeling."

"I was at Pip's, a private Club in Beverly Hills, having drinks with John DiMattia, Jack Catain and Harry Guardino. Pip's was managed by Joe DiCarlo, who was then Cher's manager, and attracted everybody who was anybody in Hollywood. From movie bosses to Mafia bosses. DiMattia and I had gone to Pip's to talk to DiCarlo in an attempt to get a guy we knew re-elected to the board of directors of the club. The guy, I'll call him Tom, had a mansion he filled with women, and he ran backgammon games out of his place. He'd take care of his customers, who always managed to lose thousands at backgammon. I'd collected a piece of stolen jewelry, a watch worth twenty grand, from one of Tom's good friends from the mansion parties. When I caught up to the thief, I hung him by his feet off the balcony of his house. The drop was about 150 feet and you'd be surprised how fast the guy remembered what he'd done with the watch. Tom was grateful and welcomed us at his place anytime. It was at Pip's I first caught a glimpse of Alana Stewart, Rod Stewart's wife. She was with her girlfriends and immediately caught my eye. It took about two seconds for us to hit it off.

"We left Pip's and went to the Beverly Hilton Hotel and got down. It was that simple. She partied all night. When I left the room, I looked like that buzzard who leaves the barn yard. I left her sleeping at the hotel. Then I went home and got some sleep myself.

"I forgot to get her number. I saw her about a year later at Morton's in Beverly Hills. My girlfriend Kathy and I went to dinner with Puggy and his girl and Ronnie Caan, Jimmy's brother. In the back of the restaurant, Rod and Alana Stewart had a table, and Ronnie said he knew them. 'I've partied with Rod Stewart. This guy's a real freak,' Ronnie said. He was trying to impress me on the way to hitting me up for a little coke. Ronnie took me over to Alana Stewart and told her I was in the Mafia and ran the town. 'Don't I know you from somewhere?' she asked. 'You swore you'd never forget me,' I told her, then whispered the particulars in her ear. She blushed, which was no mean feat."

"Being a gangster isn't about being Italian or Sicilian," Fiato said. "It's simple, really. When you're a criminal, when you have people behind you, when you're not on your own, you're a mobster. If you have a mob behind you, you're a mobster. That's what makes you dangerous. It's not one gun, it's many guns. It sends a message that's powerful: If you fuck with him, you're fucking with them.

"They saw the power I was generating and they were attracted to it. I made them powerful. I gave them a philosophy. If somebody fucks with Joe, we all come running. If somebody fucks with Hy, everybody attacks. If we make money, we split it up. If somebody slaps you in the face, you retaliate by breaking his arm. It's never an eye for an eye. You always get the best of it. And they knew I would let them eat. I gave them money, I set them up with easy scores.

"I had more money than I could spend, and Puggy and me had a million on the street, but that didn't mean I failed to share. I remembered Nicky Giso, Paulie Intiso, J.R. Russo and Larry Baioni. The best of them were generous with their men. It's something Rizzi wasn't good at. He was always stashing his money, like an old guy will. With Mike, your money was his, but his money was his, too. I set my guys up with apartments. I made sure they had clothes.

"Of course, I had plans for them too. What Rizzi called an uncontrollable hothead was a guy who wanted to get his arms around the whole package. Not just a few bookmakers. Not just one club, but a whole network of legitimate businesses. I was dreaming big, but in a matter of months I'd replaced Rizzitello, built a solid crew of a dozen men and was rolling in cash. Why? Because I enforced the principals of La Cosa Nostra. The other guys were trying to evade all the consequences. I was out to grab it all and rule by intimidation. I was willing to take whatever came. What Rizzi called an uncontrollable hothead was a man who was willing to stand up for himself. And it's not easy. You've got heat following you constantly. Back East, everyone paid off the neighborhood cops. But in California the neighborhoods were miles long, or didn't exist at all. A few cops were friendly, but there was no system in place. And I was like new blood that came along. I may have been a cowboy to Mike, but his men sure took notice. His guys, Johnny Branco and John DiMattia, got to be like Cassius and Brutus. They came to tell me about Caesar. It's 'Mike is making a ton of money and we got to starve' and 'We know Mike is a good man, but we don't understand what he's doing.'"

"In the movies, hits are planned thoroughly, and sometimes that's the way it is in real life," Fiato said. "But other times, a guy gets killed because he appears in the wrong place at the wrong time.

That's what almost happened one night at Tracton's. I was going to whack John Lantino, a small-time hoodlum with a big mouth, and saw him there. He'd been talking about Mike Rizzitello behind his back, calling him a bum.

"Rizzi told me the story over a few drinks one night. He said he wanted the baldheaded motherfucker dead and I told him I'd take care of it. So when I saw him—he was easy to spot at two-hundred-eighty pounds—and remembered what Mike had said, I was so angry with him I wasn't going to wait around. When I saw him go into the lounge, where his cousin Bobby Milano was singing, I went into a rage. I called Norman's house and told him to have the gun that killed Bomp ready. 'I don't even want to know. Don't even tell me,' Norman said.

"All the way back over to Tracton's I tested the gun. It was amazing. With its silencer, it made almost no sound. I shot at houses and trees and it was quiet as a whisper. When I got to Tracton's, I sat at the bar with Johnny DiMattia and waited for this Lantino to go to the bathroom. The last thing he was going to see was the toilet because I was going to pop him.

"In a few minutes he walked by and went into the can and I got up to follow him. I got to the door and entered, but before the door closed John DiMattia comes in behind me.

"'Don't do it,' DiMattia said. 'Jack Motto just came in and he's sitting at the bar.' Just that quick Lantino was spared. John had gotten cold feet and panicked. I was literally five seconds from shooting him in the head, and Lantino didn't even know Jack Motto saved his life.

"When I told Rizzi about it later, he pinched my cheek. 'You're Johnny on the spot,' he said. But you know something? He didn't even remember telling me to whack out the guy. He was too drunk. I nearly killed a man for him, and he didn't remember the conversation."

Although their relationship was sometimes tumultuous, Mike Rizzitello had big plans for his animal, Anthony Fiato. The closer he came to entering prison, the more Rizzitello shared with Fiato. He introduced him to Robert Kessler. Bob Kessler drove a Rolls-Royce, lived in Beverly Hills and was game for almost anything if it made money. Kessler smuggled illegal aliens, dealt in stolen merchandise, loaned money on the street and worked closely with bookmakers. He had a hand in the stock market, knew every hustler in Beverly Hills. When Rizzitello and Kessler walked into Eddie Saul's coffee shop on Ventura Boulevard, Anthony Fiato had no idea of what was to come. Kessler was tall and gawky. He was six-feet-four-inches with black hair, a pot belly and skinny legs. He was large enough to look imposing, but he was no tough guy. He was, however, endlessly ingratiating.

"People naturally confided in Kessler," Fiato said. "When I saw Rizzitello talking freely to him, I trusted Mike's judgment. Now here's a guy I've never seen before. Normally, I wouldn't even acknowledge his existence. But Kessler knew about drug dealers, bookmakers, everybody. He had cocaine connections, knew about contract murders. The guy was wired to the town, all right. I didn't realize how wired at the time. He looked like Herman Munster, but he was very smooth. He was well-dressed and gracious.

"Later, when I started loaning money with Puggy, Kessler would show up at Nate 'n' Al's. When I saw him again he said, 'Hi, you remember me. I'm Mike's friend, Bob.' And of course I remembered him. How could you forget a look like that? He sits down, orders a corned beef sandwich and a cup of coffee and chats it up like old times. When he found out I lived in Beverly Hills not far from him, he offered me a ride home and asked me if I wanted to come over to his house sometime, meet his wife and have a barbecue.

"The next day there's a knock at the door and it's Kessler. He's got bagels. He said Mike sent him over. From then on he starts coming around, visiting and bullshitting. He finds a guy in the garment district who wants to borrow $1,000 at $50 a week juice. It's little stuff, but he sort of makes himself at home. Because he

was a friend of Mike's I didn't think anything of it. He was just a
real friendly guy, an old-timer who'd been around for years."

It wasn't until 1982 that Mike Rizzitello finally caught up with the
elusive Walter Stevens, but not until the moneylender was behind
bars. But the move started years earlier, and Anthony Fiato was
behind it. While in the penitentiary, Rizzitello contacted Stevens
the old-fashioned way. He cooked up an agreement with Red
Morgan, boss of Southern California's Mexican Mafia, whose
incarceration did not prevent him from running half the prisons
in California and a sizable crew on the outside. Morgan dispatched two of his men to impress upon Stevens the importance
of cooperating with Rizzitello. Surely the ice pick they pressed to
Stevens' ear encouraged the negotiation process.

"It took years, but they finally got to him," Fiato said. "Rizzi
told me all about it. He had done time with Red Morgan and they
got along while in the joint. The deal was a good one for both parties. Stevens was to have his girlfriend deliver $100,000 to
Carmine's Restaurant. The alternative was death.

"Rizzi would find Stevens' girlfriend and get her to cooperate.
Stevens was calling James Caan all the time from prison, but half
the guys in the mob were calling James Caan in those days.
Anyway, Stevens calls his girlfriend from prison and arranges for
her to take $100,000 out of storage and deliver it to Jimmy
Coppola, one of Mike's guys. It was pretty easy, really. All that
time Stevens thought he was safe from us. The ironic thing is, it
was Jimmy Coppola, the guy who picked up the cash. He was
later stabbed and killed in prison. And all this came about because
Harvey Ross got me to pressure Marty Krause, who in turn went
to Mike Esposito, who went to his father Sal and then went to
Walter.

"Sal tried all kinds of things to get us to lay off. He called me
up one day and said, 'Butchie Peraino says to say hello.' and then
he asks, 'Is this coming from Mike?' Because if it is, they know
where to go to get it stopped. I said, 'This is coming from me.' I

know Butchie is with the Genovese people, but he's nothing to me. They were all in the porno business together. The Perainos had that *Deep Throat* movie. I told Sal, 'Well, say hello to Butchie for me and tell him to stay the hell out of my business.'

"But two years earlier I had had guys pressuring the Espositos. That was what set up the Red Morgan move. They threatened to go to everybody they knew. Sal Amarena, Jimmy Fratianno's old friend from San Francisco. They call Ronnie Rome and try to get him to talk to me, but I no longer gave a fuck about Ronnie Rome. I've bailed him out of too many jackpots in my life to listen to him.

"In the middle of it, I back down. It's my philosophy lesson coming back to me. I call them and tell them to just forget about it, and they think whatever they've been doing has worked. I was just stalling for time to let it cool off. So when I figured they'd dropped their guard, I sent Fat Steve Munichiello and Carl Cataldo over to Mike Esposito's office. And they give him the beating of his life. 'This is from Anthony,' they told him.

"At that time, there was a guy in the vending business in Southern California who went around town dropping the name of Tony Spilotro, which wasn't the brightest thing to do since The Ant man is unlikely to appreciate such a thing. So I went out and paid him a visit and warned him. I scare him silly. I told him if I ever hear that he's using that guy's name I'll rip his fucking tongue out.

"The minute I walk out, the cops walk in. And of course they interview this scared guy, who doesn't know whether to talk or piss his pants.

"It didn't take long for the Esposito beating and the intimidation of this other guy to get around town. Which is good for business in one way, but bad for business in another. It's good because my very presence was enough to have guys cough up tributes and cut me in on deals. It was bad because now wherever I go I'm leading a parade of undercover cops. I'd like to have had the gasoline concession for what they spent tailing me and my crew around California."

Joey Mangiapani was a boxing trainer who drove a limousine for a company owned by a man named Mark Kreiner, whose business interests included the Off My Back clothing company and a piece of a record company, Highrise Entertainment, in partnership with Lawrence Leal and Mike Lushka.

"After the men entered into the partnership, Kreiner determined that he was being cheated. Instead of pursuing the usual legal remedies, he contacted Mangiapani to assist him in a little persuasion. Mangiapani, in turn, reached out for Anthony Fiato after Lushka and Leal tried to back out of the new deal by disappearing from the scene owing, by Kreiner's count, more than $250,000.

"The big thing is, Kreiner promises to split the money with me if I can get these people to cough it up. We're talking about a quarter of a million, so it's worth the effort.

"Once that kind of money's on the table, the wheels start turning. We learn one of the guys is in Dallas, so I dispatch Cowboy Dave Tracy and remind him of his obligations. He gives the Texan the beating of his fucking life and reminds him that the arm of the Mafia can reach anywhere. They were trying everything they could to keep from coming up with the money. They got in touch, through Burt Young with 'Tony Ducks' Corrallo, who in turn reached Rizzitello to ask for an explanation. Mike was in New York meeting with people there on my behalf, and he contacted me and asked about it. I reminded him that we'd discussed it and that I'd sent Cowboy Dave to Texas to square it away. And when Burt Young's name came up I about screamed. What the fuck was that guy doing in my business?

"After all this starts to settle down, I make a meet with Kreiner at Ralph the Butcher's in Westwood and tell him I want $50,000 up front immediately out of the $250,000 he owes me for taking care of his business. He starts crying about not having that kind of money but eventually he gets the idea he's not getting out of this. So he agrees to work on it. I'm there with Puggy, Joey Mangiapani, and Bob Kessler, who had taken to driving me around any time I'd let him."

Somehow, the FBI had found out about the meeting and had followed Fiato. When he finished with Kreiner, agents immediately corralled the frightened limousine owner and tried to interview him. When he declined, they served him with a grand jury subpoena. The subjects of the grand jury: Craig Anthony Fiato and Robert "Puggy" Zeichick.

A day later, Burt Young called Fiato.

"That meeting you were at the other day was bugged," Young said.

Fiato soon surmised the same thing. The room had to have been bugged.

How else would the feds have known so quickly the most intimate details of the meeting?

Fiato's mind raced. He scrambled to put together the pieces. What had he said and when did he say it? Who was present when he talked about the extortion attempt? How could he walk into such a trap? Could there have been a snitch? No chance. Puggy, Kessler, Joey and Kreiner were there and all of them knew the price of even thinking of informing.

The meeting had to have been bugged.

At about that time, Anthony Fiato started to receive crank phone calls at his home. When he would answer, the caller would hang up. When he moved with Kathy to a home in trendy Benedict Canyon, the phone calls continued. Kessler, who lived only a block away, dropped by often to commiserate with Fiato. Steve Finkel came by and, ever the grateful loan recipient, dropped off hefty quantities of cocaine for the consumption of Fiato's circle of friends.

A big surprise came a few weeks later when Fiato was subpoenaed to appear before a federal grand jury in Las Vegas considering the crimes of aging Genovese crime family capo Sam Manarite. White-haired and given to a maniacal temper, "Springfield Sam" had been a loanshark from Hialeah in Florida to the casinos of Las Vegas for more than three decades. In his late sixties, he had spent much of his adult life in prison. Fiato met Manarite only

once on a trip to Las Vegas with Mike Rizzitello to meet with
Anthony Spilotro. In Fiato's mind, Manarite was a typical old-
school knee breaker. Not slick, just consistent. A dinosaur who
was destined to be sent back to the penitentiary.

But what would the feds want with him in Las Vegas?

His testimony turned out to be inconsequential. He was interviewed only a few minutes, then made the trip back to Benedict
Canyon. He was puzzled.

It wasn't until two years later that it dawned on him. The FBI
needed him out of the house in order to adjust its bugging equipment. The grand jury appearance was a ruse to allow agents time
to wire Fiato's world.

Fiato got suspicious when he dispatched his brother, Larry,
Kessler, Steve Municello, and Carl Cataldo to pay a visit on a man
named Doctor Z., a Los Angeles loanshark who represented a
group of Israeli businessmen. Fiato instructed them to hurt Dr.
Z., to kill him if necessary.

Kessler was supposed to set up the doctor with a customer who
was interested in borrowing several thousand dollars at the standard five percent per week.

"The guy never showed," Fiato recalled. "I knew something
was wrong, but I couldn't believe guys so close to me would pull
anything or talk out of school. I mean, most of these guys have
done crimes for me. And Kessler is bringing over food and all
kinds of gifts practically everyday. He and his wife only live up the
street. No way he would pull anything like that. He knows it
would get him killed."

"On May 28, 1982, I had my birthday party at Chasen's. It was a
real blowout. Everybody brought their wives or girlfriends. It was
a chance to celebrate, and it was a chance for some of the guys to
meet Rizzitello for the first time. Mike was there with his son,
Mike, Jr. James Caan was there. Burt Young, Carl Cataldo, Steve
Munichiello, my brother Larry, Steve Finkel, and a bunch of other
people.

"Rizzi got to meet all the family that was involved with me. They had been working for him and, because of circumstances, he couldn't sit down with them and hadn't met most of them. The birthday party gave us a shot at getting together. There was a line waiting to meet him. He and I sat down and I introduced people to him one at a time. All the while I figured the cops or FBI or some law enforcement was watching us, but I didn't give a fuck. I was proud of the family I had put together. Not only for Rizzi, but for myself, too."

"I was doing everything. The phone was ringing off the hook. I was constantly getting messages, granting favors, giving people permission to use my name. Puggy would show up at the door and dump thousands of dollars on the kitchen table.

"With one meeting I could straighten out a bookmaker, take over a guy's loanshark obligation and pick up the paper on some guy's restaurant. It was almost too easy. When Ralph the Butcher told me about a couple of Japanese guys who had been placing bets with a small-time bookie named Izzy, I immediately pulled both of them aside. I intimidated Izzy, made him lay off the Orientals. Then I told the Orientals I wanted the money paid immediately and I'd given them a $10,000 discount on the $40,000 they owed Izzy. Of course, they knew the alternative was to get a beating and have me and my men rob them until they'd wish they were back in Tokyo. In 24 hours, Steve Finkel shows up. He's brokered the whole thing and is laughing. The Japs gave him the $30,000 and he hands it over to me. I gave Steve $2,000 for his trouble and split the rest with Puggy. We were partners, after all.

"You're too much, Fiato," Puggy said, laughing. "You don't even have to leave the house to make money."

And for a while it was true.

Of course, Anthony Fiato's overhead grew as dramatically as his stature on the street. His terror campaign generated hundreds of thousands of dollars a month, but somebody had to pay the bills. His men received cash, thousands each week. His lifestyle wasn't cheap. Especially not after he began riding in a chauffeured limousine and eating meals prepared by his personal chef.

Larry Fiato received $1,000 a week to collect from three loan-shark customers and make a little book. But, gradually, Larry was getting the hang of the business, and that meant he would receive a larger pinch of the action he helped generate. In time, he began to take on some of his older brother's traits. He also developed a mean cocaine habit. With so much cocaine around, it was easy to forget the lessons Anthony Fiato had learned years earlier from the wiseguys in Boston. Although he personally refrained from using the stuff, it was in his house constantly. Fiato gave Finkel $500 a week to run errands. He also loaned Finkel more than $100,000 to bankroll an upstart cocaine operation. As a token of his thanks, Finkel rewarded Fiato with a 1982 collector's edition Corvette. Fiato loved the car.

"That car was some of the best fun I've ever had in my life," Fiato recalled. "I got to relive my childhood. It was everything I ever wanted as a kid. It was the car of my dreams and I cruised Hollywood Boulevard in it."

In the legitimate business world, handsome John DiMattia would have been known as a superb networker. In Anthony Fiato's world, DiMattia played a key role in finding bookmakers and digging up loanshark customers. It was no surprise that he'd played high school football and tried politics back in his home state of New Jersey. He was irresponsible in some ways, but when it came to producing bookies to squeeze DiMattia was a real pro. The shakedowns of Pete Rooney and Bobby Craig are good examples.

Alongside DiMattia, Fiato made the rounds at the hippest lounges and restaurants in Hollywood and Beverly Hills. At Mateo's, they met with Frankie Valli and Frank Sinatra. At Joe Scott's, a private club, they encountered Lee Majors, Jim Brown and Bill Bixby. At Pip's, Fiato visited with Harry Guardino and Jack Catain, both of whom he knew from the old days at the Villa Capri, as well as Jacqueline Bissett and Rod Stewart's now ex-wife, Alana. DiMattia made himself welcome on both sides of the hill.

"One of the most important people DiMattia introduced me to was an Oriental girl named Teresa, who was an agent to book-maker Earl Bayless," Fiato recalled. "She took a liking to me and we used her to work around Bayless, who's a notorious snitch like most of the bookmakers in Southern California. Through Teresa, we picked up dozens of Earl's customers. Then we used her to bet with Bayless. We'd bet thousands and thousands on games, use him to lay off bets from our other customers. When we won, we collected. When we lost, we told him to go fuck himself. Through Teresa we managed to grab a series of agents. Agents are smaller bookmakers who rope customers for a larger office. They handle the pay-and-take. By grabbing them, we got around Bayless and he had more trouble playing the snitch.

"Through Teresa we booked to guys like Murray the K., who was a big disk jockey in New York and had a house in Southern California. We booked all of Nick Arno's action. Nick was a nice guy who had been a top writer for "Welcome Back Kotter" and had MS, but I swear Nick couldn't win a bet. As the action got larger, we turned it over to my brother, Larry, who booked it out of his apartment. We're giving Rizzitello a pinch of the profits out of respect.

"That's not all I'm doing for Rizzi. Through a producer I knew, Billy Fine, I arranged for Rizzi's daughter, Donna, to get her Screen Actors Guild card. Billy put Donna in a small speaking part on one of the *Penitentiary* movies. The kid was pretty excited and Rizzi was impressed because SAG cards aren't easy to obtain. There was one thing about Mike; no matter how much I did for him, he always reminded me I could never do enough for him.

"That's the way it was with the bookmaking. We were generous with Mike. Then after our first bad week, Mike wants to stiff everybody. I couldn't believe it. He wanted to settle for the quick fucking score. We have an argument over the whole fucking thing. I gave him the money he figured he was owed for that week, and that was that. We kept working the bookmakers. The only difference is, we stopped sending Mike his money.

"When Mike finally found out about it, he was angry. He talked to DiMattia, who couldn't wait to pay him. I told John to tell Mike I was broke. I wasn't going to pay him a fucking nickel. From that point on, John, Puggy, and I worked together more closely. Puggy eventually put Mike and me on friendly terms again, which in the long run was a big mistake."

At LaMaganette, Johnny "Popcorn" Pellegrino, whose father had been a driver for "Tony Ducks" Corrallo, welcomed the wiseguys with open arms. Pellegrino also was believed to be backing crooked card games at the Cavendish Club at 9555 Sunset Boulevard. His Thousand Oaks restaurant, Porky's, specialized in ribs and was also the subject of FBI surveillance.

He had managed to open LaMaganette with financial assistance from Las Vegas entertainer Liberace, an acquaintance of Anthony Spilotro. Thanks to DiMattia and Johnny Popcorn, Fiato managed to uncover a bookmaker named Pete Rooney. The red-haired Rooney worked for Earl Bayless, who booked millions in bets out of his Marina Del Rey headquarters. Bayless was known as a snitch, and anyone who tried to put the arm on him wound up in being watched by law enforcement. So Fiato decided to work through Rooney, who might be more easily intimidated. Rooney, it turned out, was one of Popcorn's partners in the restaurant. So Fiato ordered Pellegrino to lure Rooney into a trap. They would meet at Mateo's and Fiato would surprise Rooney and scare him into cooperating.

By the time they cornered Rooney, he knew he was in trouble. So did Johnny Popcorn, who was suspected of tipping off his restaurant partner. Fiato delivered his message.

"'You Irish motherfucker, you can go anywhere in this fucking country and our hands can reach you,'" Fiato said. "You should have seen the look of terror in the guy's face. He begged us not to tell anyone that he was kicking money into us. We got up to

$2,000 a week off him. All of a sudden we were Earl Bayless's new partners."

Rooney's concern for confidentiality was genuine. If the cops found out he was paying off, they would squeeze him as a witness against the maniacal Fiato. If Bayless found out, he would no longer do business with him and Rooney would be on his own. That he was paying off La Cosa Nostra was nowhere near the top of his list of concerns.

Turning Bobby Craig proved a tougher project. He was a high-rolling bookmaker with friendships in the gambling and bookmaking fraternities. Craig was not difficult to find, but he was hard to impress. And he was known to have friends in the LAPD's Administrative Vice unit.

Craig was accustomed to mixing with actors, producers and wealthy businessmen. He often worked out of the Beverly Hills Friar's Club, where there was always a card game going on the second floor and always a collection of colorful characters holding court. When Fiato and DiMattia attempted to isolate Craig, he ran to New York bookmaker Milton Wekar, whose association with the Lucchese and Genovese crime families was the stuff of legend. Wekar reached out for mutual friends in an attempt to back off The Animal, but nothing seemed to work. Craig knew he was in trouble the afternoon he received a phone call from the lobby of the Friar's. It was John DiMattia and Anthony Fiato.

"There was a counter and John said we couldn't get up there unless we went through this person," Fiato said. "I said okay, started to walk out, then turned around and pushed John right up the stairs. He didn't want to go. He fancied himself as a guy who could hang out at the Friar's Club and pal around with the regulars. I was beginning to see that, for all his good looks and tough talk, John wasn't much of a gangster. So I gave him a little encouragement.

"When we got into the room, the card game stopped. I yelled something like, 'Where is the Jew motherfucker?'

"Bobby Craig had a bodyguard, but he wasn't much help.

When Bobby stood up and walked over, I put my arm around him. When we got to the stairs, I made sure he got to the bottom head first. When we got to the parking lot, about a thousand pounds of my crew was there: Larry, Hy and Joe. I screamed at him, told him he was showing no respect and what the fuck was he doing running to people in New York when he's got problems right here. Well, Mike had taken care of our Miltie Wekar problems and Craig was ripe for the picking. He started paying off. He thought we might actually hurt him."

While dining two weeks later at Mateo's with Rizzitello, Fiato saw Pete Rooney at the bar. Frank Sinatra's buddy Jilly Rizzo was in the house, and Mike took time to talk about their mutual friend, Sinatra. Across the restaurant, Fiato eyed Bobby Craig dining alone. One table away was a pair of LAPD organized crime detectives observing the scene. When Fiato went to the bar, he paused and said hello to Rooney, who whispered a few words of advice.

"Watch out for that Bobby Craig," Rooney said. "He's a stoolie."

Fiato smiled and returned to his table. Later he got up to go to the men's room and Bobby Craig met him at the door.

"You know that guy you were talking to at the bar? That's Pete Rooney," Craig said. "Watch out. He's a stool pigeon."

"The way I had it figured, they were both stool pigeons, but neither one of them wanted anybody to know about it," Fiato recalled. "As long as I put the fear of God into them, as long as they thought that if they talked they'd end up dead, I held an advantage over them."

"After I bailed out Harvey Ross, he started coming to the club regularly and told me all about the pornographers he knew. Now Harvey's acting like one of my crew. With his balding head, he looked something like Pernell Roberts in *Trapper John, M.D.* Sticking up for him with Sal Esposito, I gave Harvey a license to feel good about himself. He starts going around acting cocky and carrying a .45. With me behind him, I created a monster. He tells me he's working for a place called the American Video Library for Russ Hampshire, who Harvey says wants to have somebody killed. Russ realized who I was and knew me by reputation, and he's also good friends with Michael Esposito. Russ knew that Harvey was friendly with me, and he brought up this deal to Harvey that his partner, Walter, was throwing away the business by doing so much cocaine. Harvey came back and told me that Russ had told him he wanted to have his partner killed.

"So I send Harvey to Radio Shack for a seventy-eight-dollar pocket recorder and arrange a meeting with Russ. I told Harvey, 'Get him alone again and get him to repeat what he'd said. Harvey goes to the meeting, follows him into the men's room and asks him if he was really sure he wanted to go through with this. Harvey gets him to say he wants his motherfucking partner dead and is willing to pay Anthony fifty-thousand to do the job. Half up front and half when it's done. We take the half up front.

"After Harvey met with him, we made another meet, this time at the Tail 0' the Cock on La Cienega. Harvey, Puggy, John DiMittia and I were at the meeting. When Russ walked in I could see the fear on his face. He only expected to be meeting me and Harvey. Russ was carrying a briefcase and sat down. He appeared to know everybody at the table. I told Harvey to take out the tape and play it for him.

"Russ's eyes almost popped out of his head like a frog. I gave him the tape. I said, 'Here, you're lucky this came to my attention because this motherfucker Harvey was going to blackmail you.' He was so happy, he slid the briefcase over in the booth and handed over twenty-five thousand cash, just like that. We're not going to kill anybody for this guy. And we don't have to. He can't go to the cops. He can't do anything. It was sweet.

"When he left, we just laughed. I'd had Harvey make six copies of that fucking tape. Russ kept paying for two years until finally after the fifth or sixth time he turned his pockets inside out and said, 'All I've got left is lint. Tell Walter, tell the cops. Tell anybody you want. I don't care what you do.'

"At that point we'd taken thousands from the guy and we didn't need to hurt anyone."

Jack Catain was different. He was an experienced wiseguy who had managed to grow rich in Los Angeles over the past forty years. Although in semi-retirement, Catain's contacts were impeccable. His ability to work his way inside legitimate institutions was unprecedented in Los Angeles organized crime.

So when Fiato heard that Catain had an inside man loaning large sums of money to the aging racketeer's friends, he jumped at the opportunity. The only problem, of course, was that Fiato was not friends with Catain.

"I'm looking to grab a hundred thousand off Jack Catain, who had a big connection with a bank on Sunset Boulevard. Jack was able to give out loans of more than a hundred thousand dollars to independent producers. I didn't want to make a movie. I just wanted the money.

"So I have Harry Guardino lure him for me to the Polo Lounge in Beverly Hills. This guy Jack is a long-time Los Angeles hoodlum who'd had trouble with Rizzitello and Jack LoCicero. Rizzi and LoCicero were trying to extort money from Catain, who was Milano-friendly. Catain and Johnny Lantino had even gotten the best of Rizzi and LoCicero in a fight one night at Tracton's. But there weren't many fights at the Polo Lounge, unless it was between producers and starlets. Everybody who was anybody in Hollywood has lunch there.

"I'm supposed to meet Jack with John DiMattia, who he's on good terms with, and instead John backs out at the last minute. He knows what I'm after, and I think he didn't want to lose the friendship with Catain. I later found out he owed Jack money. It was a typical move by DiMattia. You can always depend on John DiMattia. He'll always let you down. He pulled the same stunt when we were supposed to collect some money from Lou Alexander and Frankie Avalon. Lou was a bookmaking customer, but he had also loaned money to John, who disappeared when it came time to collect the debt.

"So I take my brother Larry with me and we tip the maitre d' to tell us where Catain's table is. He was obviously suspecting trouble because he's with a big heavyset guy, a football player-type. I introduce myself and tell him that an emergency came up and John couldn't make it.

"He starts to stammer an fidget and says that he doesn't think he can help me, that his contact has dried up or some such bull-shit, and I get angry with him. 'What the fuck do you mean you can't do it?' I ask him. 'You're giving money to these broken-down valises. You know we're good people, and I know your banker will do anything you tell him. So tell him to wake the fuck up and come up with the cash.

"Then the football player gets excited and pats my hand, tells me to settle down. I tell him the words of Larry Baioni: 'What are you, a tough guy? Let me tell you something. All the tough guys are dead. We do away with them all.'

"Then I took a fork and stuck it in his face. I tried to poke out his eye, but I missed and hit his cheek bone. Blood was gushing everywhere, and everybody in the place was staring at our table. A woman started to scream, and all hell broke loose. A guy tried to stand up, but my brother Larry backed him off.

"I told Jack Catain, 'You made a big fucking mistake. You haven't seen the last of me.' A week later, he came up with fifty thousand as a tribute to our new found friendship. It wasn't the hundred grand, but it wasn't bad."

Once Fiato's crew got rolling, violence was an everyday occurrence. They cleared out bars, intimidated restaurant owners, shook down bookmakers. They even worked on Sunday morning. When a degenerate gambler fell behind on his juice, Fiato staked him out early Sunday outside a North Hollywood taco stand. When the man saw Fiato waiting, he made a run for it to a nearby Catholic church. Carrying a baseball bat, Fiato followed him inside and whacked him over the head in the middle of morning mass.

"We thought the guy was a snitch for Jack Motto from Administrative Vice, and we made sure he didn't remember our names,"

Anthony Fiato recalled. "We wanted to make sure no one thought they could find sanctuary from us, and as soon as he woke up he found a way to pay his debt without opening his mouth."

When Anthony Fiato received a nervous phone call from Norman Freedberg asking him to come to his house in Panorama City, he presumed it had something to do with loansharking. By late 1981, Puggy and Anthony had loaned Norman thousands of dollars and expected the broken-down actor to remember his obligations.

"When I get out there with my brother, Larry, we're met at the door by Norman's nephew. Norman comes up to me and asks me to excuse Larry, and so Larry and Norman's nephew go into another room. Something's obviously bothering nervous Norman.

"We go out into his backyard by the pool and he's acting stranger than usual. He tells me a story about how Frank Christi has been fucking his girl, Jan. He said he saved $5,000 to have Christi killed and would I arrange it for him. At this time, I've probably got $25,000 in my pocket. When I hear the words I really get pissed off. I tell him, 'You mean you had me drive all the way out here so you could ask me this? You don't kill a guy over a fucking broad. Are you crazy? If you're mad at him go get a baseball bat and break his legs.' I mean, Norman was like a cartoon character. I never thought in my wildest dreams that he would ever kill Frank Christi.

"On the way home I told my brother Larry about it and he nearly fell out. I told him, 'Can you imagine this fucking guy wants to kill Frank Christi over that whore of his.' And Larry said, 'This guy is a fucking moron. He really takes himself serious.' And we laughed our asses off."

In early July 1982, Anthony Fiato, Kathy and Larry were sitting at home watching television when a news reporter began talking about the sensational murder of *The Godfather* actor Frank Christi. Shortly after midnight on July 9, a witness observed at least two men scuffling with Christi outside his home on Woodrow Wilson

Drive in the hills above Studio City. He was later found lying in his carport next to his red 1974 Datsun car. He had been shot to death.

The mystery surrounding Christi's death was compounded not only by his known underworld ties, but also by the fact his divorce lawyer, Frank Salitieri, was murdered the same week at his nearby residence.

To Anthony Fiato, there was no mystery. The mob hadn't killed Frank Christi. Norman Freedberg had.

"I looked at my brother and my girlfriend in disbelief," Fiato said. "I said, 'Can you imagine that motherfucker had it done.'

"And a couple days later Harvey Ross came over and tells me he did it with two other guys. He's puffing out his chest, really proud of what he'd done. He thought I'd be impressed.

"All I wanted to know was whether he used that .22 pistol with the silencer that was used in the Bomp murder, and he said he hadn't. Before Harvey told me I pretty well figured out who was with him. It was Alan Betts and Ronald Coe, two guys I'd hooked him up with. They were pulling jewel heists and B&Es together.

"I said to Harvey, 'How much fucking money did you do it for? Not the five-thousand?' He nodded and said yes. I found out later it was really seventy-five-hundred. 'You mean to tell me you split five-thousand three ways and killed this guy for that?' Harvey could tell I wasn't impressed.

"The next morning I get a call from Puggy, who naturally starts talking about the news. He wants to meet to figure out what to do about everything. He sets up a meeting at a Denny's restaurant and we meet over there. But the Denny's is too wide open and we get up and decide to move to a place called Frankie's Pizza, a little restaurant Puggy and I had taken over. On the way over, we ride over in Harvey's black Cadillac. Harvey and Betts are in the front seat and Puggy, Coe and me are in the back. Larry is following us in my car. On the way over I laid down the fucking law. 'You know what happens to fucking tough guys,' I told them. 'We do away with them. Everyone wants to be a tough guy. Well all the tough guys are dead.' In my voice I heard the words of Larry Baioni and J.R. Russo. Needless to say Harvey, Betts and Coe were none too pleased to be sitting with me."

Jimmy Caan has made no secret of his friendships with organized crime figures. Caan grew up in Brooklyn and ran with the Corona Dukes street gang before going on to stardom in Hollywood. It was only natural that he would want to meet the new powerhouse in town.

"I first met Jimmy through a drug dealer named Mike Liszt," Anthony Fiato said. "Mike was bankrolled by Puggy in a drug deal. Mike started dropping by the house because he owed Puggy money. He mentioned to Caan that he knew me and Caan wanted to meet me. So one night Mike shows up at the door with the guy, who was a little nervous at first. But he was a good storyteller. He immediately started telling war stories about guys he'd had fights with on subways, that sort of thing. He's trying to impress me. Right away he started talking about the people we had in common. He knew Andrew Russo, Alley Boy Persico, Joey and Lenny Mangiapani, Joey Isgro. He was joking and talking about the Jews and the Italians and asked me if I knew his friend Joey Ippolito, and I said I did.

"But I also knew that he was a big drug user at the time, so I took out some cocaine and dumped it on the table. The more coke he does, the more he talks. Then he called up his wife, Sheila, and before we knew it, we had a party going.

"He kept making fun of Mike Liszt, a small man, and he kept saying, 'I didn't believe a little fuck like Mike Liszt would know a guy like you. I had to come see for myself.' Mike had said he'd done business with Caan in the past.

"At that time he talked about Burt Young and other guys he knew, and he'd helped Burt get a part in a movie. He mentioned Joey Mangiapani, a friend of Burt's, and asked whether I knew him. Then he talked about the time he got into a fight back in New York with Joey's brother, Lenny. He was telling small world stories.

"Blockhead Steve Monaco was over the house when Jimmy was there, and he couldn't believe he was seeing a movie star up close. He wasn't the brightest guy in the world to begin with, and Jimmy saw he was nervous, so he attempted to lighten him up."

Fiato said, "Blockhead Steve, I want you to meet Jimmy Caan."

Monaco said, "It's a pleasure to meet you, James."

Caan said, "Please, call me Jimmy."

Monaco: "All right, James."

Caan: "No, you don't understand. Call me Jimmy."

Monaco: "Okay, James."

Caan to Fiato: "Now I know why you call him Blockhead."

"After a while we decided to go to a night club, and we caravaned over to Westwood," Fiato recalled. "He was driving a Mercedes with his wife, and Blockhead Steve was driving me. On the way over, Jimmy has to stop for gas and pulls in quick to a station. Steve pulls in right behind him and winds up ramming his Mercedes. I was embarrassed. And Blockhead Steve could barely speak. We had a great time, but, man, that Jimmy could party.

"And the next morning I get a knock on my door at the crack of dawn. It's Jimmy and he's asking for more stuff. I went back inside and found some for him and he went away happy."

Over the next few months, Caan and his younger brother, Ronnie, were frequent visitors to Fiato's home. Ronnie had just gotten out of the hospital, where he had donated bone marrow to a critically ill family member. When they were getting along, Jimmy and Ronnie Caan were like a pair of New York-bred comedians. They played off each other and could draw a crowd and then make it bust up laughing.

Ronnie Caan's mood shifted constantly. He smoked cocaine and was in the throes of severe addiction. He would brag about conning drug dealers into providing him with product by convincing them that he was the executive producer of his famous brother's latest movie and that he was empowered to sell points in the project.

"He was a fast talker," Fiato said. "This is the kind of guy Ronnie is. If he told you that he just had lunch with Jimmy Hoffa, you'd look at him like he was crazy. And by the time he got through talking, you'd ask him what Hoffa ate. That's how good he was."

In short order Jimmy Caan met Mike Rizzitello and later called Fiato to assist him in straightening out one of Ronnie's debts to mob drug dealer Louie Ippolito. Fiato cooperated, and placed intimidating calls to Ippolito, whose brother, Joey, also was known as a mob-linked drug trafficker.

In time, Caan partied with Fiato at Hugh Hefner's Playboy Mansion, and Fiato introduced Jimmy Caan to a trustworthy bookmaker. He also visited the actor on the set of *Kiss Me Goodbye*, a movie also starring Sally Field and Jeff Bridges. Caan, whose many roles included playing gangsters, cowboys and even a half-back with a fatal disease, danced and carried a cane in the movie.

One morning, Fiato received a phone call from a frantic Jimmy Caan.

"Antony, my man. I just got a call from this motherfucker who's got my brother," Caan said. "He wants fifty thousand my brother owes him."

Fiato told Caan he'd take care of it. Within five minutes, he had assembled his brother, Larry, "Fat Steve" Munichiello and "Cowboy" Dave Tracy. They drove to Beverly Hills and met with Caan near a park on Rexford Drive. Fiato set a plan in motion: He stashed himself and his men out of sight.

When the kidnapper's car pulled up, Caan, who constantly held a cane to prepare for his role in his latest movie, would get out of his own vehicle, then signal when the deal was ready to take place. What would happen next would likely lead to gunfire, and Fiato and his boys were armed.

"Jimmy had a .45 himself. And, sure enough, these guys pull up. One guy gets out of the car. The other guy stays in the car on the passenger side, which was strange. Ronnie is in the backseat. Once the first guy gets close enough to Jimmy, we jumped out and I start beating the fuck out of the guy. I expect to hear gunshots from the car, but there's nothing. Instead, the other guy gets out of the car and starts running down the street. We're beating the fuck out of the first guy, and all of a sudden Ronnie comes out of the car yelling, 'Anthony, no, no, no.'"

"The bloodied man on the ground cried to Ronnie, 'What did you get me into?' Then, to Jimmy he said, 'Your brother put me up to this.'"

Cowboy Dave and Larry caught up to the guy who ran away, gave him a beating and left him sprawled out in a palatial front yard like a broken lawn jockey.

Within minutes, police sirens filled the air. The Caan brothers drove away slowly with Fiato and his crew trailing. When police pulled over the actor, Fiato parked within earshot and heard, "Can't two brothers argue on a Saturday morning in Beverly Hills?"

The cops laughed. One said, "I loved you in *The Godfather*" as they drove off. Only an actor could get away with such a disturbance of the peace. If the police had been a little more observant, they might have caught a glimpse of a real godfather.

Fiato and Caan maintained constant contact, and often spoke in street language on the telephone. One day the actor dropped by Fiato's place for cocaine and favors.

"It was a typical night. Jimmy was telling war stories, shoving coke up his nose, and calling me Ant-ny," Fiato said. "He'd finished *Kiss Me Goodbye*, the movie where he'd taken me on the set and showed me off as one of his Mafia friends. Over at my house one night Jimmy says this guy Gene Kirkwood is producing a movie, *The Pope of Greenwich Village* and it would be perfect for him and Al Pacino.

"He asked me if we knew anybody who could get in touch with this guy, Kirkwood. I immediately thought of Aaron Russo and told Jimmy at that time I'd reach out to someone.

"The next day I called Aaron Russo and asked him if he could get this guy Gene Kirkwood in his office for me to talk to him. What I didn't tell Jimmy was that Joe 'Fish' Gruppa had told me about this guy Kirkwood, that he had been a friend of Tommy Ricciardi, an associate of mine in the L.A. mob. So I figured I'd have an in because I'd heard Tommy Ricciardi had helped Kirkwood out when he came here from back east. Tommy helped feed him and put him on his feet. That's all I needed to get my hooks into him.

"I set up the meeting at Russo's office at Paramount Studios in Hollywood. When I got there with Mike Lizst, Aaron Russo was behind his desk and a young, good-looking guy was sitting in a chair looking bored. It was Kirkwood. I brought Mike Liszt with me because he wanted to meet these Hollywood types. Aaron had that big smile on his face that he always had when he used to see me. He introduced me to Gene Kirkwood, and I told Kirkwood that we had a friend in common, Tommy Ricciardi. I said, 'Well, I'm not going to beat around the bush. My friend Jimmy Caan is looking to be a part of this project, and he says he can guarantee Pacino.' Kirkwood said, 'Jesus, it's too late now. I got Mickey Rourke and Eric Roberts for the part.' I said, 'As far as we're concerned, it's never too late.' He started giving me some legal mumbo-jumbo that I didn't understand, and Aaron Russo confirmed what he was saying was true about how he was locked into the contract. I said, 'The most important thing is that Jimmy Caan understands this, that he understands that this deal is etched in stone and can't be broken.' So I asked Aaron if I could use his phone. I had Mike Liszt dial Jimmy's number. I took the phone and said, 'Hey, Top Cat, I'm at the meeting. I'm listening to all this lawyer talk. I know you can understand it.' And Kirkwood explained to Jimmy how production had already started and Jimmy told me. 'He's telling the truth. Thanks for trying. Give the guy a break, but not in the legs.'"

Caan tabbed Fiato for several favors, including an attempt to collect an $8,000 debt from another tough-guy actor. The actor stayed

at Donny Soffer's Turnberry Island resort and left the hotel without closing out his account. Soffer had made millions building
shopping centers and owned the boat "Monkey Business," which
had been the site of presidential candidate Gary Hart's notorious
liaison with Donna Rice. He also was Caan's friend, and Caan
was attempting to do him a favor.

"Jimmy used to go to Turnberry to rest, fish and party," Fiato
recalled. "I sent Fat Steve, Larry and Carl Cataldo to Nate 'n' Al's
to find the guy, but he wasn't there. They came back three straight
days. The actor was always there when he was in town, but then I
learned he'd gone back to New York for a while."

During their conversation, Caan also had unkind words for producer Dody El Fayed, the son of the Egyptian millionaire who
had invested a fortune in Hollywood. He'd also reneged on a deal
with mob drug trafficker Mike Liszt.

"I told my guys to stick a fork in the actor's face if he didn't
come up with the money," Fiato said. "He fancied himself as a
tough guy because he knew people with the Genovese family in
New York. A lot of people knew Dody. He used people all over
Hollywood and left a trail of debts."

When a 1982 federal grand jury met to probe Fiato's criminal
enterprise, the government called in his associates and friends,
including Jimmy Caan.

"Jimmy really helped me, which I appreciated at the time," Fiato
said. "I knew they were onto something, but I didn't know what.
Then everything went quiet, and I figured they'd gone away. At the
time, I was too busy making money to worry about it."

Larry Fiato's take on Caan was different.

"I didn't like Jimmy Caan that much," Larry said. "He was my
brother's friend. Just another user. He was like a lot of the people
we knew who said they were our friends, but then would deny
they ever knew you. Unless he needed me to deliver drugs to his
house. He wants to be a tough guy, and to other wiseguys he always
wanted to be known as a connected guy, a worker, someone who
was capable with his hands. But he was just a wanna-be guy."

Anthony Fiato could always rely on his little brother for backup, but good help was not always easy to find. For every scheming professional like Pete Milano, for every genuine tough guy like Mike Rizzitello, for every slippery whisperer like Luigi Gelfuso, there are dozens of guys who have great difficulty putting their shoes on the proper foot, much less carrying out a job. Many are just plain stupid, but few of even the dimmest bulbs rivaled "Blockhead Steve" Monaco.

How dumb was the Blockhead?

When he hooked up with Fiato in Los Angeles, Monaco was wearing a Navy uniform. He said he joined the Navy but had decided to quit.

"Why did you join the Navy?" Fiato asked.

Deadly serious, Monaco replied, "I joined the Navy to see the world."

"But just like that he decided to quit the Navy," Fiato said. "He didn't get the idea that they might want their uniform back and even come looking for him. He just walked away from the base."

Fiato liked the Blockhead, but he didn't trust him for important jobs. Instead, he sent him out for pizza. After waiting for his food for more than two hours, Fiato called the pizza parlor and asked if a guy had come by in a Mercedes to pick up the pies.

"He was here, but he left," the parlor's cashier said. "He drove the wrong way into the parking lot and punctured all four tires on the tire guard."

When Monaco came through the door, Fiato asked him where he'd been.

"The craziest thing happened when I went in to get the pizza. A bunch of black guys knifed the tires and flattened them," Monaco said.

Fiato recalled, "The guy was not only dumb, he was a terrible liar."

Once, when Fiato, DiMattia and Monaco were arrested on a petty bookmaking charge, the former Navy man was apprehended for being Absent Without Leave. He went stir crazy inside of a day and attempted to commit suicide. But Blockhead Steve failed at that, too. He tried to slash his wrists by scraping them against the cell door lock. In effect, he was attempting to rub himself to death. He received only a mild rash.

The Fiatos were used to spotting cops in the bars and nightclubs they frequented. They understood their activities would be frowned upon by the local authorities, but it took months for them to appreciate the scope of the investigation they were under.

"When I first found out we had a problem, I was driving across town from some business to a meeting with my brother and Puggy," Larry Fiato said. "I noticed I was being followed by three cars, whose drivers weren't even trying hard to disguise what they were doing. I called my brother from the car phone and told him I was being followed, and everyone said I was paranoid. We were meeting on the ninth floor of a building on Ventura Boulevard, and I told them to go to the window when I pulled up and they'd see the cars. 'Watch when I pull into the driveway.' They weren't even trying to hide while they were following me. After that, they knew I wasn't paranoid. But we didn't miss a beat. We kept operating and we got work done even with the tails on us."

By early 1983 Bob Kessler had become Anthony Fiato's constant companion. So it was only natural that when Kessler heard about $1 million in stolen bearer bonds floating out there for the taking he would tell his good friends, Mike Rizzitello and Anthony Fiato. On June 1, 1980, Montgomery County Maryland issued 199 consolidated public improvement bonds worth $1 million. With an interest rate of 6.4 percent, they were due to mature in early 1983. They were stolen from Manufacturers Hanover Trust, and the endlessly resourceful Kessler knew plenty about them.

"Kessler starts telling me about these bonds," Fiato said. "They were stolen and some of them were cashed. Mike was on the phone talking about them. Now a million dollars is a lot of money and Mike can smell the money. We sent Finkel east to make an exchange."

Kessler had come into his knowledge through Jack Feinberg, a lifelong scam artist whose own story read like fiction. When it came to his role in organized crime, he was Unlucky Luciano. For all his angles, Feinberg, who also was known as Jack Fine, had an uncanny knack for attracting the attention of law enforcement. His arrest record spanned four decades.

"Fine was a con man who worked for Mickey Cohen and talked about the Mick fondly," Fiato said. "He also was an associate of Mike Rizzitello. Jack was always coming up with scams. He knew people in the movie business and the banking business. Puggy and I would run into him at Nate 'n' Al's and he knew Bob Kessler. We used to make a joke out of Jack. He was around 60 years old and had been in the can so many times he must have been the worst thief in the world.

"He was a bustout guy, a guy who would take a business and drain it of its assets, then make it go bankrupt. Rizzi came to me and asked me to loan him thirty-thousand. He said Jack would pay two-and-a-half percent a week. Fine was involved with Lenny Aron in a deli in Palm Springs. They both were attempting to work a deal on Jacob Zemer, who knew all about the bonds. Fine and Aron were trying to shake down Zemer, who was looking for help from them and ran into my man, Steve Finkel. Finkel worked Zemer for information and gave him jewelry as a tribute. The whole idea was to get the inside track on the bonds, which we knew could be redeemed for cash.

"Zemer wanted help to get Fine and Aron off his back and I was glad to oblige him for $5,000—and a piece of the action. I tell them that from then on they had to do everything through Finkel and cut everyone else out. Finkel got access to the bonds, which were held by a New York company.

"I coordinated everything. I asked Puggy to get on the phone. We sent Finkel to New York to establish ownership of the bonds and his end went off without a hitch. Puggy was nervous. He was afraid to talk in case the phone was tapped, but I didn't care. I was smelling that money, too. At one point, to lighten Puggy up while we were talking on the phone, I said, 'Whoever's listening, Puggy Zeichick's my partner,' which he didn't appreciate. To establish ownership of the bonds you had to have the serial numbers. We bought the numbers for $1,000 apiece from Zemer, and Finkel took care of the rest. We cut out Fine and Aron, plugged in Finkel and were on our way to a huge payday.

"But it got interrupted along the way."

CHAPTER 7

The dog wouldn't stop barking.

It was early, almost 6 a.m., and Anthony Fiato lay in bed listening to the yap of Tony, his Lhaso Apso. Obviously, something was irritating the dog, even scaring him. Benedict Canyon was full of coyotes. Perhaps one had wandered near the back fence, Fiato thought. He had been up most of the night partying, and could hear his wife and bodyguard, Fat Steve Munichiello, talking in the living room. They had been doing cocaine for hours.

The pounding at the door jarred Fiato from bed.

"Kathy," a man's voice called, "open the door right now."

When Kathy opened the door, law enforcement agents poured into the entryway and into the living room with guns drawn. They had a search warrant and they weren't waiting around for a guided tour. Fat Steve managed to dump the cocaine he had into a flower pot near where he was sitting.

"In comes the FBI agents, federal marshall's office, LAPD, DA's investigators, the LAPD organized crime squad, the state police. There had to be twenty law enforcement people in my house. I was naked and, frankly, stunned.

"Before I could say anything, an FBI Agent named Andy Stefanich said, 'Anthony, put your pants on.' I watched them move and it was obvious they knew the location of everything in the fucking house. I was dead, I knew I was dead. I had a pistol at the time, but I'd given it to Carl Cataldo to keep at his house. I had fifteen-thousand in my pants pocket, thousands more on my dresser and stuff all over the house. They were having a field day.

"I always thought that my phone might have been bugged, but I never believed it, really. Something big was going on, and I was in the middle of it.

"I tried to remember if I'd said anything having to do with a gun or talked about clipping somebody. Everybody's gun was drawn, as if I was going to shoot it out like Dillinger. I was frozen. Remember, I'd been pinched before, but nothing like this had ever happened to me."

Jim Nelson, the former Major League baseball player who became a big hitter with the Los Angeles office of the FBI, sat at the fireplace and said, "It's going to be a long year for you, my friend."

Another agent, Bob Hamer, added, "You look bad, Fiato. You look like you're ready to have a heart attack."

Nelson said, "Shut up and do your work."

But Anthony did look sick. His chest was heavy. He couldn't get enough air. No arrests were made and, after turning Fiato's house upside down, the swarm of law enforcement left almost as suddenly as it arrived.

While searching Fiato's residence, FBI agents discovered a half-dozen video copies of *The Godfather* and wondered whether life was imitating art. Perhaps they did not realize that Fiato had been part of an operation that had bootlegged thousands of videotapes over the past three years. As they eavesdropped on Anthony Fiato's world from their listening post in the old garage at the federal courthouse in Los Angeles, agents were constantly entertained by the tough guy's way with a one-liner. They also were impressed by his penchant for violence.

Agents Hamer and Chris Spilsbury continued to try to rattle Fiato. Having had access to nearly every word Fiato had uttered in his home and on his telephone for the better part of a year, they knew that he had recently been to the doctor for a heart checkup. Hamer was especially cruel to Fiato, noting time after time that the tough guy did not look well. Jim Nelson finally put a stop to the chiding. Nelson, described by fellow agents as a walking encyclopedia of organized crime information, knew well the importance of maintaining communication with the Fiatos. If turned, the gangster brothers would be invaluable to the government's investigation.

At the moment Anthony Fiato's house was being raided, Larry Fiato heard the government at the door of his apartment.

"They came to my apartment," Larry said. "I was in bed naked with my wife and I had got up when I heard a noise. I saw the lock on the front door fly across the living room. I thought to myself, 'What the hell is this?' All of a sudden fifteen cops walk in. They treated us like Dillinger. They put a gun to my wife's head."

Soon after the first search warrant was served, the law returned to remove its bugging devices and wiretap equipment from Anthony Fiato's house. Five agents were at the back gate. Others crowded around the front door.

"I came out of the house in my bare feet," Fiato said. "They were all over the place. One of them, agent Mike Wacks, handed me a piece of paper. It was a notice of intercept. I'm thinking I'm going to get pinched right then and there, but they're at the house to pick up their recording equipment. They had the house bugged. I was reeling, wondering about all the conversations I'd had in my own living room."

Then Wacks said, "Hey, Tony, you're stepping in dog shit."

"It doesn't matter," Fiato said. "I'm dead. It's all over with."

Three agents passed Fiato and he knew they'd been listening to all his conversations. They knew all the extortions he had arranged, all the beatings he had sanctioned and performed personally.

"'It takes five of you motherfuckers to come into my house,'" Fiato recalled saying. "I spent the rest of the day agonizing over everything I'd ever talked about. I'd planned murders, big scores. Everything. I'd planned to whack Steve Finkel and Harvey Ross,

who Puggy and I thought were snitches. The FBI had warned
them, and they still didn't believe them. I'd even contemplated
killing Mike Rizzitello. There were so many people who came
and went from the house, so many things that were said."

But the agents weren't talking just to hear themselves speak.
They were planting seeds of doubt in the minds of their cocky
targets.

"One of the things we used to do with Anthony, they'd be in a
very good conversation, criminal conversation, they'd say, 'let's go
outside, I'm not sure about the house,' and we'd place a phone call
to them and hang up, you know," agent Mike Wacks said. "And
he says, 'These fucking cops are out here again, we can't go out,
we've gotta stay here.' So they'd keep the conversation going. All
we had to do is call them up and hang up on them.

"When we served the search warrants, we still had a couple
weeks left on the Title 3 (the federal wiretap permission statute).
And after all these months, we kind of got to know Anthony and
Larry, and being the sleazy persons we were, we started punching
a few of their buttons, you know, doing this and that to make
them even more paranoid. After that point we started, uh, we
started playing with him even more. Especially Larry. Well,
Anthony too. Because his friends really left him at that point. His
backers, the Cosa Nostra guys were all in jail. The only guys who
were out there were the Jewish backers. And that's what it came
down to. I think the expression is, 'While the Jews play, the
Italians pay.' And that's what we used to stress with Anthony, and
say hey, man, these guys aren't going anywhere. You're the one
gonna go to jail."

Bill Weichert said: "At this point, Mike and I certainly didn't
have to be concerned about making the case. God we had enough
evidence. And the reason we kept pimping them; there was a reason. It wasn't just to be facetious. We thought in time that maybe
we could approach these fellows, probably after an indictment,
and say, look, we have got you so good you only have one way to
go and that's to help us. Our objective of course was the mob, the

family in Los Angeles, and anywhere else we could go. We knew they were from Boston."

In a short time, the agent's psychological games began to have their desired effect.

A federal grand jury had been convened, and Fiato's name was at the heart of the government's case against the Los Angeles mob. It was only a matter of time before Anthony Fiato was named in an indictment. His amazing run of luck was ending. Fiato had managed to stay on the street more than eighteen years without taking a hard fall. He spent the next three weeks sewing up business deals and wondering about the strength of the government's case. The FBI had to have informants to make a case. No one could get a conviction just with wiretap material. They needed eye witnesses, and that meant they needed rats in his organization.

Fiato also learned just how much the government knew. They had been working his crew since the fall of 1982 and had found the apartment Kathy Villa had rented for Anthony and herself at 1115 South Elm Drive in Los Angeles.

"We discovered through several confidential sources . . . that they were running with a capo of the Los Angeles family named Michael Rizzitello," FBI Agent Bill Weichert said. "And they had a rather extensive loansharking operation then, and we culminated the investigation, thank God, in time for the search warrants, and that's when these fellows began to realize what had happened.

"As a matter of fact, when we searched their homes, Anthony's home, Larry's home, and one other guy, Puggy Zeichick, the partner, it became obvious to them that they were had. We told them we'd been wiretapping for seven-and-a-half months, and all the different crimes and violations of the law we intended on indicting them on, and so on. We didn't arrest them at that time because we had seven-and-a-half months of tapes to prepare and weren't anxious to rush into court."

Give or take a decade, the Fiato brothers faced 400 years in prison if the government moved on every deal that had taken place the previous year. That also meant something else: Someone in his midst was an FBI informant.

Who? Friendly Bob Kessler would have been a likely candidate, but he came to Fiato through Rizzitello. For some reason, Kessler was always reluctant to discuss business in Fiato's living room.

If the brothers were looking for support from their criminal compatriots, it would be a long time coming. Everyone scattered in the wake of the search warrants.

"The most damaging part is that after we got word about it and everything was in confusion, we didn't know what to do. The customers we didn't want to go near, and with all the income stopped, you're left wondering what the hell you're gonna do," Larry Fiato recalled.

Anthony: "I'll tell you exactly what it feels like. It feels like, see, guys like us want to go through this life getting everything for nothing and never paying a tab. All right, that's what it really amounts to. And it seems like I had a great banquet, these many many years, I'm thirty, forty-two years old, and I finally get hit with the tab all at once.

"It was too much for me. Almost every thought, I could remember, almost every thought I had for seven months was like a shiv going into my heart. I'd be up all night and it had its effect on my wife and my marriage. Then seeing the so-called loyal trust that you imagined this Mafia has, and these types of people have, which vanishes immediately when there's a little trouble.

"You know, in on the scores, and out on the beefs. That's what it really comes down to. I never experienced that before; I had guys tell me about people like this. But it was my experience in this particular time to find out that the people around me ran for the hills, and I was so disappointed, so hurt, confused, and scared. I didn't want to go to jail.

"I always had a suspicion that something was going on because I would say, well, go over here and meet these two guys in a car at Fifth and Elm. But 20 minutes later, two cops would be at the corner of Fifth and Elm.

"I had a suspicion, but you never really want to believe it can happen to you. That's the advantage the FBI has over everybody. Nobody believes that it can happen to them. Nobody.

"You have to be a real extreme, consummate paranoid to believe something like that. You know your house is bugged, phones and everything. I used to make jokes on the phone. I used to say, 'If the FBI's listening, go fuck yourself' and I'd hang up. I used to say that, but I never really believed it."

The agents also got lucky.

"During the initial search of his apartment, we found a gun, and we got Larry busted on a probation violation," Mike Wacks said. "He went away for 30 days."

Larry Fiato: "During this time, I was talking to my brother, and he was saying about how everything is starting to come down, and the FBI's all around, and everything is lost, and it was in jail then that I decided I'm not gonna spend 20 years in jail, no way. So when I came out, you know, I saw that everything was in such a disarray, I had nothing left. They took everything. My car was gone, my apartment, everything. No income. That's when I decided to do something about it. And my brother didn't know a thing."

Larry Fiato worshipped his big brother, but he was a wreck. He also had a major cocaine habit. The collections Larry made on Anthony's behalf were a tangled mess of missing cash. At one point, Anthony had to kick in $10,000 because Larry had blown that much on drugs. For all his faults, he still had an instinct for survival.

"I was in jail and I was thinking about all the stuff that they had on us. I just knew that we were in a lot of trouble and my brother, for the first time, was confused. Well, because of the wiretaps and everything, we knew what we did, and we thought that they had all of that. I mean we didn't know exactly. All I knew is that I was going to go away and do some serious time. This time it wasn't no more 30 days or four months. This was serious shit.

"All the people that we were associated had run. Our money dried up. I mean we had nothing left and the people that we still had around us were not that strong. I thought there'd be a big line. We'd go down and go down hard. So I just walked in there. I didn't even tell my brother I was going in there. I just walked in.

"In other words, I felt like I had to make a move. I had to do it because I knew that my brother would never do it and that was the only way we're going to get out of this. And me and my brother were the ones who were going to go. Not Puggy, although he was involved, he was the money man, he had his lawyer, he had everything. We were the Italians and we were going to go. So I just took it upon myself to do it.

"I got along fine in jail. I was the only white guy in a cell and didn't have a problem. But that didn't mean I wanted to spend the rest of my life there. I was fearful of going to jail for a long time, and I was paranoid from all the cocaine. To this day I remember perfectly what I was thinking when I decided to make a deal. I was thinking, 'My brother got us out of everything my whole life. He always had a way out, was always thinking two, three steps ahead. Puggy had an army of lawyers. But for the first time in my life my brother was absolutely doing nothing. He was waiting for something to happen.' I knew when I went in there he would either have to kill me or come with me, and either way I wasn't going to do four hundred years in the penitentiary."

Anthony recalled, "Larry wound up moving into my house with his wife. I was paying him thousands, and he couldn't pay his fucking rent because of that fucking cocaine. He starts disappearing, and you have to understand, when something like this happens everybody goes underground until things cool off. They're looking to me for leadership and I have to keep up a strong front. Larry tells me he's looking for a job and needs to borrow the car. And he disappears for a few hours. I think he's out using that cocaine, but when he returns he's acting strange and it's not from the drugs. I sense something's wrong with Larry, but I had my own problems to contend with.

"After a while he finally sits down and says he wants to talk. Then he says he wasn't out looking for a job but instead met FBI agents at a hotel. 'They got us,' he said. 'I've seen what they've got on us and they've got us for a hundred years. I'm telling you they got stacks and stacks and stacks of evidence against us. I saw it.'

"And my eyes are about popping out of my head. I can't believe what I'm hearing. 'What do you mean you saw it?' Then he told me he met with two FBI agents and they showed him a ton of stuff against me.

"And all the time he's talking I'm thinking, 'The kid knows everything about me and the people I've dealt with. He knows every crime I've committed here and in Boston.' It scares me that he did this and that I don't know for sure how far he'd gone with them.

"If someone that you love betrayed you and you can't believe that it's happened, you become overwhelmed by this, paralyzed. You're in a state of shock. I'd never hurt my family. I'd die for my family, but my own brother is sitting there telling me he's met with the enemy.

"I had to keep my head together. My heart was racing. I went to the bathroom and took a handful of valium and slowly my heart rate starts to slow down. I've got to slow down my thoughts, got to arrange them in the right order, got to maintain my control. I can't let Larry know how angry I am, how close I am to killing him right then and there. I know I've got to kill this fucking kid, my own kid brother. It's for more than my own self-respect. I've got to kill him for self-preservation. He's hurt all my friends, and if I don't kill him right away they'll kill me as soon as they find out. And they're bound to find out. The feds will leak it just to watch what they do. I didn't know how far he'd gone. So I started trying to con him by asking him questions. How much did he say? Did he talk about anything in Boston? I'm doing the acting job of my life. Kathy is hysterical, but I'm calm. And he keeps telling me we're dead, that we're going away for a long time. 'They got you tied up in knots,' he says. 'You're going away for the rest of your life. They told me I wouldn't have to testify against you.' But I can't trust a word out of his mouth. My heart was jumping again and I realized the pills I'd taken had had almost no effect on my heart. His words keep tumbling over and over in my head. My own brother has ratted me out. That's what cocaine will do to you, make you rat out your own brother. I'm instantly humiliated at what my brother did. Look, I'd violated every fucking law there was. RICO, Continuing Criminal Enterprise, you name it.

"I'm a fucking dead man. This fucking kid has put a death sentence on me. He's hurt Rizzitello. He's hurt everyone I know. He's got to die. He put me in a fucking spot with these people and they'll expect me to kill him. But who do you go to to talk about killing your own brother? I already know there's a grand jury indictment pending with my name on it. And finally the valium kicked in and I started thinking about everything that had gone on.

"I look at my brother and he's so pathetic, sniffing and sniveling and he has to know what I'm thinking. I know he'd never do something like this to me if he wasn't on drugs. I think it over for a while and a couple of days later I tell him to arrange a meeting with these fucking guys. I'm so humiliated, but my sense of self-preservation is starting to kick in. I know I have to do something, even if it's wrong. When he told them that he'd talked to me, they went crazy. But the meeting was arranged."

Larry and Anthony drove to a Ramada Inn and went to a pre-arranged room. Once inside, he met the enemy face-to-face. There was agent Michael Wacks, who had made Fiato a special project. Wacks was a veteran street agent who had gone undercover against the mob in the BRILAB case involving Louisiana's Carlos Marcello crime family. There was his partner, Bill Weichert, who visibly shook when Fiato entered the room. Wacks and Weichert had been working Fiato for months. Wacks was the most experienced undercover agent on the Los Angeles squad and personally spearheaded the bureau's Operation Rising Star.

Then Los Angeles Organized Crime Strike Force Chief James D. Henderson arrived. Henderson was known nationwide as the man who turned Aladena "Jimmy the Weasel" Fratianno. He was one of America's premiere mob-busters.

"Henderson couldn't look me in the eye," Fiato recalled. "He started asking questions about me. I couldn't believe this guy couldn't look me in the face. I thought, 'What the fuck is this guy trying to do, insult me?' Then I figured it out. After listening to all those tapes of me, he must have thought I'd go berserk or something. They asked about my relationship with Mike Rizzitello. From their questions I could tell my brother had told them everything about me, all my past, Boston, the whole works. I realized that if I act like a fucking wiseguy we're not going to get along. My brother was a lie-detector for them. They asked about all my dealings and were interested in my relationships with all the mob guys. They knew that Pete Milano wanted to make me in his crew, and they knew Rizzitello had already put me on record with Neil Dellacroce. They knew everything, including a lot of things Larry didn't tell them. My brother was right. I hated what he did, but he was right. They had me by the balls."

Henderson recalled, "Anthony Fiato had a reputation as a real tough guy. He was the real deal. And unlike a lot of the people in that world, he was smart. He had managed to elude law enforcement for many years. And in Los Angeles at the time, Anthony and his brother, Larry, were true enforcers."

Once Anthony Fiato started talking, the room went quiet. The agents knew they had a potential gold mine of information on their hands. They also knew they would ask him to wear a wire against his friends. Once the process was begun, Fiato had no choice but to cooperate.

In a subsequent meeting, Anthony Fiato worked with agents James Nelson and Chuck Jones. Nelson was a big man who had played first base for the Minnesota Twins.

"Nelson reminded me of a John Wayne-type of character," Fiato said. "And then he goes and pulls a John Wayne right at the table we're sitting at. He reaches down to his ankle and pulls out a gun and slaps it on the table, and he's looking at me real tough."

The FBI agents' instructions sounded simple enough. The Fiatos were to continue business as usual inside the Los Angeles mob. Had they been low-level hoodlums, the job might have been easy. But Fiato was the ranking underboss of Rizzitello's crew, and Larry Fiato was a trusted associate who had entrée into every corner of the Hollywood underworld. Wearing a wire on a few bookmakers is one thing: The Fiatos were being asked to betray the biggest mobsters in Los Angeles.

They were outfitted with recorders for their home telephones and supplied with body microphones. They were to collect as much incriminating information as they could and remain in daily contact with their FBI handlers. Court-authorized wiretaps of Los Angeles Godfather Peter John Milano's Westlake Village home and vending machine business, as well as mob capo Luigi Gelfuso's Encino home, would assist the government's game plan.

The timing could not have been more fortuitous for the government. Only two weeks before the brothers approached the FBI, Puggy Zeichick had brought Anthony Fiato the good news he'd heard: Fiato was going to be made into the Milano family.

John DiMattia had been told to deliver the message to Fiato, whose initial reluctance—he already considered himself proposed for membership in Rizzitello's faction of the Gambino crime family—was overcome by his curiosity. Shortly after he heard the good news, he had become a government informant. DiMattia planned to use Fiato's fearsome street reputation to propel himself into membership.

"You have to have been on the street at least ten years so they know you," DiMattia told Fiato during their meeting over drinks at Tracton's Restaurant on Ventura Boulevard in Encino. To a traditionalist like Fiato, the thought of being sanctioned in an inferior outfit such as Milano's was a comedown. He preferred the powerful reputation of Dellacroce, or the consummate wiseguy Joe Russo. But Milano had come calling, and Fiato would be wise to accept the invitation from the boss of the city's rackets. Milano was in the midst of something of a Mafia recruiting drive, and mob associates from San Diego to San Jose were being considered for membership. Fiato knew or had heard of all of the new soldiers, and he winced at the thought of so many semi-tough characters carrying the mantel of a made member of La Cosa Nostra.

"It was pretty pathetic, really," Fiato recalled. "I mean you're talking about a lot of drivers and bookmakers and broken-down valises. There was Dominic the Pig and "Fat Stevie" Cino, Rocco Zangari, who people called Big Foot, and a few other names. But for crying out loud, Cino and Zangari were bookmakers. They weren't guys who could do any real work."

But he had struck at the heart of why Rizzitello held such low regard for Milano's stewardship of the family. While Big Mike was the consummate man of action, and was rumored to have killed a dozen men or more, Milano's boys were bookmakers and loansharks who hired out their collections. They ran vending machine companies and coffee distributorships and shook down bookmakers when they could. DiMattia, for one, recognized the potential of having Fiato on the team.

"We're going to take over all the Jews and bookmakers in this town," he bragged. "It's gonna be just like back East. Everybody's gonna pay their taxes."

A few days later, Fiato heard from Gelfuso, the experienced Mafiosi who had been so loyal to Milano over the years. Their meeting was set up for Santo Pietro Pizza Parlor in Westwood. At a table in the back, Gelfuso told Fiato that New York mob bosses had approved Pete Milano's plan to reorganize and strengthen the Los Angeles family, to finally make it worthy of respect and to make people forget its Mickey Mouse moniker.

"We're going to grab all the bookmakers and all the independent guys who are operating in this town," Gelfuso said. "That Johnny Popcorn and that Lenny Bayden, them too. We're taking a piece of them. We've got our mitts into plenty."

"Even narcotics?" Fiato asked. "Guys are getting whacked out all over the country for dealing dope."

"Out here, we do what we want," Gelfuso replied. "Any way we can make money is okay as long as it isn't broadcast."

On March 5, 1984, Fiato sat down with Gelfuso at the Melting Pot on Ventura Boulevard. He was more nervous than usual, which Gelfuso mistakenly assumed was due to the conversation they were about to have. It's not every day a guy goes over the ground rules for membership in La Cosa Nostra. Fiato was on edge for another reason; he was wearing a bulky recording device strapped to his body.

"It felt like I was wearing a refrigerator," Fiato said. "I was sweating my ass off. All the time Louie was talking I was imagining he could see the recorder, or that someone would pat me down and find it. I was sweating like hell, but I couldn't let him see that. The funny thing is, I'd grown up around movie actors and had met plenty of movie stars in my life, and all of a sudden I was giving the performance of my life.

"Rizzitello had already started his own family, sanctioned by Neil Dellacroce, and made me a lieutenant in that family. Now Louie Gelfuso was approaching me to be made in the Milano crew, which as far as I was concerned was made up of a bunch of do-nothing bookmakers. I never would have agreed to sit down with Gelfuso if I hadn't been working with the FBI. In fact, I was angry at the idea that I was going to sit down with this fucking loser. Normally, I would have killed the motherfucker for trying to get me to go against Mike. But now I had to pretend I was grateful to this guy. Now that I was working with the FBI, I had to sit and take it. And so I did."

After exchanging pleasantries, Pete Milano's trusted messenger got down to business. Gelfuso was obviously nervous.

Gelfuso: I just want to ask you a couple of questions. First of all, how do you spell your last name?

Fiato: F-I-A-T-O

Gelfuso: And your first name, what gives?

Fiato: Anthony. Craig Anthony.

Gelfuso: Craig Anthony.

Fiato: Right.

Gelfuso: All right now. Your father was full-blooded Italian.

Fiato: Yeah.

Gelfuso: I knew your father.

Fiato: Johnny Fiato.

Gelfuso: Yeah, I met him. I knew him. He was the bartender at the . . .

Fiato: Villa Capri.

Gelfuso: That's right. Because . . . you know Skyball. You know Sky.

Fiato: Well, I told you how it went the last time when Mike had that, ah, that call back East.

Gelfuso: Yeah.

Fiato: It went through Skyball. Skyball knew my father.

Gelfuso: All right, now you know, you understand this whole thing . . .

Fiato: I know, I know.

Gelfuso: You know that it's for the rest of your life. Make sure you want to do it.

Fiato: Louie, if I'm here I want to do it.

Gelfuso: There's no backing out. Well, these are just things I got to say to you, you know, 'cause it's going to be said again.

Fiato: All right.

Gelfuso: I want you to think it over.

Fiato: No.

Gelfuso: Make sure.

Fiato: There ain't nothing for me to think over.

Gelfuso: Because, ah, something like this, you know, you've been around long enough, it comes before fucking, I think you know . . .

Fiato: Comes before your family, I know.

Gelfuso: Yeah.

Fiato: I know the whole thing.

Gelfuso: All right, if there are any questions you want to ask, you're welcome . . .

Fiato: There's nothing I should ask. I know, I know the ball-game and I know you're in for good and that's it.

Gelfuso: You understand my position and we're going to do this right, not like it used to be with fucking everybody running in different directions. Ah, if you're going to do anything, you got my number. Check with me.

Fiato: All right.

Gelfuso: Because, ah, I talk to him [Pete Milano] almost every day, but rather than get a lot of heat on him, just let somebody know what you're doing. It's not because nobody don't trust you.

Fiato: Right.

Gelfuso: It's because you're doing something with somebody and one of the other guys is doing something with the same guy, we want to know so we can tell one guy to either back off or, you know, you know what I'm saying.

Fiato: Right.

Gelfuso: It's not going to be that I made a fucking score and I put it in my fucking pocket.

Fiato: I like that, Louie.

Gelfuso: You got the okay to do what the fuck you want right now. . . . When you do it, you know what to do. If there's a situation that's not right, just back off for a minute and we'll sit down. Just call and say you know what, let's get together. We'll meet somewhere but we'll stay away from joints where we see each other.

Fiato: I don't run around. I don't hang out. I don't do any of that shit. I just do my own thing.

Gelfuso: I'll never ask you to do anything that I wouldn't fucking do myself. If I thought it's wrong, I'll say to you I think you should leave it alone. We'll get to it a different way. Nobody needs to go to jail. Pete's out of trouble.

Fiato: That's the one thing I learned. Before I was cocky, I knew everything. That's one thing I learned the last three or four years. I learned to pick my spot. That's what I learned now. Instead of the other way, rushing in like a fool and fuck everybody, all that stuff is gone. You got to know where to go, know where to eat and that, that's what I am going to do.

Gelfuso: Because we don't need anybody in jail. We don't need anybody in jail.

Fiato: And you don't have to do it, like you said. If anything, I'm a little over aggressive.

Gelfuso: Yeah. When I was young, I was a motherfucker. I was like you.

Fiato: Crazy, yeah.

Gelfuso: You already got your reputation.

Fiato: Now I can put a little polish on it.

Gelfuso: You got it. You got it all. You don't need anything and, listen to me, you got all the backing you want. With a couple of phone calls, I can have ten guys right at your doorstep. Come and help you whatever you fucking want to do. I know you're capable of doing it yourself. It's just that, if we need help, it's there. That's why I wanted to spend a few minutes with you alone.

Fiato: Before I was a short score guy and Mike was always like that. I got somebody now with a little money behind me and I want to do the right thing and just let him use it, and he'll enrich this family. He'll enrich it. Ten thousand couldn't do nothing for me. I live good and if I keep my guy it stops me from being a desperado.

Gelfuso: That's it. That's the reputation you got.

Fiato: Yeah, desperado. I know, I admit it.

Gelfuso: No disrespect for Mike, but he had you running and doing things that made you a real bad guy.

Fiato: Now the fucking heat hates me.

Gelfuso: Keep in mind these fuckers, they got all the money and all the time in the world . . . if they really want you, those cocksuckers. We got to outthink them.

Fiato: I like your sense. Hey, listen, if I were with a different guy before and I had that kind of intelligence talking to me, I would have done things a lot different and I would have been a little more successful than I am now with grand juries and shit like

that. I would have been a little more successful. You know where
I am getting lucky here. Most of the people they're trying to get
against me are scared to death of me. I got fucking lucky. They
are terrified of me. I told them I'd blow their fucking houses up.

Gelfuso: You'll win in the long run because they won't testify. . . .
All right, if there are any questions you want to ask.

Fiato: I got nothing to ask. I liked the way we talked the other
day and this just adds to it. I already expected to hear something
like this and I am ready for it, and that's what I want.

"I had to be sponsored by another made guy. J.R. Russo was on
the lam at that time, and I couldn't get him. I had to wait until
Jack LoCicero got out of prison, but that wasn't for four months.
Jack was a consigliere to the family.

"We waited until Jack LoCicero got out of jail and Luigi set up
a meeting between him, me and Jack LoCicero. We arrived first.
I hadn't seen Jack in a few years because of the Forex beef, and as
he approached the table he said, 'I know thisa guy. Your father he
work at the Villa Capri. You like this fuckin' life. I tole you many
times to be careful.'

"Jack tells Louie in front of me, 'You wan' him in? He's in.' At
that point I'm part of the family. At that point the ceremony was
a mere formality."

But everything was not all right with Anthony and Larry Fiato.
Anthony had to work constantly to keep his anger toward the
Milanos buried. He would have preferred to skip the investigative process and pick up the gun. Gelfuso would have been out
of the way.

"We were in this thing all the way," Anthony said. "We didn't
have the benefit of being trained as FBI agents, we didn't have the
benefit of knowing the laws of entrapment. We didn't have the benefit of knowing society's right from wrong, as opposed to our value
system. I dreaded every time that phone rang. You know, it was
either the FBI or a Mafia guy calling me to meet him. I dreaded it,
because I mean, the wire was going on and I was going out there.

"My disappointment was in my ideal of what I always believed in. See, where I come from, I mean, these people, the same way the FBI agents might look up to . . . Ronald Reagan or whoever the hell they look up to, I looked up to Lucky Luciano that way as a kid. Well, in my neighborhood, it was natural, my value systems, I kept them intact, I was honorable to the family. The same way the FBI keeps the law, I broke the law faithfully because that was my nature. And those value systems, you know, can really cross you up you know, in some very serious ways. I found out."

"Every time you put that wire on, you die," Larry said. "Because you're tape-recording these guys. I mean these are guys that you've grown up with, that you've admired all your life. And it might not be the immediate faces in your scope. You're seeing people from the past. When you wear a wire, you're outside your body. You completely shut down and go on instinct. It's horrible. You go into a permanent state of shock because you're not really you. You get paranoid. It wasn't hard to do this in the sense that taping those people was really pretty easy. But you're always afraid and you're always acting like you're not afraid. Wearing the Nagra wire is like wearing a watermelon. You think everyone can see it."

Anthony: "You're seeing your father, who may be turning over in his grave, looking at you. You're seeing guys that knew you as a kid, that came to your father's wake and gave an envelope to your mother, that looked out for your family. I mean, when I was a kid and I saw Mafia guys walk down the street, I'd look up at these guys and, oh my God, I'd get such a good feeling when they'd just acknowledge me."

That's where Weichert, and especially Wacks, came in. Wacks had been undercover in the Marcello mob and knew much of what the Fiatos were experiencing. He maintained daily telephone contact with the brothers. The agents and operatives often talked several times a day.

"With us, they had to do an even bigger turnaround," Mike Wacks said. "We're talking forty years in Anthony's case and for Larry thirty years of doing nothing but illegal activities. So we had to teach these guys, luckily we had a little bit of background. We knew where they were coming from. To get them to change their life over, it was like changing my life back over to being an FBI agent. And it was very, very hard at first.

"When they went out, it was very hard to make that adjustment. . . . And the next thing we know we've got people beat up all over Ventura Boulevard in Los Angeles. You got a card club in Los Angeles where Larry goes in with another guy and they beat a guy with a pipe. So right away we've got problems. . . . We got off to such a fast start with these guys. We thought down the line we might get into the capo or DiMattia, but right away we were, boom, in there and this guy's giving marching orders. Boom. I want this guy whacked. I want that guy beat up. I want this guy collected from. . . . They were more physical in the old sense. If they had a problem, they'd just whack a guy, or whatever. Now they have to be somewhat smoother, but they still had to make a point. Because we told them initially, which was maybe our mistake, we said, 'Go out and act yourselves.'"

With that, Anthony Fiato returned to work, this time as a nominated member of the Milano crime family. He had direct access to Milano and was on a par with Luigi Gelfuso. Fiato's problem was simple: In order to impress his Mafia sponsors, he had to continue his impressive earning spree, and sooner or later that would mean beating up a slow-paying loanshark customer or instructing his brother or one of the members of his crew to do the same.

His FBI sponsors frowned on such activity, and with rare exceptions the Justice Department never allowed its witnesses to commit crimes of great violence while working for the government. Lesser offenses were tolerated, and law enforcement commonly turned its head to crimes committed by its snitches. But they drew the line at shattering a man's kneecaps with a blunt instrument.

Wacks and Weichert would help with Fiato's dilemma when they could. In early April, Fiato received $5,000 from his government handlers to produce as a tribute to Gelfuso and the Los Angeles family. Anthony and Larry met Gelfuso in the parking lot of the Beverly Glen Shopping Center, where the gift was given. With Gelfuso looking on, the Fiatos kept $3,000 and gave $1,000 each to their new sponsors Luigi and Pete Milano. The $3,000 was later returned to the FBI.

"I took it off a coke dealer. He didn't need it," Anthony said. "I want you and Pete to have it as a sign of my affection. The guy is going to pay five thousand a month for the privilege of dealing coke in Los Angeles. And I'll take care of that Spike McShane, too, the guy who books out of Santa Anita and has been kicking in to Vito Spillone. He'll be kicking in to us soon enough. I'll ask him who gave him permission to book at the track, and he'll cooperate. I know that Vito is with the Chicago Outfit, but that Spike is in our town. I'll take care of him."

"That's right," Gelfuso said. "Unless it's cleared with this family, it's not cleared. Just so you know, I put the word out to Skyball and haven't heard back from him. I sent word for you under another name, ah, Anthony Fortunato, and I had to give them your real name. We'll get it straightened out. And don't forget that Lenny Bayden, he owes us two thousand a week through that Mario.

"You tell him to stay close to that Mario, 'cause he don't want no trouble from us. You whack him around if you need to. You know that Ronnie Rome, he knows Pete, and that Ronnie says Joe Russo knows you and will vouch for you. That Skyball's not easy to reach, so we'll go with this Joe Russo. He's all right. Pete knows him. I want you to know something. Pete likes what you're doing."

At the office of the Los Angeles Strike Force, Attorney-in-Charge James D. Henderson was less comfortable with what Anthony Fiato was doing. Reports of the Fiatos terrorizing bookmakers and slapping around customers threatened the government's rapidly expanding case. As friends of the government, the Fiato brothers had to live up to a minimum standard of behavior. At the very least they were not supposed to bust heads and break knees as part of their undercover work. Their FBI handlers wanted them to be convincing, but not quite that convincing. As the attorney responsible for ushering the organized crime cases into court, Henderson became alarmed by the Fiatos' activity.

Henderson voiced his concerns in an April 12, 1984 memorandum to Tom Kubic, the Supervisory Special Agent of the Los Angeles office of the FBI:

"The purpose of this memorandum is to reiterate my previously set forth views expressed at the recent meeting between yourself, Bill Weichert, Michael Wacks, and Blair Watson in my office. It had been my initial impression (and that of Mr. Watson) that the Bureau's use of the Fiato brothers would be essentially two-fold. First, it was my understanding that the Fiatos would be generally debriefed by the Bureau with regard to matters currently under investigation and being handled by the Strike Force and as to other matters in which prosecution might be warranted and of which we were previously unaware.

"Second, the Fiatos were to be equipped with electronic surveillance equipment for the consensual recording of conversations with subjects of current investigations which might be generated as a result of the Fiatos' cooperation. As one of your legal advisers in Bureau organized crime affairs, it is the latter area which the Strike Force believes should be of substantial concern to you. It was my original impression that the Fiatos would be among a group which was going to be sent on a series of assignments by Los Angeles organized crime leaders and that they would engage in no violence and would assume basically a passive role in things like extortion activity and that they would later provide testimony as to the course of events as they unfolded.

"It has come to my attention, however, (and this was the reason for the meeting which I called on April 5, 1984) that the role assumed by the Fiatos has hardly been a passive one and, in fact, has been an extremely active one. Not only have they engaged in physical violence but they appear to have led the way in some instances of extortionate activity as I informed you at the meeting. This presents a number of problems. The most apparent, of course, is that if the Bureau can't control the Fiatos' activities then serious questions as to whether they should be utilized on the street in any capacity are more than apparent. Under such circumstances it is our legal recommendation that they not be so utilized."

Problem was, the Bureau had gained unprecedented access into the workings of the Los Angeles mob. At the time, the description of La Cosa Nostra's induction ceremony was extremely rare, and it was clear that if everything broke right, Anthony Fiato might take them further than anyone had been inside the mob.

By the early 1980s, the government had turned plenty of mobsters, but no one had come this close to tracking a Mafia rising star. Wacks and Weichert worked overtime to appease the strike force and keep the Fiatos from getting blood on their investigation, but with volatile men like the Fiatos there were no guarantees. And the action was only increasing as Fiato worked into the good graces of Gelfuso and Milano.

On May 17, 1984, Anthony, Larry and Bob Kessler met at Gelfuso's Encino apartment. In the back bedroom, Gelfuso spoke privately with Anthony Fiato.

"I want you to move on that Mondavano kid," Gelfuso said. "Pete's given the okay. It took a while because that Jimmy [Caci] was supposed to take care of it."

Gelfuso handed Fiato a photograph of Danny Mondavano and a scrap of paper with an address on it.

"Here's the fucking kid," Gelfuso said. "We want the kid grabbed, but leave the old man alone. The kid is causing trouble like you wouldn't believe. He's the problem. Beat him to a pulp. Slap the fuck out of him. He'll give up the money. It's Four-hundred-sixty-eight thousand. I don't do nothing without telling Pete. As soon as you beat the kid, we'll tell that father of his, 'Now you see what happened to your son and next time we are going to bury the whole fucking family.' And you know that we'll whack up this money evenly."

With the FBI picking up the tab for the cash tributes, on May 17, 1984, the Fiatos again produced the $5,000 score from the unnamed cocaine dealer and met at Gelfuso's apartment to divvy up the money. When Gelfuso asked about the status of the Danny Mondavano extortion, Larry said, "We're going over there tomorrow morning at five. Somebody's watching the house for us today. We'll get it done."

Through Gelfuso, the Fiatos were gradually meeting other members and associates of the Milano crew. On June 1, they met Albie Nunez. Albert Jesus Nunez was born in 1931 in Bayonne, New Jersey. His father was Mexican, his mother Italian. He had been working the streets all his adult life and had never been convicted of a felony. He had been suspected of many and arrested for auto theft, but never nailed.

Louie Gelfuso loved Albie Nunez. Nunez provided undying loyalty and plenty of muscle for Gelfuso, who in turn treated him like an Italian and even served as the best man at Nunez's wedding. How respected was Nunez? Pete Milano thought enough of him to serve as an usher at his wedding. Albie was a trusted messenger, who often sent word back and forth from Gelfuso to Milano. Although he worked at a Budweiser brewery, Albie's real job was to act as a loanshark and collector for Gelfuso. Albie's life's dream was simple: to one day become the first exception to La Cosa Nostra's rule that a member had to be full-blooded Italian.

From that point on Nunez often worked with Fiato, who began to pick up thousands of dollars in outstanding loans that had gone uncollected since the government's intent to bust up the multimillion-dollar Fiato-Zeichick money lending racket. It became clear to Fiato that not everyone in the Milano crew was pleased to see him arrive on the scene. For the previous four years Fiato had shown nothing but contempt for the Milano "bunch of bookmakers" whom, he thought, were only posing as gangsters. He had been a man of action, and considered them inferior and unworthy of respect.

But now that he was joining their family, he had to get along.

Thanks to a growing dispute over ownership of Zeichick and Gene Holden, Fiato's patience was being sorely tested. Gelfuso's job was to resolve family disputes, so he called for a meeting at the Valley Hilton in Sherman Oaks between the Fiatos and Jimmy Caci's crew.

Born in Buffalo, Jimmy's birth name was Vincent Dominic Caci. In 1984, Caci was a capo based in Palm Springs, and his associates included Milano soldiers "Fat Steve" Cino, Rocco Zangari, and Johnny Vaccaro. Caci's younger brother, Charles James Caci, who was known as Bobby Milano, was a singer and actor married to Keely Smith.

At the Hilton, Zangari wasted no time with small talk.

"We got a couple of things," Zangari said. "First of all, Puggy. You got to leave him alone. Puggy don't belong to nobody but us, that's number one. He don't belong to you or nobody else. . . . This is final, this is the way he wants it, the old man, this is the way it's gotta be. This kid belongs to us."

"All right," Fiato said, the body mike catching every word.

The conversation returned again to Puggy Zeichick and the $5,000 he owed Fiato as well as Gene Holden's loansharking contacts in Los Angeles and Las Vegas. And Fiato's patience was wearing thin as he listened to the two-bit tough guys talk their talk.

"Can I speak here?" Fiato fumed. "I am a right guy. I am not a wrong guy here, how I left off with Puggy. We had a business going before everything like that, and we might have some court troubles and stuff coming down. He owes me five thousand, which I want."

Zangari and Caci agreed, and Fiato left the table boiling mad.

"I never would have taken that shit from those guys if I wasn't cooperating with the FBI," Fiato recalled. "I was ready to kill them. I was seething. It was all I could do to curb that fucking appetite for violence. If I hadn't been cooperating, they'd have been fucking dead."

Even as a kid at the Villa Capri no one had shown him disrespect and gotten away with it. He ached to retaliate, but as he reached the car a thought crossed his mind. He already was retaliating.

Danny Mondavano had been a slick-talking thief his whole life. He was a loanshark who muscled his customers and cheated his partners. He was raised in Boston and hustled with "Fat Vinny" Teresa, a mob hanger-on who gained national notoriety when he turned informant for the government and penned a best-seller called *My Life in the Mafia*. In the book, Teresa said, "Danny became the most valuable property I had in my stable of hustlers. We worked dozens of deals together, all of them profitable." From casino skims to loanshark operations, in "Fat Vinny"'s eyes Mondavano was "one of the best thieves in New England."

He was also one of the most hated. Cheating both sides of any deal is a good way to make enemies in business, and on the street such activity can get a person killed. Mondavano had talked a group of wealthy businessmen, including Roy Elson, into investing in his hard-money lending program. Mondavano collected nearly half-a-million dollars from his investors on the promise that their money would double and triple over the course of a year or two. He appealed to their sense of greed, and they were more than happy to participate in the loanshark program.

In his role as a Washington, D.C. lobbyist, Roy Elson was accustomed to meeting all sorts of characters, not all of them savory. Elson had been a top aide to Arizona Senator Carl Hayden and had been the chief lobbyist for the National Association of Broadcasters. He ran for the U.S. Senate in 1964, against then-Arizona Governor Paul Fannin, and in 1968 against Barry Goldwater. He had navigated treacherous political waters and had managed to thrive.

As experienced as Elson was, he was ill-prepared for a wiseguy the likes of Danny Mondavano, who had been pulling white-collar cons most of his adult life as an associate of the Patriarca crime family. Mondavano had served time in federal prison for securities fraud. He was nothing if not relentless. He had been pulling street scams since he was a kid, and phony loanshark investments were a favorite. Simply stated, Mondavano found willing "investors" in his supposedly thriving Mafia loanshark business. He embraced their investments and then simply refused to return their money. When they argued with him, he reminded them of his affiliations.

By late 1980, he found a willing investor in Roy Elson. The deal was simple: Elson would recruit investors, and Mondavano would loan their money at two-percent interest per week to businessmen and flea market merchants in the Boston area who were idea-rich but cash poor.

With Elson's colorful assortment of contacts, Mondavano was soon receiving money from a former Assistant Secretary of the Interior, an ex-bank president and a dozen other legitimate citizens who were only too willing to risk scads of cash with their lobbyist friend's street contact.

Elson managed to gather $300,000 for starters, which properly loaned amounted to $6,000-a-week interest. For his part, Elson invested $32,000.

Mondavano carried thick wads of cash and talked in astronomical sums, but when it came time to pay his investors Mondavano provided one excuse after another. He had to pay street taxes in Boston and Los Angeles, he said. He owned money to Carlo Mastrototaro, a Boston-based Genovese crime family member working in concert with Francesco "Frankie Skyball" Scibelli. Elson wanted to believe Mondavano was sincere; after all, the lobbyist had plenty of his own money and more than $300,000 of others' cash invested. Negotiations continued through January 1984, when Elson began discussing the matter with his longtime friend, San Fernando Valley resident Edward Byles. Byles, a trusted associate of the Lyndon Johnson administration, was through much of his career one of Las Vegas casino operator Morris Shenker's many attorneys.

Byles reached out to mobbed-up singer Bobby Milano in Palm Springs, who set up a meeting. Was Mondavano connected to Mastrototaro?

"If he isn't connected," Elson said, "then you don't even know what the hell is going on in your own territory."

The Milano visit resulted in the roughing up of Mondavano and his coughing up $4,500, but that left Elson thousands short of the money owed him. The job had been performed poorly by Jimmy Caci and "Fat Steve" Cino. And so the responsibility for the Mondavano job came to brothers Anthony and Larry Fiato, who made half-hearted attempts to find their man. After all, if the FBI wasn't going to let them beat him up, what was the use?

Besides, by then not only were they cooperating with the government, but they learned that Roy Elson was as well.

By the spring of 1984 it had become clear that Danny Mondavano had no real money on the street. Whatever money Elson's friends had invested with him had, in all likelihood, ridden away on the back of a Santa Anita thoroughbred—Danny Mondavano was a gambling degenerate. Others taken by Mondavano had attempted to call in markers in Chicago and elsewhere to collect the debts.

Gelfuso made it clear that approval for the Mondavano grab had come from Pete Milano.

"Pete gave the go-ahead," Gelfuso said. This is the kid that's giving everyone a bad time. Now you live it up. I'll work with you or whatever we do, but we just want to beat him. If anything comes, just like Pete, Pete says if anything comes, I want you guys to know that it's cut up, everything is cut up evenly with whoever is involved."

"I am with this family?" Fiato asked.

"You are," Gelfuso replied.

It was the least Gelfuso could say to a guy who was on the verge of bringing the family close to half-a-million dollars.

In no time Pete Milano's curiosity overcame him, and he had Gelfuso set up a meeting with his new street enforcer, Anthony Fiato.

"I can only say that I heard a lot of things about you, and they seem true because you've got a very nice manner about you," Fiato said.

"I been through so goddamn much that when you see people that go out and cowboy, you say to yourself, 'these guys, if they only knew how it really is," Milano said.

In the course of conversation, Milano gave his philosophy about creating an air of legitimacy. He owned pizza parlors, a vending machine company and a coffee distributorship.

"You gotta have a place to hang your hat. I've been impressing that on all of you—even if it doesn't make any money. Then you got the cash flow. You can manipulate it. Louie thinks a lot of you. He recommends you very highly, so I say this: stay close to him. I impress upon you to try and use your head, both of you. Take a little surveillance of the situation. Especially when these here deals come from out of the blue. You never know when there's something else behind it."

Louie was quick to remind his boss that Fiato had plenty of experience doing work on the street. Fiato commanded the kind of respect that was hard to find in the Milano family.

"See, Anthony's already proved himself," Gelfuso said. "He did all that a long time ago. When he was running with Mike, he did all that because when he walked in that fucking club, as soon as he walked in the door you could hear a pin drop in the place. They all know he's it."

While going after anyone tied to the Milano crew was not as difficult to take for Fiato, who despised several members of the family, he hated wearing a wire on street guys such as Joey Mangiapani, who were tied to Mike Rizzitello. Trouble loomed for Fiato as Mangiapani continued to approach him unsolicited. He obviously saw what others saw in Fiato: a man capable of violence on the rise in a family that shied away from real work.

"Joey Mangiapani was a great kid," Fiato said. "He was tight with Jimmy Caan and trained a hot young fighter named Mark "The Bounty" Hunter.

Wearing a wire looks simple enough on television cop shows, but it can be a complicated matter. When Anthony and Larry Fiato first began cooperating with the government, each wore a small transmitter instead of a conventional Nagra recorder. The transmitter was small enough to fit into a cigarette pack, but it had its drawbacks. Agents monitoring the conversation had to remain close by in order to pick up the signal.

During the extortion of Lenny Bayden, Anthony and Larry Fiato and "Fat Steve" Munichiello were scheduled to meet the bookmaker at Monte's Steakhouse on Ventura Boulevard. Agents Wacks and Weichert, meanwhile, set up their listening post in the parking lot at Monteleone's.

It's probably for the best because what the agents would have heard might have made them cut short their investigation. Bayden brought reinforcements in the form of Jerry Quintana. But when Quitana atempted to impress the Fiatos by name-dropping Pete Milano, the brothers started swinging. End result: Larry punched out Quintana and Anthony KO'd a restaurant employee.

Following the Fiato brothers' lead, Albie Nunez began shaking down bookmakers for his mentor, Gelfuso. In early July, 1984, Nunez finagled a meeting with longtime Los Angeles bookmaker Lenny Bayden and, true-to-form, began whacking the old man around in the name of the Los Angeles family.

Nunez was partial to using a tightly rolled newspaper to punish his weaker victims. It could be used as a blunt instrument and, once unrolled, could not be deemed a concealed weapon. When Nunez delivered the news, ribs were cracked and eyes were blackened. After repeated visits from Nunez and Gelfuso, Bayden came up with a $5,000 tribute. Death threats will do that to a guy, especially when he knows he is breaking the law and is unlikely to be taken seriously by law enforcement. That is the mob's true strength.

True to his word, Gelfuso split the Bayden score with his partners, including Anthony and Larry Fiato. Of the $5,000, $600 went to Anthony, $300 to Larry and $400 to Bob Kessler. The rest was divided between Gelfuso and Nunez, or kicked up the ladder to Pete Milano.

"It went all right," Gelfuso later told Larry. "Albie grabbed him and whacked him four or five times."

But as loyal as Albie Nunez was, he could still count. By late summer, he realized he had taken most of the risks in the Bayden extortion and complained that he'd only received $400 for the job. Luigi Gelfuso cut up the score, but he cut his boys' slices paper thin.

"I only got gas money," Nunez said to Larry.

In time, the government was to get far more mileage out of the Lenny Bayden extortion.

Despite the heat all three men were receiving from law enforcement, Milano, Gelfuso and Anthony Fiato found time to meet in May, 1984 in Westlake Village. Once together, Milano reiterated how pleased he was with Fiato's performance.

"You whack anybody who uses my name," Milano instructed him.

Fiato agreed and reminded the boss of bookmaker Lenny Bayden's loose lips. Gelfuso said the Bayden matter was being worked on.

"We were shaking down bookmakers and betting into them," Fiato said. "We got ahold of Al Lazar, an ex-Brooklyn cop, and Nick Dio, who had taken over the bookmaking for Bobby Craig. Craig had a wife named Esther, who was acquainted with Bob Kessler. Esther gave Bob Al Lazar's number. With Lazar we could bet three thousand a position, which means we could bet $3,000 on every game. Johnny Vaccaro used his son-in-law, ex-Ram football player Fred Dreyer, who was giving Johnny hot games. We followed Johnny's lead and bet the games.

"We collected when we won. We stiffed them when we lost and they were looking to recover about fifteen thousand. They were sore as hell, but I laid down the law with them. I told them I represented the family over here and we weren't giving them a nickel. They wanted their money, but they weren't going to get it. I said, 'Before you get out of line and say something you'll regret, you better ask around about me.'

"Johnny was out on a bond posted by his son-in-law, and when he got busted later he blew the bond. I heard Dreyer went ballistic. He lost thousands thanks to his father-in-law."

Weeks after Anthony Fiato began cooperating with the FBI, it became clear the government was getting more than it bargained for. In Fiato they had a one-man clearing house of crime. His phone rang constantly with propositions for investment, requests for high-interest loans and messages from Luigi Gelfuso and the Milano family.

John DiMattia delivered one message in early March. A meeting was arranged for the Encino Hilton, and Fiato and Kessler met DiMattia, Dino D'Agostino, real estate broker Art Bishop and his Philippino associate, Rick Domingo.

Once everyone had gathered around the table, Domingo was called a thief. He had stolen jewelry and valuable documents from Bishop. Domingo broke out in a sweat, and Fiato went into his Animal mode. He grabbed the Philippino and dragged him through the lounge and into the men's room, then opened a stall and shoved the frightened little man inside. Fiato searched Domingo, threatened to tear him to pieces. It was real bully work, but the point was not to shed the little man's blood but to extract the truth from him.

Fiato came away convinced that there had been a liar at the table, but it wasn't Domingo. It was his accuser, Art Bishop.

On cue DiMattia began accusing Bishop of lying. Then he said, "Don't you know who this is? This guy will take your fucking eyes out. He's one of the biggest guys in this town and it's going to cost you fifteen thousand just for getting him out of bed at this hour and making him come down here for nothing."

Bishop was given a choice: He could pay with a check, or pay with a cracked skull.

From that moment forward the heat was on Art Bishop. Mob extortions are seldom subtle.

On March 13, "Fat Steve" Munichiello and Bob Kessler paid Bishop a visit at his Inglewood office, where the realtor was threatened again. Within four days, Dino D'Agostino called Fiato to report that Bishop had run to some wiseguys out of Providence for protection. Over the next two weeks, Anthony and Larry Fiato recorded their mob associates making plans to separate Bishop from his money. In no time Luigi Gelfuso was more than happy to lend his opinion on how to extort cash from Bishop, and by now Gelfuso often dropped Pete Milano's name.

"Fat Steve" Munichiello eventually delivered a two-punch message that began the money trickling from Art Bishop. Hours of taped conversations revealed one of the resounding ironies of traditional organized crime: As many as six men were willing to scheme day-after-day to find ways to get out of working a straight job. After more than a month, the take on the Bishop extortion was little more than $1,000.

The moves against Art Bishop continued into the heart of the summer, and by mid-July Munichiello was paying regular visits to the real estate office. Bishop, who suffered from cancer, feared for his life but refused to go to the police. Informed of Bishop's delicate physical state, Munichiello just laughed.

"I could give a shit," he said.

"You'd fucking hit a nun," Anthony Fiato said in a recorded conversation.

"Yeah, but only if she got out of line," Munichiello said, laughing.

By this time, Art Bishop received regular beatings to encourage him into paying the balance of the $15,000 tribute.

During one of their many meetings, Bishop confided to Fiato, "I'm 65 years old. I'm trying to raise some money because I don't want any fucking trouble from you guys, okay? I'll do the best I fucking can, you know, because, hey, I'm scared."

Fiato arranged a payment plan for Bishop that enabled him to pay $500 a week and still keep his teeth in his head. Bishop, who had been raised on Federal Hill in Providence, Rhode Island, in the heart of the Patriarca family's influence, was relieved. It was clear to Bishop that Anthony Fiato was the reasonable one in his crew. Where he called Kessler and Munichiello "Frankenstein and Igor," Bishop was comfortable with Fiato. So much so that he asked him to slap around his former friend Rick Domingo. Bishop also offered to launder the mob's money through his real estate business, and gave Fiato information that would enable him to shake down a million-dollar cocaine dealer who operated out of a foreign car dealership in Hermosa Beach.

The FBI let Anthony Fiato keep the cash he collected from Art Bishop, the proceeds of felony extortion, to cover expenses.

Anthony and Larry Fiato worked day after day for Gelfuso and members of the LA crew. They collared tardy loanshark customers and reminded them of their obligations. They helped plot the murder of Mike Andes, a San Fernando Valley bookmaker and scam artist who was a government informant. Andes had approached Pete Milano and attempted to sell him a few thousand dollars worth of stolen coffee coupons. The LA mob's police insiders managed to obtain a list of snitches, and Andes' name was near the top of the list.

Not only did Milano distance himself from the bookmaker, but his trusted gofer, Albie Nunez, vowed to take care of the snitch. Nunez's words were heavy with irony considering the presence of Bob Kessler and the Fiato brothers in his life. But when it came time to act, Nunez began thinking of his freedom.

"I gotta have a confrontation with a guy and have a fucking murder beef," Nunez lamented.

"In other words, you have to leave him alone or whack him out, that's what you're saying if you get involved with this guy," Fiato said.

"I can't leave him alone cause it's just a matter of time," Nunez said.

"That's what I'm saying so let's be compelled into a strong move, not a beating or a fight," Fiato said. "It's like a junkie. Either you leave him alone or you whack him up."

"Yeah," Nunez replied. "Louie says to me, `Well, you know we'll get a lot of heat.'"

"From who? From the local law?"

"Louie don't want to do it because he figures the guy is a rat and it would cause too much heat," Nunez said.

Nunez was relieved when Anthony Fiato volunteered to take

care of the business with Mike Andes. Nunez provided two pistols. Once he no longer faced the job of murdering Andes, Nunez' confidence returned.

"Boy, I love it," he told Larry Fiato. "I'd love to be with you, you know what I'm saying?"

Before the Andes murder contract was carried out, Larry Fiato was arrested on an outstanding traffic warrant. He told Nunez he ditched the pistols and used the arrest as an excuse to delay the hit, confiding to Nunez that he was certain Andes must have been a snitch.

Someone close to Nunez and the Fiatos was, but who?

As the Fiatos grew more comfortable in their roles, Wacks and Weichert added new twists to the case. One arrived in the form of Mark Legere, a Boston-based cocaine trafficker who Fiato introduced to Luigi Gelfuso. In reality, Legere was an FBI undercover agent named Vincent De La Montaigne. Fiato informed Gelfuso that Legere owed the family $25,000 for a cocaine deal, and Gelfuso immediately accepted the tribute payments. Gelfuso also proposed that Legere use his cocaine contacts to help set up a deal in Las Vegas with Johnny Vaccaro. While Legere was working, he learned about Albie Nunez' New Jersey cocaine source, Artie Fraconeri. Legere and Larry Fiato chased the multi-kilo deal from Los Angeles to Bayonne, over to Boston and down to Miami. Although the cocaine deal was never consummated, Legere uncovered an intricate distribution network that led him to some of the biggest traffickers in Florida's multi-billion-dollar drug trade.

The only thing bigger than Mike Murray's mouth was his ego. Murray, who hung out with Johnny "Popcorn" Pellegrino, specialized in stiffing bookmakers and lining up crooked card games. He was a small-time hustler, but when he took advantage of Jimmy Caan's cousin he made an enemy of Anthony and Larry Fiato. So it was with a sense of delight that the brothers sat with Luigi Gelfuso and John DiMattia at the Melting Pot Restaurant in March 1984 to discuss Murray's future. It seemed his big talk had gotten all the way to Las Vegas, where Anthony Spilotro's people overheard him criticizing Italians. Gelfuso received the message, and passed it along to the Fiatos, who were then faced with something of a dilemma.

As government informants, they were not allowed to participate in violent crimes. As lifelong mobsters, they found it difficult to resist pounding Murray into a bloody pulp.

Mike Murray was nothing if not predictable. Anthony Fiato dispatched his brother and Steve Munichiello to the Cavendish West Bridge Club, where Murray was busy working one of the tables.

"Murray, hi. I'm a friend of Johnny Popcorn's," Larry Fiato said. When Murray looked up from his cards, Fiato nailed him with a stiff left hand.

A thug not given to understatement, Munichiello pulled out a pipe and began beating Murray with it.

"This is for bad-mouthing Italians," Fiato said.

Murray staggered away from the club and went underground. Once word of the Murray beating began to circulate on the street, Gelfuso called the Fiatos to report that the con artist and his associates had beaten a friend of Bobby Milano's out of $45,000 in a card game at the Cavendish. That meant more work for the Fiatos. Milano was involved, as well as Steve Cino. And the LA crew spent the next several weeks squeezing various parties until the money appeared.

Although his job title was bartender, Richard Alicate was no stranger to organized crime. He worked the bar at Tracton's Restaurant on Ventura Boulevard. The restaurant was popular with actors, socialites and the boys in the Los Angeles mob.

Fiato had known Alicate for several years, so it was hardly surprising to learn that the bartender was augmenting his income with a low-key loansharking business. What was of greater concern was the fact that Gelfuso wanted Alicate closed up immediately. Fiato took the call and delivered the message to his acquaintance.

"It's come to the attention of some serious people that you're shylocking out of this place," Fiato said. "You know I represent those people, and so you know what comes next. We have a problem that's going to be solved one way or another. We want you to stop shylocking."

Alicate reached out for his senior partner, a Southern California Chevrolet dealer, who got in touch with Gelfuso. In time, the bartender wisely opted out of the moneylending business.

Anthony Fiato was relieved.

"We know the street, and the street is ours, and people on the street respect us," Fiato told Alicate's partner. "We know how to loan money and more than that we have it to loan. I've got six or seven guys that go out and collect money and we always get paid. All I have to do is look at people; I get it done.

"He'll tell you that because it always gets back to Tracton's whenever there is an episode that I'm involved in and somebody got his fucking head split open. I've got a nice crew. All I can tell you is I do what I do and I do it well and I make a lot of money doing it and I have a bad habit. If somebody fucks me, I get them. I am a consequence man. I am a consequence to the people that fuck me."

Gelfuso was not as easily impressed by Alicate's promise to quit the business. If the bartender had money on the street, it was Gelfuso's for the taking. In the spring of 1985 he dispatched the Fiatos with a list of loanshark customers, but the extortion plan went no further. In order to collect the thousands, the Fiatos would invariably be forced to rough up a few customers and intimidate others—acts that were sure to jeopardize the government's case against Milano's Los Angeles mob. The Fiatos quietly let the matter drop and Gelfuso barely noticed.

By then, Gelfuso's attention was focused on Bob Kessler.

On August 6, 1985, Robert Kessler and a Hollywood producer friend arrived at the Tail O' the Cock Restaurant for a meeting with Luigi Gelfuso and Albie Nunez. The subject was labor peace and how it could be ensured through Gelfuso's influence for a movie Kessler's friend was producing.

As the two men approached Gelfuso's table, they were met by Nunez, who patted Kessler on the back and felt something bulky. It was a Nagra recording device. Bob Kessler was a government informant. The producer was an FBI undercover Agent named Garth Schweickhardt.

Once the men were seated, Nunez asked to speak to Gelfuso in private. Sensing his cover had been blown, Kessler excused himself and went out to his car. Once outside, Kessler quickly removed the recorder and hid it under a dumpster next to the restaurant. He made it to his car just as Gelfuso and Nunez came out looking for him.

Gelfuso immediately confronted Kessler, who claimed he was only out to get a couple packs of cigarettes. A search of Kessler's car turned up no recorder, but Nunez and Gelfuso were not easily persuaded. Kessler returned to the restaurant and retrieved an envelope containing $3,000 from Schweickhardt and handed it to Gelfuso, who was momentarily appeased. Nunez was livid.

"You've got my number," Nunez told Kessler. "Tear it up. I don't ever want to hear from you again."

Gelfuso whispered, "It's a good thing we didn't find nothing, or we'd leave you dead right here in the parking lot."

Albie Nunez left the parking lot and drove to Pete Milano's place to explain what had happened. Nunez then went to the home of the one tough man he knew could never be a snitch. Anthony Fiato. By the time Nunez finished explaining what had taken place, Fiato was seething. He suddenly knew that it had been Kessler who had put the FBI on him. In that moment, Anthony Fiato felt like killing Bob Kessler. It was all he could do to contain himself and remember who he now worked for.

Later that night, Fiato received a phone call from Albie Nunez, who wanted Kessler's home address. Nunez knew Kessler lived near Fiato, but Fiato couldn't bring himself to provide the address.

Nunez's malice toward Bob Kessler was quite genuine. If he found him, he would kill him. For the next few days Nunez called everyone he knew who had had any contact with Kessler in an attempt to locate him. But Kessler was nowhere to be found.

Around Fiato, Nunez could barely contain himself.

"Pete himself, Pete himself, the day I went to see him, that night he called me after supper, after I told him at the vending machine company, he called me after supper," Nunez stammered. "We were talking' 'that motherfucker, fuck' he says, 'You, me, Rusty, go kill him.'"

Although Nunez didn't know Kessler's whereabouts, he did know one of his scams. Kessler purchased high-mileage used cars, turned back their odometers, and sold them out of his home through a series of advertisements in the Los Angeles *Times*.

"The L.A. *Times* is going to help us get him," Nunez said to Fiato.

"The idea is good," Fiato replied. "Great minds think alike."

All the while the government was listening.

For Fiato, the wondering was finally over. He finally knew for sure that Kessler was a government snitch.

"I was still devastated by it," Fiato said. "I wanted to choke the bastard. But then I think to myself, 'How can I justify that feeling? I'm doing the same thing he's doing.'"

Kessler's future was far from the only order of business.

Kept apprised of his status with the mob by his FBI handlers, Kessler insisted on returning to the street and arranged a meeting with Gelfuso at the Tail O' the Cock. Kessler was kept under surveillance by two FBI agents. Once he got next to Gelfuso, he poured on the charm. How could his dear friend Luigi think he would do such a terrible thing as inform for the government? Hadn't they known each other for years? Hadn't they made money together?

"We thought maybe the government had something on you and were forcing you to do it," Gelfuso said.

"Oh, that's bullshit, Louie," Kessler said. "You know me better than that."

Later that night, Gelfuso met with Fiato and assured him that he had squared away the problem with Kessler. If Kessler got into trouble, he was to tell Gelfuso immediately. If Gelfuso had other plans for Bob Kessler, he wasn't tipping his hand.

In truth, Luigi Gelfuso had little time to worry about Kessler. Thanks to the new members in his crew, he had more action than he could handle and was riding the highest wave of his criminal career. His days as a small-time hood who struggled to shake down bookmakers appeared to be over. With the help of the Fiato brothers, Gelfuso was fast becoming the biggest earner in the city.

"We got it here," underboss Carmen Milano confided to his devoted captain, with the Fiatos recording every word. "We got the town, absolutely we have it. Louie's responsible. I got to hand you to Louie."

Anthony Fiato said, "We got a hundred things going here." Gelfuso added, "I've been holding these guys back. I can't hold them anymore."

Part of Gelfuso's strategy was to have his men bet into bookmakers across the city. When they won, they would collect. When they lost, they would stiff the bookies and remind them who they were dealing with and what right did they have to operate in this town? It was a scam as old as the games themselves, and it worked because of the intimidating qualities of the Fiatos and the inherent cowardice of illegal bookmakers.

Between the betting scam and collecting outstanding loanshark debts left over from Fiato's operation with Puggy Zeichick, the mobster brothers had plenty of work to do. And the government was quickly developing its case.

Luigi Gelfuso espoused old-school mob philosophy, but he was anything but a traditionalist. He was, in fact, a devoted drug dealer who trafficked in large quantities of cocaine. Far from staying away from dope like a true Mafiosi, surely one of the mob's greatest myths, Gelfuso enlisted his crew and even his son, Michael Gelfuso, in the highly lucrative racket.

"Everything you do with my son is with my blessing," Gelfuso told Fiato.

The Fiatos had little difficulty getting Gelfuso to participate in any cocaine-related setup.

Larry Fiato approached Gelfuso with an offer to purchase an ounce of cocaine, but Gelfuso was prepared to buy it by the kilo. With the contact made, Bobby Bourne entered the scene. Bourne was a Hollywood producer who claimed to have drug connections throughout the movie industry. He was, in fact, undercover FBI Agent Bob Hamer, a Bureau street legend whose activities resulted in indictments across the nation. The Fiatos' jobs were simple: introduce Bourne to the Gelfusos and let the agent do the rest.

With Larry Fiato in tow and recorders capturing the moment on tape, Bourne met with Michael Gelfuso at an Orange Julius in the San Fernando Valley. After some small talk, the three men went to Fiato's car, where Bourne paid Gelfuso $9,000 in cash for five ounces of cocaine.

Not long afterward, Larry Fiato paid Gelfuso $5,000 for a sample in anticipation of a much larger shipment. Fiato turned over the dope to the FBI, and a routine lab analysis provided a reminder that there is no honor among thieves. Michael Gelfuso had sold Larry Fiato a mixture of baking soda and mannitol, not cocaine.

Posing as Bobby Bourne, agent Bob Hamer grew closer to Gelfuso as the Fiatos worked him into the conversation. The faked tribute payments helped cagey wiseguys Luigi Gelfuso and Albie Nunez warm up to the mild-mannered stranger. Hamer began meeting with Nunez at the Universal Studios commissary, often arriving just minutes before the hoodlum pulled into the parking lot. Nunez, of course, believed Hamer had been on the lot all day.

An experienced undercover agent, Hamer appreciated the Fiatos' ability to blend him into their world. Without a duke in, he would be on the outside looking in and might never be able to get close to the hierarchy of the L.A. mob.

One night at the popular Palm Restaurant, the case came seconds from falling apart. Fiato had set up a meeting among himself, brother Larry, their friend Bob, Michael Gelfuso, and Albie Nunez. Agents Wacks and Weichert would be in the room watching the scene. The purpose for the meeting was twofold: First, Hamer would attempt to secure a kilo of cocaine for resale from Gelfuso. At the same time, a team of FBI surveillance specialists would be entering Gelfuso's apartment and planting listening devices throughout the place.

The evening began well enough, with the group assembling and ordering cocktails. Hamer, who drank very little alcohol, nursed his cocktail while the others had a couple belts. At the bar, taking in the scene, Wacks and Weichert ordered drinks as well.

After an hour, the group ordered dinner. When the food came, Hamer ate as slowly as he could to drag out the meeting and give his cohorts back at Gelfuso's apartment time to set up their bugs. He chewed each piece of steak twenty to thirty times. At one point near the end of the meal, he excused himself and called a contact number. The surveillance agents hadn't even entered Gelfuso's apartment. It would be another hour before they were ready.

In a panic, Hamer signalled to Wacks and Weichert, asking them to pretend they were television producers who knew "Bob" and wanted to visit. Anything to stall the dinner check.

Problem was, Wacks and Weichert had been drinking heavily for the previous two hours. They were ill-prepared for an acting job. Still, they approached the table and grinned as they took seats near the men they had been trying to put in the penitentiary for years.

"It began all right, but these guys were really wasted," Fiato recalled. "They were introduced to Al, Michael, Larry and Anthony. Wacks had been undercover in the Brilab case and knew enough to keep his mouth shut, but Weichert was especially out of it. In a few minutes he's calling Al `Albie' and me `Craig.'

"Gelfuso got suspicious right away, and Hamer and I had to

work like hell to confuse him. The case was sitting right there at the table and Weichert damn near boozed it away. I was scared and angry at the same time, and I thought I saw Hamer's life pass before his eyes."

If Weichert hadn't almost blown the case, the night at the Palm would have been a real comedy. Larry Fiato recalled Weichert saying, 'We're going to send Albie to his room for twenty' loud enough for Nunez to hear him."

Anthony Fiato reacted quickly to attempt to save the play, calling Wacks and Weichert a couple of aging homosexuals who were looking for their next television project. All the while Fiato was charging bottles of Dom Perignon on Weichert's credit card.

"They were suspicious, but they took my brother's word for everything," Larry recalled. "That's how stupid they were. For weeks afterward Michael Gelfuso kept trying to get me in touch with those directors. He wanted to be in the movies."

By December 1984, Michael's father Luigi Gelfuso appeared to take Bobby Bourne into his confidence. He was willing to finance multi-kilo deals from Bourne to Johnny Vaccaro in Reno, who was said to have all the buyers anyone could want. To Anthony Fiato, that sounded like something he pulled a few years earlier in Las Vegas through Jerry Matricia. In the months to come, Gelfuso and Bourne would switch roles as buyer and seller.

Ever suspicious, once when Bourne was slow to pay, Luigi Gelfuso immediately went on the defensive.

"We want to see him this afternoon," Gelfuso told Fiato. "Fuck this tomorrow, tomorrow, tomorrow. You call him right now and tell him I want to see him right away."

Whenever the money came through, it always found its way into Pete Milano's pocket. But in the 1980s the Milano family was not the government's only target. The FBI also was investigating the mob's presence in the movie industry, and agents and prosecutors often used Fiato as a sounding board. Fiato was interviewed by Marvin Rudnick, chief prosecutor in charge of the MCA investigation, and confirmed Sal Pisello's status as a made member of the Gambino crime family.

"I grabbed him in the Palm Restaurant one night to shake him down," Fiato said. "He ran to his people in New York and after a phone call we stayed away from Sal."

CHAPTER 8

With their street undercover work in full swing, by late 1984 the Fiato brothers found themselves in demand outside Los Angeles. They had only begun to trust Wacks and Weichert, and now they were being asked to meet with agents from Boston. Escorted by their FBI handlers, the Fiatos were introduced to James Ring, who headed the FBI's organized crime squad in Boston, in a case that was making use of the undercover expertise of Vince De La Mantaigne.

"They were interested in three or four guys that I might know, who had been listed on my surveillance records when I was in Boston," Anthony Fiato recalled. "There was Biaggio DiGiacomo, Dominic Isabella, Vinny Nip Ferrara and a face I hadn't seen in a few years, Nicky Giso.

"I identified Biaggio right away, but I wondered why they were so interested in him. He was a guy who was very friendly with Joe Russo, but Biaggio was a greenie, a Sicilian who spoke broken English and on Sundays used to hang out around my shop on Hanover Street because he knew I was tight with Joe Russo. He'd get me coffee, offer to do odd jobs, always treated me with the highest respect because he knew I was going places with Joe Russo and the family.

"In that sense, Biaggio was a lot smarter than he looked. He worked in construction in those days. Biaggio was in the Sicilian Mafia, and his brother was a top figure who had been murdered

195

back there, but in America he was just another scuffler, a guy who dressed like he was just off the boat. I knew plenty about him. When he came over to this country he lived in East Boston, which was Joe Russo's territory.

"When I found out he had become a capo through the war of attrition the FBI was having with the Mafia, I couldn't believe it. I asked them if they were sure they had their information right. The FBI had destroyed the Angiulos on the North End. The guys who were left had scattered all over the city or were on the lam. This is how I became a part of Operation Chokehold.

"Biaggio, Nicky Giso, Paulie Intiso, these guys had escaped the investigations that had nailed almost all of the rest of the family. I mean, Raymond Patriarca Jr., Jerry and Danny Angiulo, Larry Baioni, Ralphie Chiong, Johnny Cincotti, they were all in trouble, either indicted or on the way to being indicted. Joe Russo was still on the street, but everyone knew he was a target. The government had been trying to grab him since I was a kid."

Once it was clear to Ring that Fiato had had a relationship with DiGiacomo, De La Mantaigne joined the conversation. On first blush, the play was simple. Use Fiato to introduce undercover agent De La Mantaigne to DiGiacomo, and let nature take its course. De La Mantaigne had been eating regularly at DiGiacomo's restaurant in east Boston, but had gotten nowhere with the extremely suspicious Mafia man.

But that meant Fiato would return to his hometown and wear a wire against the very people he had grown up with.

"I didn't want to do it, but Wacks and Weichert harassed me," Anthony Fiato said. "They said the more cooperation I gave them the better it was going to look with a judge. They told me I really didn't have to do much, just go around with the undercover agent, let the guy be seen with me, and then leave. In and out. No sweat. That was easy for them to say. They didn't know, and would never know, what I knew about the people in Boston."

From the moment Anthony and Larry Fiato stepped off the plane, they felt like spies in their own country. By the time they drove down Hanover Street, they were certain they had made a terrible mistake allowing the feds to talk them into coming back home. The sights and smells were achingly familiar, but they had changed in ways few people from the old neighborhood would understand.

"When I got there I felt disoriented," Anthony Fiato said. "Me and my brother went to my house. Then we met with Vince, who came around and picked us up in a Cadillac. I thought we were going to spend a few days knocking around the neighborhood, easing into the act. But then I found out that these mutts want me to walk in right out of the blue and start wearing a wire on some of the sharpest guys in the history of the mob.

It was beyond absurd, and I was pissed off about it. But guess what? I didn't have a choice, not with prison hanging over my head. I was arguing with everybody, really on edge. And it didn't help that the agents in Boston were treating me like some two-dollar snitch. At one point I called them all a bunch of cocksuckers and challenged them to step into the closet to see who'd come out alive. I guaranteed them they wouldn't walk out of that fucking closet. I said, 'Fuck you and fuck your surveillance.'"

Wacks took Fiato aside and reminded him that the game was almost over. "Do what you have to do to survive," Wacks said. "Do it your own way."

With that, the agents backed off. Instead of fitting him with a bulky Nagra, which fits at the base of the back, Fiato was given a smaller recording device, which he wore down his pants. Then, with Nicky Giso's address, he and his brother took De La Mantaigne's Cadillac and drove into the city. Instead of heading to a restaurant in East Boston, where Giso met daily with his crew of bookmakers and strong-arm guys, the Fiatos drove to the North End.

"And who do I run into? My old pals Sonny Polosi, who still owes me money from Las Vegas, and his running mate Bobby Luisi. They've heard I'm a made guy now and that I'm on top in L.A. I haven't seen Sonny since '79, but he knows exactly what I'm thinking. He owes. He owes.

"I say, 'Did you hear about your pal, Costanza? He got whacked. Guess he must have owed somebody some money, you know what I mean?' And the poor guy turned white and changed the subject."

Polosi said, "Did you hear Nicky Giso's got throat cancer? He tells everybody it's polyps, but it's throat cancer. He talks like he's really sick."

Anthony knew Polosi would immediately begin spreading the word that the Fiato brothers were back on the North End. Before nightfall, their cover would be secure.

"We're driving around the North End and I see Pegleg, the old bartender from the Coliseum, hobbling down the sidewalk. I stopped the Cadillac and got out. It was beginning to feel like old times, and I almost forgot the reason I'd come back to Boston.

"Pegleg sees my diamond watch and the way I'm dressed and says, 'I heard all about you in California. You're doing pretty good. The boss is hanging in Revere now. The feds are putting everybody in jail, and Nicky's running around with some fucking young broad who's barely out of junior high.'"

With that, the Fiatos picked up Giso's address from Pegleg. When Giso inquired about how two guys who hadn't seen him in five years found him so easily, as he surely would, Fiato would have a verifiable story.

But it didn't make walking into the restaurant any easier.

"My heart's beating out of my chest," he said. "I haven't seen this guy in fucking years, guys are getting busted left and right, and I walk in on Nicky as he's sitting with three or four book-makers, including a guy named Spucky, who I knew. Nicky didn't even recognize my brother and asked who he was. I was ready to die, but I couldn't let on. They asked about Ronnie Rome, whether I was still seeing him, and I told them he was running with Anthony Tumac's people and in business with Marty Taccetta. Ronnie Rome owed everybody money, so he was always the first guy people asked about. I made sure to tell them I'd seen Pegleg and that that was how I got Nicky's address."

Nicky Giso, in a raspy voice, said, "Hey, Tony Rome. He eats the chicken, leaves the bone. How are you, kid?"

But Fiato could feel the tension in the room. He stood by Giso's table.

"Nicky gets up like he's going to hug me, then steps behind me and starts massaging my shoulders. He pats me on the back and says, 'You put on some weight' and pats my stomach. "You're nice and strong' and feels my arms. He pats my left pocket, and the microphone is in my right pocket.

"I know what he's doing. He's frisking me. So I take out a wad of hundreds from my right pocket that would choke a fucking pig. I said, 'When I was with you I had lint in my pocket. But I'm doing all right now.'

"The guys at the table laughed and that threw him off. I'm with him for forty-five minutes and every second of the time I'm afraid the wire is going to show. He's frisking me, checking me out. He did everything but pat my crotch. I had to piss and I was afraid to go to the bathroom. I was really scared. I was showing a photo of Kathy and my house in Beverly Hills. I can tell they think I'm big time in the drug business. 'I'm not doing too bad, Nicky,' I told him. 'Me and you are friends, but we haven't been formally introduced.'

"At one point I whispered to Nicky, 'Tell Joe Russo to get in touch with Frankie Skyball.' Nicky whispered to Spucky, who sent the message to Paulie Intiso, who would relay it to Joe Russo, who would contact Frankie Scibelli, who was one of the most powerful men in the Genovese crime family.

"Frankie Skyball is from Springfield. The Genovese family oversees the Patriarca family on the commission, and Nicky knows that if I'm using Skyball's name I'm doing real well on the West Coast. I looked at Nicky, and saw that I'd gotten over on him. He was impressed. And then I started thinking about him. He was the guy who got me started in this thing. He came to my father's funeral. It really made me sick to my stomach what I was doing to him."

"After Larry and I left the restaurant, we got about twenty feet down the road and I had him pull over. I threw my guts up."

That night, Anthony and Larry Fiato arrived at Biaggio DiGiacomo's restaurant with undercover agent De La Mantaigne. Biaggio immediately recognized his old friend, Tony Rome.

"He comes over, puts his arm around me and gives me a hug," Fiato recalled. "But he's immediately interested in how I know this guy who has been coming into his restaurant. 'Oh, I did a few things with him,' I told him. Biaggio starts talking about Ralphie Chiong, J.R. Russo and the rest of the guys, just like old times. He's not talking about criminal activity, but he's comfortable enough with me to mention those names in front of a stranger. He looks at my gray hair and says, "Hey, you beginning to look like a Joe now.'

"He was really happy to see me, told me to watch out because the FBI was all over the place. And he brought up Ronnie Rome and the money he owed everybody. That Ronnie Rome was going to get me killed yet.

"When De La Mantaigne, who used the name Mark Legere, went to the bathroom, I whispered to Biaggio that I'd only be in Boston for a short time. He knew that I had the reputation as a guy who made a killing with drugs and loansharking, and I knew that he was thinking this other guy, Mark, must be a partner or something. I let him think that.

"When we got back to De La Mantaigne's motel room, I told him not to offer anything to Biaggio. To let him come to you. The bait was planted, and, sure enough, that's what happened. The agent told Biaggio that he was into me for a lot of money and that he had access to a ton of coke. That got Biaggio's interest. And those conversations were enough for the government to get a wiretap on all these guys, and that got Operation Chokehold moving. I'd betrayed some of the best friends I'd ever had."

But the FBI wanted more. Paulie Intiso had died a couple days prior to the Fiatos' trip to Boston, and the federal agents insisted Anthony Fiato wear a wire to the funeral. It was a line he would not cross.

"These were the men I had respected my whole life, men who gave envelopes to my mother when my father died," Fiato said. "I hated the fucking FBI for what it was making me do. Sure, I was out of prison, but who was I? I was a man without a country. I told Wacks no. They could throw me in jail, but I wasn't wearing a wire on those guys anymore. I later heard the FBI offered Biaggio a deal to allow him to remain on the street and keep operating—anything short of murder—if he cooperated with them and provided them solid information. That's the problem with the Boston FBI guys. They're so anal retentive. The Los Angeles guys are a lot more laid back, and they're more effective because of it."

Larry Fiato: "When the FBI wanted my brother to wear a wire into Paulie Intiso's funeral, that was it for him. He'd been searched by Nicky a couple of times. But the FBI didn't care if they put him in danger. They were using him and didn't give a shit. At that point, they were just as bad as the mob guys, if not worse, because they think they're on the side of righteousness, especially that De La Mantaigne. They'll do anything to get the people they want, and they don't care how they do it."

"If I thought introducing an FBI agent to the Boston people was a nightmare, it was nothing compared to what happened the night Bill Weichert brought over a female FBI agent to our home to explain what the future held for us," Fiato said. "The pressure had taken its toll on all of us, and one night, while I was still married to Kathy Villa, it all fell apart.

"After she started going with me, Kathy's Beverly Hills friends turned on her. They didn't like her going around with a Mafia guy, and Joey Villa didn't help when he started bad-mouthing her and me around town. Kathy really tried to stay with me while I was working undercover. She tried to understand but the pressure was getting to her just like it was getting to me.

"But what really broke it with Kathy was the night Bill Weichert got drunk at our house in Beverly Hills. Weichert came over with a female agent, and we all had drinks and talked about the idea of entering Witness Protection. Kathy hated the idea, and

Weichert wasn't helping matters by telling her she'd have to leave Beverly Hills for good and freeze her ass off in Butte, Montana. I didn't have a choice, but Kathy did.

"Then the conversation went from bad to a real nightmare. While I was in the kitchen talking to the female agent, Weichert, who was loaded with Jack Daniels, made a move on Kathy. I didn't find out until later or I would have torn his fucking head off. He grabbed her, tried to kiss her and made a complete jerk of himself. He was drunk, but that's no excuse. He was filling his hollow leg with Bourbon and what he did helped ruin my marriage.

"It scared Kathy. She stopped trusting the FBI at that moment, and without that trust she had nothing to lean on. It was a real mess, and when she told me later what happened I was ready to kill the guy. People don't know how much trust you put in the hands of the FBI when you decide to cooperate. Betraying that trust ended the whole fucking thing.

"I knew at that moment Kathy was going to leave. And, to tell the truth, I couldn't blame her.

"When I found out, I called Mike Wachs screaming and yelling. He knew that giving the guy liquor was like giving a blind man the car keys. Wachs talked to him, and Weichert later apologized. But it was too late.

"Kathy went to school to study real estate. She became a successful agent and started making some of the highest residential sales in the country. She was on her way."

CHAPTER 9

Thanks in part to Anthony and Larry Fiato, by the spring of 1987 the FBI and Los Angeles Strike Force had the Milano crew investigation nailed tight. Although cases in New York were bound to grab larger headlines, the shattering of the Los Angeles mob was in some respects more intriguing because of the use in an undercover capacity of the so-called Gangster Brothers.

Anthony Fiato's defection so rattled Mike Rizzitello that he lost trust in even his closest associates. If Fiato, who had sat on Rizzitello's knee, could betray him, then anyone could.

Lack of faith in his own men was a key reason Rizzitello decided in April to pay a visit to Mustang topless bar owner Bill Carroll. Rizzi had met Carroll while in prison in 1970 and had been attempting to acquire a piece of the club for months. He had warned Carroll repeatedly to come up with part of the $150,000 the Mustang generated each month. Carroll refused.

"This is for not letting us eat," Rizzitello said as he pumped three bullets into Carroll's head. Although critically injured, he did not die immediately. Just ten hours later, bar bouncer George Yudzevich, who had bragged that he had disposed of the gun and bloody clothes of Carroll's attackers, was found dead. Yudzevich had been shot in the head.

It was just Mike Rizzitello's luck. Although blinded, Bill Carroll recovered and testified about his old acquaintance. Rizzitello was sentenced to 33 years in prison.

On May 22, an 18-count federal indictment was unsealed against Peter John Milano and 14 other men, including Carmen Joseph Milano, Luigi Gelfuso, Vincent Dominic "Jimmy" Caci, Rocco Zangari, Steve Cino, Johnny Vaccaro, Charles James "Bobby Milano" Caci, John Patrick DiMattia, Albert Jesus Nunez, Stephen George Munichiello, Michael Gelfuso, Robert Ralph D'Agostino, Arthur Franconeri, and Abraham Anthony Prins.

"The prosecution, developed by the Organized Crime Strike Force program, is the most significant organized crime case on the West Coast in a decade," Attorney General Edwin Meese III said. "The indictment, and others to follow, will involve as defendants virtually all of those, the government charges, make up the membership of the Cosa Nostra organized crime family in Los Angeles."

Added U.S. Attorney Robert C. Bonner, "With this prosecution, the main body of the Los Angeles family as a viable criminal enterprise has been gutted."

Not since the Forex case, which netted boss Dominic Brooklier, Sam Sciortino, Louis Tom Dragna, Mike Rizzitello, Jack LoCicero—and nearly Anthony Fiato—had the L.A. mob been hit so hard.

But the rich material the Fiatos had helped generate was only beginning to bear fruit.

A week after the Milano indictment, Mike Rizzitello and a half-dozen others were indicted for attempting to acquire one million dollars in stolen municipal bonds. The indictment alleged the seven men had tried to broker the bonds, stolen from Manufacturers Hanover Trust in New York City in 1983, by claiming they had been acquired in exchange for 80 acres of land in Alaska. They managed to cash in $300,000 worth of bonds before the deal broke down. Wiseguy restaurant owner Lenard Aron was named in the indictment, as were Thomas Saullo Jr., Steve Finkel, Puggy Zeichick, Jack Fineberg, and Jacob David Zemer.

Four days later, it was Joey Mangiapani's turn. The boxing trainer and pal of Jimmy Caan was indicted along with clothier Mark Kreiner and "Cowboy" Clyde David Tracy for attempting to strong-arm their way into a better arrangement with record company owners Lawrence Leal and Mike Lushka.

In July, Robert Ralph "Dino" D'Agostino was indicted. A restaurant owner and chef by trade, the affable D'Agostino cut a deal with prosecutors and avoided a racketeering conviction by agreeing to plead guilty to charges he sold 83 grams of cocaine to undercover FBI Agent Bob Hamer.

D'Agostino, who was later sentenced to six years, had tried to solicit the Fiatos to assist with a slow-paying customer. At sentencing, D'Agostino admitted to Organized Crime Strike Force boss Richard Small that the Fiatos' fierce reputations were widely known: "They're capable of blowing you away, sir. I know their neurotic conditions, of talking with them and telling me some of their fanatic stories. 'This mother so-and-so, I'll break his legs, I'll break his arms, I'll blow his eyes out.' I don't need to get involved with those types of characters."

But he was more than happy to get involved as long as he believed he was going to benefit by the connection.

In the last weeks leading to the Milano indictment, and for weeks afterward, the Fiatos were hidden from sight as they prepared to testify at trials to come. But by the time the government began turning over its voluminous evidence to the defense, it was clear the Los Angeles mob was as stuck as a fat man in a phone booth.

Mike Rizzitello, Puggy Zeichick and Thomas Saullo were acquitted in the million dollar bond case. A jury convicted Steve Finkle and Jack Fineberg of conspiracy and deadlocked on the remaining defendants.

As the main trial drew near, Bob Kessler lay stricken with terminal cancer in a room at New York's Mt. Sinai Medical Center. His deathbed testimony was videotaped; it would provide devastating evidence against Luigi Gelfuso, John DiMattia, Johnny Vaccaro and Albert Nunez. Combined with the Fiatos' personal experience with the mob, and FBI undercover agent Bob Hamer's testimony, the portrait of criminal activity was as comprehensive as it was devastating.

Perhaps the oddest reaction to the prosecution came from DiMattia, who had been the subject of a hit ordered by Pete Milano, who believed him a snitch. DiMattia had been warned by the FBI in keeping with the agency's policy, but he was still reluctant to believe the truth. "These are my friends," he said. "They wouldn't hurt me."

A few weeks later, Nunez bailed out and pleaded guilty to extortion and cocaine distribution conspiracy charges. He received a 10-year sentence, the longest hitch of anyone in the Milano crew.

Pete Milano took a plea-bargain and accepted a six-year sentence; underboss Carmen Milano received a two-year deal. Bobby Milano, Jimmy Caci, and Big Steve Cino also pleaded guilty under the weight of evidence. The case against Rocco Zangari was weak, but Milano instructed him to accept a guilty plea. In exchange, federal authorities were willing to not go for the throat on the rest of the crew. Zangari got five years probation, but the government got its conviction.

"I think it puts them out of business for a while," Former Los Angeles Strike Force Chief James Henderson told the *Los Angeles Times*. "The government does this once more and there's not going to be a La Cosa Nostra in Los Angeles."

"It was a package deal that saved the government hundreds of thousands of dollars in trial costs and four to six months of trial time," Strike Force Attorney Richard Stavin said.

Days later, street boss Luigi Gelfuso, Johnny Vaccaro and John DiMattia confessed to a variety of extortion-related charges. In court, DiMattia admitted his role in attempting to collect money on behalf of former U.S. Senate candidate Roy Elson in the $480,000 Mondavano scam. He also admitted influencing Sunwest Bank officials to obtain credit lines in excess of $100,000.

While Rizzitello and his cronies enjoyed a short-lived celebration in the bond case, taunting police surveillance teams and cursing the Fiato brothers' names, by far Anthony's biggest disappointment came when he entered court to testify in the extortion case of Puggy Zeichick and Gene Holden. Zeichick would be convicted and Holden acquitted at trial, but the real confrontation took place outside of court, where Fiato faced down his former loansharking partner.

"To give you an idea of the kind of FBI protection I got by then, an agent dropped me off in front of the courthouse," Fiato said. "In the hallway, I ran right into Puggy, whose trial was in recess. I thought we might get in a fight, but instead he ducked past me, gave me the finger and went into the bathroom. I was angry as hell. I'd avoided wearing a wire on Puggy for months, and the FBI had trouble building a case against him because of it, and he was angry at me?

"I followed him into the bathroom and said, 'You stupid motherfucker. I'm not testifying against you. I did nothing to hurt you and you want to blame me for your problems? In all the time I was working undercover I never wore a wire on you. Why wouldn't you take the deal they offered? Haven't you listened to the surveillance tapes they have on us? You said we could beat any case in front of a jury because juries are stupid. They're going to play that in the trial, you idiot.' But he wouldn't listen.

"At trial, they played the tape and Puggy put his hands on his forehead and started shaking his head. He knew he was dead in the water. That's what convicted him. Gene got acquitted and Puggy got convicted, and Puggy walked around afterwards and talked about how I had ruined his life. It got back to me, of course. After all that talking, when Puggy went into the can he immediately contacted the FBI about becoming a rat. They didn't want him."

By late April 1987, the heart of the Los Angeles Mafia investigation had fallen out of the newspapers. It was finally Danny Mondavano's turn to get his. Backed by the Fiatos and Elson, Mondavano, his wife, Rose, and son, Dennis, were indicted on tax charges. True to his nature, Danny Mondavano was long gone by the time the government got around to indicting him.

After the commotion died down, Anthony Fiato was back to

thinking about his old life. He missed it and felt ashamed of what he had done. Not to the Milano crew, but to tough old Mike Rizzitello.

"Rizzitello never had a clue about what I was doing," Fiato said. "I mean, I grew up at his knee. He was my father's good friend. Never in his wildest dreams would he believe that I would do this to him. And that hurt to think about. I was like a man with two faces. I'm laughing. I'm joking and inside I'm dying. I changed my whole personality around.

"I had to do something that I don't know if a lot of people can do. I only know what I did because it was sink or swim. Because I was a very black and white person; I had to learn what gray meant. Gray didn't exist for me. I had to adjust and I had my conscience, which is the square person's conscience turned inside out. Every time that I put one of these people in a situation of recording them, my conscience was working against me, not for me. I was saying I was doing a wrong thing, not a right thing, and it was like death to me. I used to go home and I'd throw my guts up. And if it wasn't for the agents helping me, telling me over and over that what I was doing was the right thing, telling me that I was just an instrument of justice, that I was just getting these people out of the way and this was just a mechanism that was going on. I was just an instrument of justice for the FBI."

Larry Fiato recalled, "That's the big difference between an FBI agent wearing a wire and one of us wearing a wire. It's because we have the conscience that we have to fight all the time. When the FBI guys do it, that's their job. That's what they're schooled to do. We have to fight that all of the time. It was especially hard on my brother."

But Anthony Fiato had long since stopped kidding himself about his motivation for working with the government. The image he had grown up watching on the silver screen, on Hanover Street and Hollywood Boulevard, was shattered forever.

"I did it to save my ass, man," he said. "I didn't want to go to jail. You understand? That's what it really boiled down to. Mike

Wacks and Bill Weichert both told me, 'Hey, what are you going to do? If you go to jail, you're going to come out in ten, fifteen years and they're going to say, hey, you're a stand-up guy.' So I looked at it in terms like that. I looked at it in terms of survival."

In his way, Anthony Fiato had become a mob star. He was so popular within the FBI, in fact, that he and his brother were invited to Bureau headquarters at Quantico, Virginia along with agents Wacks and Weichert to tell their incredible story. With a video camera capturing the scene, the four men informed and entertained an auditorium of FBI agents for more than five hours. An edited version of the videotape was later used as a confidential FBI training film titled, "The Gangster Brothers." Wacks told Fiato he considered the video unprecedented in its candid illustration of the relationship between agents and informants. The Fiato brothers were credited with helping convict nearly 70 members and associates of organized crime.

"I felt like a star," Anthony Fiato recalled. "Everyone looked at me, and I felt like a star. We checked in and went to a barracks, where we stayed. There was a cafeteria where all the agents ate and law enforcement from police departments all over the country. The cops were distinguished by their red shirts. There were large rooms with all kinds of classes going on, from handcuffing perpetrators to climbing ropes, and we were given a tour by one of the senior agents.

"As usual, me and my brother stuck out like sore thumbs. I had a cashmere sport coat worth fifteen hundred bucks, diamond and gold jewelry. Obviously, I wasn't one of the agents and everyone saw that. When we started to tell our story, they were fixed on us, like they were watching a movie. They weighed every word that was coming out of our mouths. Me and my brother both felt important, like we had done something special. For one of the few times in more than a year, I felt really good about what I had done. We poured our hearts and souls to these people and were scrutinized like two bugs. They asked us everything about everything: What was attractive about the life, did we know people in

Cleveland? Agents from all over the country were asking us about the mob guys in their city. There were seasoned veterans and new trainees, people from other law enforcement agencies. They all wanted to learn more about how they could develop sources like us. By then we were well versed in all the legal expressions, and it surprised the other agents that we sounded so much like them. But we had the experience that a lot of them didn't have. By then we had learned the intricacies of their business. I had lived in two worlds and I explained that to them. I told them I didn't know who I was anymore, that I had left the only world I'd ever cared about. I was insecure about the whole thing even after all those months.

"At the end of the program, one of the senior agents thanked us and then the applause started. We were all caught off guard by the show of emotion from these guys who are usually so stoic and serious. They gave us a five-minute standing ovation. All four of us had tears in our eyes. I knew right then and there, maybe for the first time, that I had done the right thing. I had truly been respected."

CHAPTER 10

With the Los Angeles mob shattered, Anthony and Larry Fiato faded from the Southern California scene. They spent a few months in Bakersfield, then made plans to leave California entirely.

Although they had repeatedly been offered status in the government's Witness Protection Program, which would have meant a steady paycheck from law enforcement as long as they produced useful information, they hated the idea of spending the rest of their lives in hiding.

They accepted relocated witness status, and prepared for a life they hadn't known since childhood: ordinary citizenship.

For Anthony Fiato, there was still unfinished business. He hated the fact that the men he believed were responsible for the murder of Frank Christi had not been punished. In fact, the murder investigation hadn't been touched in years.

"I let the FBI know immediately in 1984 of the Christi murder, but it was a state beef," Anthony Fiato said. "Compared to the Mafia, it was the lesser of two evils. They were concerned with the Bompensiero weapon, which Norman Freedberg had told me he had in his possession, along with the L.A. mob's arsenal. I called on the phone to Norman and he told me that he'd explain it to my brother. I had Larry go and speak to him and he told Larry he broke the gun up and threw it in a lake. And the talk about Norman went no further."

Once the Milano family was out of the way, Mike Rizzitello

had been on an attempted murder charge, and the Boston mob was on the run, all that remained was the Frank Christi murder. As a liaison between the FBI and local law enforcement, it was the job of Agent Mike Wacks to persuade Anthony and Larry Fiato into cooperating with police detectives in the Christi investigation.

"Do me a favor," Wacks said to Fiato. "Talk to these guys from robbery/homicide. Just tell them what you know about the Christi murder."

"I was reluctant," Fiato said. "The agents were talking about using me in an undercover operation in San Diego, where I act like a biker hooked up in the drug trade. I was ready to play the part, especially since it meant I'd be able to earn a living for a few more years. I stood to gain nothing from the Frank Christi case.

"Christi was a tall, odd-looking guy with a real caustic wit, and if he took his wig off he looked like a death camp survivor," Fiato said. "He was an arrogant guy, and not a likable person. He was always knocking people. But he didn't deserve to die. He was writing a screenplay with Norman. They were the best of friends until Frank started messing around with Norman's girlfriend.

"At first Harvey told me he shot the guy, but Betts and Coe told me he only drove. They said they used a shotgun and a fucking pistol. Betts told me he shot Christi in the chest with a pistol. Christi was coming out of his car when they approached him. They told me he said, 'What did I do? What did I do? Why me? Why me?' They were laughing about it, smirking about it, making the gestures with their hands like they were shooting. They bragged that they'd never be caught. It was their first time doing a piece of work and it went to their heads."

Although Anthony Fiato knew there would be little or no compensation and his story was bound to get him dragged back into court as a key witness in a murder trial, he agreed to assist the detectives.

Once the call was made, LAPD Robbery/Homicide Detectives Enoch "Mac" McClain and Tom Lange knocked the dust from the seven-year-old Christi file and acquainted themselves with the scant facts available on the murder. They could see why the case had gone nowhere.

Although Christi had performed in "*The Godfather*," he wasn't exactly the violent type. Some of his associates had criminal backgrounds, but they weren't hit men, and this had the makings of a hired job. What had Christi done to anger someone enough to shoot him with at least two weapons?

"Normally, what happens when you get a case like that is you work on it until all the leads die out," Mac McClain said. "With other cases coming in all the time, you don't have the luxury to continue to dig up leads. The case isn't closed, but it's dormant. Until we got that call, it wasn't going anywhere."

They drove downtown for a meeting with the FBI and were introduced to Anthony and Larry Fiato.

"Anthony basically said that a guy attempted to hire him to do a murder, and that he and his brother refused to do the murder," McClain said. "Later on, the guy they had been solicited to kill was actually killed, and he said he knew the people involved because they had bragged to him about doing the murder.

"The Fiatos played an integral part. Prior to them coming up, we had nothing and nothing was being done on the case. To this day Anthony will call and we'll talk about the case and ask whether I think we'll ever be able to get this guy. Anthony Fiato was a very personable guy, but he was involved with the mob and a lot of things, and you have to remember that. It's hard not to like him, but in the back of my mind I know he's capable of doing a lot of things and has done a lot of things. I liked him, but on the other hand I knew I had to keep a certain distance. I respect him for what he did and I appreciated what he did. There's no way we could have forced him to do it. I think the basis for our friendship is mutual respect.

The Fiatos provided the detectives their first solid leads in the Christi case. The information had been in the FBI's possession since 1984, but agents had kept quiet in order to protect their ongoing organized crime racketeering investigation. Now that the Milano family was shattered, the Christi case information resurfaced.

Anthony Fiato identified Harvey Ross as one of the shooters. Ross had failed in an attempt to impress Fiato with his skills as a desperado years earlier. Fiato didn't believe Ross was capable of pulling a trigger and ending a human life, but he had listened to Ross brag about killing Christi.

Harvey Ross was not alone. He was accompanied by a couple of hulking lumberjack types who appeared to be twin brothers, men later identified as Ronald and Donald Coe. It was Ronald Coe along with Alan Betts who Fiato believed had accompanied Ross on the Christi hit.

At the time, Detectives McClain and Lange were unaware of the identity of Harvey Ross's cohorts. Because Ross, whose real name was Harvey Rosenberg, was known as a burglar who frequented Torrance, California, McClain contacted Det. Mike Terry of the Torrance Police Department. Terry was familiar with Ross, and he also had seen him in the company of the men Anthony Fiato had described: Ronald and Donald Coe.

Once mug shots were obtained of the three men, Anthony and Larry Fiato easily identified Ross and Ronald Coe. Donald Coe was not one of the shooters.

No one knew their whereabouts.

In time, the detectives contacted the "*America's Most Wanted*" television program, whose producers agreed to cut a segment on the Christi murder case. The program included mug shots of the Coes and Harvey Ross/Rosenberg. Living under an assumed name and attending college in Florida, Ross saw the segment and realized he couldn't continue to hide.

His conscience also had begun bothering him. He called McClain shortly after the program aired and left a message. By then, he already had been identified by the photographs, and the authorities took him into custody. Ronald Coe and Alan Betts were picked up in the Northwest.

Ross confirmed the Fiato brothers' story. He also implicated
Alan Betts as one of the shooters. The confession may have been
a way for Ross to ease his mind as he faced an even more stressful
and painful reality: terminal cancer. In a tearful videotaped confession, Ross admitted taking part in the murder of Frank Christi
for $5,000 to be split three ways with Ronald Coe and Alan Betts.

"It was amazing to me that they would do this," McClain said.
"Harvey stated that they were all hooked on dope. They were
down-and-out and owed money to mob people. They all had families. Even though they wanted to get more money initially, and I
think Harvey at first said no, they later figured that five-thousand
was better than no dollars. Harvey said he changed his mind at
the very end, but it was too late. It was one of the things that bothered him the rest of his life, that killing."

As Anthony Fiato completed his testimony before the grand
jury, prosecutor Dale Davidson was surprised to see the normally
taciturn group stand and applaud the reformed mobster. The
grand jury later indicted Rosenberg, Ronald Coe, Alan Betts and
Norman Freedberg for the murder of Frank Christi.

Superior Court Judge Paul Flynn presided over the first trial,
which found the Fiatos in fine form. They had prepared well for
their testimony, arriving early in Los Angeles. Normally, the
Christi murder trial would have been front-page news in Los
Angeles, but by 1995 it had been eclipsed by a double homicide in
Brentwood and the trial of the football star O.J. Simpson.

But they were too busy to be concerned about the Brentwood murders. Anthony and Larry Fiato concentrated on the business at hand.

Harvey Rosenberg died of lung cancer before trial, but not
before he gave an extensive, videotaped statement. As devastating
as Rosenberg's words were, they could not be cross-examined.
Anthony Fiato remained the key witness, and three defense attorneys attempted to carve him to pieces. After all, he was a mobster
with a reputation for violence who had ratted out his best friends
to save his skin. Surely the jury would look upon him with jaun-
diced eyes.

However, once the trial started, the Fiatos spent each recess in the witness room, where Patty Jo Fairbanks, who was in charge of corraling witnesses, had her hands full with those scheduled to testify in the sensational Simpson trial.

"I was up in the witness room and there's a nice-looking black guy sitting there," Fiato said. "It was Ron Ship, an ex-cop who was one of O.J.'s best friends. He was well-dressed, but he was really nervous. He was watching the proceedings from inside the witness room, which they weren't supposed to do, and he said, 'Oh, it looks like I'm next.' I said, 'Hey, man, they're going to try to make you fold. The minute they try to disrespect you, you fight back. Don't let them show you any disrespect; they'll be wanting you to fold. You have to fight back.' He thanked me.

"When he came off the stand and came back in the witness room, he came over and gave me one of those hip-hop brother handshakes. He couldn't thank me enough for getting him through it. The best part is, the guy thought I was a cop!"

It was in the witness room Anthony Fiato first met Nicole Brown Simpson's sister, Denise Brown.

"I had just gotten off the stand from testifying and we were taking a break," Anthony said. "She was there in the break room with one of her girlfriends. Everyone was going through the room. Marcia Clark, Chris Darden, Lange and Vannatter, Brian Kelberg, Shari Lewis. I was joking around, just trying to relieve the tension, which was pretty thick. I told Marcia Clark she looked just like a young Susan Sarandon, and she said, 'I'm glad you said young.' The truth is, we were so focused on our own trial testimony that we didn't realize the intensity of the Simpson trial. As we walked in for lunch after I'd testified all morning, Denise Brown was sitting there with her girlfriend, Betsy."

As Fiato entered the room, Betsy said, "Your name must be Vinny. The way you're dressed, you look like a Vinny."

"The way you're dressed, sweetheart, you look like you work for Heidi Fleiss."

The room erupted in laughter, but Betsy was nothing if not persistent. She continued to chat with Fiato.

"This is a real drag," she told him. "We're not supposed to laugh. We have to go around with long faces."

At one point, she told Fiato she was a radio operator whose handle was "Hot Beaver." When Brown saw Fiato's facial expression change, she laughed.

"You're laughing now, but if you come home with me tonight you'll be smiling in the morning," Fiato said.

Brown laughed again, but saw that he was serious.

"You remind me of some guy I used to go with a long time ago," she said in a quieter moment. "I really liked him."

The next day, Fiato bought Brown's lunch and made small talk. She talked about how nervous she was to be experiencing the trial and all the publicity. She laughed at his jokes, and he began to think he might get lucky. He didn't know it at the time, but sexy Denise Brown was the kind of woman who rarely brought luck to her men.

Instead of looking down on Fiato, over the course of a week on the stand, the jury came to like him. Fiato answered questions honestly, didn't flinch when he was called a snitch and a turncoat. Instead, he reminded all present that he had played an important role in putting most of an entire crime family in prison. True to his pugnacious nature, he began to enjoy sparring with the defense.

"They were so anxious to nail me, they were easy to lure," Fiato said. "I'd been playing that game since I was a kid, allowing them to think their thoughts and express them, then surprising them. They tried to trip me up on the twins, Ronald and Donald Coe. I told them, 'Ray Charles could tell the difference between these two,' and the jury laughed.

"They tried to confuse me about the number of people present at the meeting that Betts, Coe and Harvey admitted killing Christi. I said, 'How many people do you have sitting down at that table? The way you're adding guys to the meeting, you might as well throw in Jimmy Hoffa. I'll bet you think your client is innocent.' When he said he did, I said, 'Counselor, your nose is growing like

Pinocchio's.' And the jury laughed some more.

"When I was asked how I could possibly identify the defendants from the photos I was given, I said, 'When I saw their pictures, they jumped out at me like the face on a bottle of poison.' And the jury laughed again.

"At one point, we discovered that the defense had a tape which they were going to claim was me saying I owed Norman Freedberg a couple hundred bucks. This was going to be their 'gotcha' evidence, where they would catch me in a lie. I said, 'If you've got a recording of me saying that, then everything I've testified to is a lie.' And the mutt jumped at the chance to expose me. He goes and gets the tape and pushes a button.

"I couldn't help smiling. I said, 'That's not me, you moron, that's my brother.' He complained to the judge that I'd called him a moron, but the judge was laughing and told him he was a little thin-skinned."

By trial's end, Ronald Coe and Alan Betts would receive life sentences without the possibility of parole. Norman Freedberg would be more fortunate when a jury would be unable to decide his guilt or innocence. A new trial would be ordered.

After more than a week on the witness stand, Anthony Fiato finished his testimony. Larry Fiato followed his brother. In a move meant to raise the specter of deception and attack the credibility of the prosecution's key witnesses, defense attorneys immediately asked Larry Fiato whether his older brother had talked to him about their testimony.

Assuming the brothers had discussed the case, the lawyers went into bulldog mode.

Had Larry Fiato spoken with his brother prior to his testimony?

"I couldn't even if I wanted to," Larry said. "My brother's too busy trying to make a move on Denise Brown."

CHAPTER 11

In the witness room, Denise Brown approached Larry Fiato and whispered softly as she slipped something into his palm.

"She wrote her numbers on a piece of white paper and asked me to give it to my brother," Larry said. "I couldn't believe it. My brother had been talking that talk to her, and she obviously liked him. In the witness room, everyone treated Denise like a goddess. They had built this picture shrine to Nicole in the office with various sayings from the Bible about death and about how she was this flower and all that kind of stuff. There wasn't a photograph of Ron Goldman, and his family saw that when they gathered up there. I watched Fred Goldman struggle to keep himself and his family together and I was awed by his courage. He was a real man among a bunch of hypocrites. That poor heart-broken man who loved his son so genuinely and had such faith in the system, and he fought like hell to get it. But he didn't know what he was up against. When I saw that they didn't even have a photograph of Ron in the room I about died. I felt so ashamed for those people, who were all supposed to be the good guys. It was such an insult to the family. The next day the hypocrites put up a picture of Ron Goldman. It was a surreal room, and Denise was the princess."

A few minutes later, Anthony Fiato and Special Agent Mike Wacks entered the witness room. Handing his older brother the slip of paper containing the phone numbers, one to an apartment near the courthouse and another that rang at Brown's home in

Monarch Bay, Larry Fiato grinned like a kid.

"For everything that I've ever done against you, tell me that we're even," Larry said. "Denise Brown gave me these numbers to give to you."

"He gets every damned broad," FBI Agent Mike Wacks said.

Anthony Fiato had bedded Playmates and party girls, but was especially taken with Brown's obvious beauty and apparent vulnerability. The world was focused on the sister of Nicole Brown Simpson. But even Fiato was surprised when Denise Brown made the first move.

"I was dying to get to know her," Anthony Fiato said, "but there was no way I was going to call her the first night. I mean, every guy in America is after her. I'd heard Geraldo Rivera had his hooks in Denise and had put her up in that condominium near the courthouse, something she later confirmed. All I knew about Rivera is that he was the tabloid TV guy who'd found the pocket lint in Al Capone's safe. The cops and lawyers at the courthouse were all eyeing her. So I figure I'd better play my cards right.

"So I wait a day and return to the witness room again. As I walked in, I saw Fred and Mrs. Goldman and their daughter, Kim. I offered my condolences to them. I really felt sorry for those people. They appeared to be grieving terribly for their son.

"Then I saw Denise, and she looked especially good. She sort of scowled at me, but she warmed up quick enough. She told me, 'I've been thinking about you. And I said, 'I woke up at two in the morning thinking of you and couldn't go back to sleep.'

"She was testifying then and was obviously nervous. Outside the witness room, I told her I was sorry I hadn't called her and that I'd like to take her out. She was staying close to home because of her testimony, but I called her that night and we talked for three hours on the phone. I told her to hold the cross she wore around her neck and take the strength from it. The next night she called me from the condominium and admitted Geraldo had rented the place for her. There was a girl staying there with her, acting like her secretary, who screened all the calls and reported

back to Rivera. It was pretty weird. Denise told me not to use my
real name when I called there. So I told the secretary I was
Downtown Vinny Brown. Denise and I laughed about that.

"With the Christi trial wrapping up near the end of the week,
my brother and I were scheduled to leave Los Angeles on
Saturday. I figured Friday night was my last chance to see her, but
she said she had to be with her father.

"By the end of the week we found out that we'd nailed Betts
and Coe, and we were ready to celebrate. My brother Larry,
Wacks and Dale Davidson and his wife, Vivian, who were both
excellent prosecutors, Tom Lange, Enoch McClain and his wife
went out and had dinner and drinks.

"We were pissed that we hadn't gotten Freedberg, but everyone
knew the judge would set a new trial date and we'd get another
chance. They were putting us on the back burner, telling us what
good guys me and my brother were, really pouring on the charm.

"At one point I told Lange that I really had a thing for Denise
Brown and that I had her number and was going to call her. I
could see the panic in his eyes. I told him I really liked her and he
said, 'You and a million other guys.' Then I showed him I had her
phone numbers and said, 'This is your worst fucking nightmare. If
you had hair, you'd be pulling it out.' He kept telling me she
wasn't your average beauty, that she lived in the fast lane and that
she was high maintenance. I was just trying to give her a tuneup.

"We were originally scheduled to leave on Saturday, but we
missed the flight. When I called home, Denise had called and left
a message, so I called my little raven-haired sweetheart to see what
was on her mind. Me, I hoped. We talked for a while and made a
date for Monday night.

"I had to play it right. So I told Wacks that Denise and I were
getting together finally. I said we needed someplace special, someplace like the Ritz Carlton.

"We had a rented car and my brother and I picked her up at her
apartment near the courthouse. We went to the lounge at the Ritz
and were met by Mike Wacks and his wife. Denise's not drinking,

and nobody likes to be the only sober guy at a party, so I decide to drink sparkling water with her. The dining room is fabulous, and she's just been on television that day.

"Every human being in the United States had been watching her. Who was out with her? Tony the Animal Fiato. I'm with her and feeling like a million bucks. Everyone else was drinking and I picked up the tab. We had a great time, and after everyone finally went their own way I took her back to her apartment in a taxicab. It was a $60 ride one-way. Once we get in the cab we immediately start going at it. She took my hand and placed it on her breast and I was about to explode. I felt like a school kid.

"As the taxi drove on through the night, I thought how many men in America wanted to have their hand where my hand was.

"Tom Lange was right. This was one fast woman. We were making out like high school sweethearts. When we finally got back to her place, we kissed again outside the cab. I leaned her back against the car, pressed against her and planted the old Valentino sorrento. She grabbed my arms and I said, 'Take my strength. Don't let them push you around.' She said she wanted me to come upstairs, but she had two other women staying there."

By the time Fiato left Los Angeles and returned home the next day, Denise had left half-a-dozen messages. They talked night after night for more than a month, made love over the phone.

"We built our desire for each other. By then Denise was starting her domestic violence foundation and was touring the country and being interviewed by newspapers and magazines. She was going to Florida for a *Vogue* magazine photo shoot, and then was scheduled to be in New York.

"We made a date for a weekend in Boston. I booked a room at the Copley-Plaza Hotel and rented a limousine. We were finally going to be together after too many hours of x-rated phone calls, and I planned to make it memorable. When I met her at Logan Airport, the press photographers and TV cameras came out of the woodwork.

"This woman was front-page news everywhere she went, and that meant my face was going to be plastered from coast-to-coast in the press. That might have been good for my image as a Romeo, but it didn't do much for my life expectancy considering the number of Mafia guys who wanted to see me dead and were eager to do the job themselves.

"In 24 hours I went from Denise Brown's mystery man to her hit man, but I didn't care. It didn't even bother me that the press had reported that she'd been partying the night before with Geraldo Rivera in Manhattan at the Shark Bar and Tatou.

"She gave herself to me in our suite and we didn't come up for air the first night. She was as sweet as she'd told me on the phone. We had talked about what we would do to each other, and when we met we did it.

"By morning the word was out. We had plenty to read."

The *Boston Herald*, March 3, 1995:

Nicole's Sister Met with Ex-Mobster in Boston

By Ralph Ranalli

Denise Brown, sister of O.J. Simpson's slain ex-wife Nicole Brown Simpson, met socially with a former Mafia enforcer turned FBI witness during her recent trip to Boston, the Herald has learned.

Brown, 37, hugged a man later identified by sources as C. Anthony "Tony the Animal" Fiato, 50, when she arrived at Logan International Airport Wednesday for television interviews on domestic violence. She had said she was meeting her "boyfriend" in Boston, sources said. . . .

Not that they were spending a lot of time reading.

"From the moment she entered the limousine we were at each other," Fiato said. "We made love like two maniacs. Our lovemaking was so loud that the people next door called down to the desk and complained about the noise. The desk called our room in the middle of the night. I was in paradise.

"After the first day, we slipped out of the hotel. Denise needed some things from the pharmacy. She's a real health nut and wanted some vitamins. By the third day we were together, I was the one who needed vitamins.

"On the street, people pointed and waved and asked if I was the mystery man. Passing cars honked and it was like a parade everywhere we went. We shopped on Newberry Street, which is the Rodeo Drive of Boston, and a guy opened his restaurant early just so we could have a romantic lunch alone in a private booth. I tell you, it was like *The Lady and the Tramp*. And back at the hotel, she was no lady.

"The next day we went shopping at the Prudential mall. There were thousands of people there and she was really soaking it up. I was a big hit with the brothers who were telling me, 'Hey, man, you got it goin' on. You got the girl. You got everything.' And I just laughed. I was enjoying the ride.

"Denise wasn't amused when people seemed to appreciate me more than her. I just tried to keep a sense of humor about the whole thing. Don't get me wrong. I really liked her. She was the kind of wild woman I could fall in love with, but I could hear the clock ticking.

"That afternoon she got a call from Gloria Allred, the attorney, who was advising her on the domestic violence business. Allred asked Denise to tell me to leave the room. We'd been together three days straight, hadn't been out of each other's arms for more than a few minutes, and she wants me to stand in the hall with the maids and room-service waiters. But I just stood there next to her as she was told she was throwing her life away by being seen with me. The domestic violence gig was going to collapse because she was doing the mambo with Tony the Animal.   "Denise was told to call me an acquaintance, not a friend or lover. Which was interesting since I could barely walk after three days with this sex machine."

The couple quickly made tabloid headlines around the country. TV's *A Current Affair* ate up the story of Nicole's sister and the Mafia enforcer.

Never subtle, *The Star* tabloid made much of their relationship from its March 21 edition:

Nicole's Sister Caught in Secret Romance with Mafia Hitman

"Denise Brown has flipped for hit man Anthony "Tony the Animal" Fiato—and now the one-time-killer-turned-FBI stool pigeon fears Denise's life is in danger from vengeful mobsters.

Turncoat Fiato's evidence has put up to 70 mobsters behind bars, and he knows the godfathers of the Los Angeles mob would love to see him dead.

"I worry about Denise. I've told her I don't want to put her in any danger. But I love her and I don't want to stop seeing her," Fiato, 50, has told friends. . . ."

The weekly tabloids were still hitting the streets with news of the couple's romance, but Fiato knew deep in his heart the day she left Boston that they'd never see each other again.

"When she got back home, she told me she gave a story to the *National Enquirer* and they were saying I used her to get publicity. What I'd need publicity for is anyone's guess, but that was the gist of the story.

"I know it sounds corny, but it hurt my feelings. I really liked her. She was gorgeous, but damned if Tom Lange wasn't right. She was a fast one, all right. What it all meant was, I'd seen the last of Denise Brown, who was not the kind of woman who let love get in the way of business."

By the time the Fiatos returned to Los Angeles to prepare their testimony in the second Christi case, the Simpson trial was in full swing. Having shared drinks with the sensational murder investigation's lead detectives, Tom Lange and Phil Vannatter, the Fiatos had some insight into the case against Simpson.

Just when Anthony and Larry Fiato figured they had seen the last of Los Angeles, word of their conversations with Detective Vannatter began to circulate through the courthouse.

CHAPTER 12

The Fiato brothers were confident as they prepared their testimony for the second trial of Norman Freedberg for the murder of actor Frank Christi. They had carved out a solid relationship with Detective Enoch McClain, but as they entered his office for a strategy session they knew something was wrong.

As usual, McClain was blunt.

"You two guys got yanked off the case," he said.

"We're yanked off the Christi case, for what?"

"You're being investigated," McClain said. He was joined by Dale Davidson, who added, "As far as we're concerned, you guys can just walk out of here."

It was that innocuous conversation they had shared with Wacks, Lange and Vannatter over beer in late January at the hotel. Fiato had been joking with Wacks about being able to ruin Vannatter's credibility by reminding the world of his remark that O.J. Simpson had been a suspect from the start of the investigation, which began in the early morning hours of June 13 after the bodies of Nicole Brown and a young man later identified as Ronald Goldman were found stabbed to death outside her Bundy Drive condominium in exclusive Brentwood.

Vannatter had testified that Simpson initially had not been a suspect, and that detectives chose to enter his home and search it out of a concern for the safety of the football star and his children. Wacks had informed his FBI supervisor, who had gone to the prosecution and set in motion a potentially calamitous series of events.

Vannatter's remark, taken out of context, could accomplish in a finger snap what Simpson's Dream Team had failed to do in months of digging: Put a crack in the homicide detective's testimony.

Anthony Fiato was livid, but he volunteered to give a statement clarifying his impression of the detective's remarks. McClain just shrugged. He was angry at Los Angeles District Attorney Gil Garcetti.

"This DA will do anything to win this O.J. Simpson case, so you guys are out of it," the detective said. "They're going to try to get as much as they can on you, and cross-examine you."

But the Simpson case wasn't the only one in jeopardy. The convictions of Betts and Coe potentially hung in the balance, and the Freedberg case would be lost without the Fiato brothers' testimony. Was the district attorney willing to set the stage to allow two killers to go free in order to salvage the so-called Trial of the Century?

"What about Betts and Coe?" Fiato asked. "You mean to tell me all these people are going to come after me and attack me when, based on my testimony, these other guys got put away? You're going to risk all that to try to damage my credibility? If I'm saying something in this Christi case my credibility is tremendous, but it's terrible when it comes to Vannatter."

"It's their decision," McClain said.

Anthony Fiato: "Now I'm really pissed off. We got up to leave and who do we run into but Phil Vannatter. He turns and walks away. We were laughing and partying a few weeks earlier, now these motherfuckers are putting me on. By the time we get back to the Doubletree in Marina Del Rey, all of a sudden my name is being blasted all over the fucking television. There I am, the Mafia hitman again. What's worse is, I passed up a chance to go undercover as a biker right in the middle of the dope trade in San Diego—I even got a tattoo on my arm—just to help with the Christi case."

O.J. Simpson's attorneys hinged much of his defense on the credibility of the Los Angeles Police Department homicide investigators. Detective Mark Fuhrman's career was destroyed when he was exposed as a racist who was willing to perjure himself on the witness stand. Tom Lange and Phil Vannatter proved far more difficult for the defense to discredit, and as the summer of 1995 wore on, it was clear to most observers that the lead investigators in the Simpson case gave real credibility to the evidence presented. Whether Johnnie Cochran, Robert Shapiro, F. Lee Bailey or Barry Scheck, the defense questioned each bit of evidence at great length and treated each prosecution witness with utter contempt.

The case continued to grind on, thanks in large part to Judge Lance A. Ito's inability to control his courtroom. Simpson paid millions for his defense, and was getting his money's worth and more.

After months in the courtroom, the defense thought it had received a gift when Deputy District Attorney Bill Hodgman approached Shapiro to inform him that three men had heard Vannatter discussing details of the Simpson case. It was Hodgman's duty under the rules of discovery to inform the defense and the judge of the information learned by the prosecution. To do less could be grounds for a mistrial. The issue came to a head Tuesday, September 19 in Department No. 103.

"And that basic information concerns statements that are attributed to Detective Vannatter made in the presence of at least three people who say they heard the statements and two other people who were present who may or may not have heard those statements," Shapiro said. "And those statements were made in January and February of this year. The first statement concerns a conversation that took place with Detective Vannatter, Detective Lange, Deputy District Attorney Davidson, Larry Fiato and Anthony Fiato. They were meeting in a hotel room going over testimony for presentation on behalf of the witnesses for the District Attorney in a homicide case known as the Christi case."

A member of the United States Attorney's office met with the judge and requested that the Fiatos' faces not be shown on camera. Anthony Fiato laughed when he heard the news. He'd been a newspaper and television tabloid feature numerous times over the past seven months. His face had been plastered on the front page of the Boston Herald. But he chose not to argue the point after it became clear that Larry was concerned about his own identity. Larry had managed to hold down a straight job for several years and lived under a new name. One glimpse of his face on the television screen and it would force him to move.

"The world wasn't watching," Anthony said. "The camera wasn't on me, and that was fine with me. But let me tell you something, it was powerful, being on that stand with the reporters. I got treated as an enemy by the cops. They thought that I was going to dime out Vannatter. When I first cooperated when I was helping them put away Christi I was Sunny Jim. I could do no wrong. I was the best guy in the world. I got introduced to Marcia Clark by Dale Davidson, who told her how well I had testified, that if I was a witness in the Simpson case they'd be sure to win it. Well, suddenly I was a witness in the Simpson case."

The defense and prosecution both recognized the potential danger the Fiatos presented. Shapiro attempted to frame the issue.

"A conversation allegedly took place in a hotel room where Detective Vannatter was allegedly quoted as saying, by Mr. Larry Fiato, that regarding the O.J. Simpson case 'We went over to Rockingham because he was a suspect. The husband is always a suspect,'" Shapiro told the court. "He was interviewed, upon getting that information, in the last week or two, by Mr. Hodgman and Mr. Kelberg, and he made those statements to these members of the District Attorney's office in a tape-recorded interview. . . .

"He also said that at a later time, perhaps in February of that year, he was having a cigarette on the 18th floor in an area known as the smoking area, with Detective Vannatter, and at that time Detective Vannatter repeated the same phrase, that O.J. was a suspect and the husband is always a suspect.

"Two other people came out during that conversation. One was

Anthony Fiato who confirms that he heard Detective Vannatter say those words, and the second is Special Agent Wacks from the Federal Bureau of Investigation."

Anthony Fiato's innocuous conversation with Mike Wacks had spiraled out of control. Fiato had kiddingly told Wacks about leaking information to investigative producer Vic Walters, and Wacks had reported the comment to his FBI supervisor, who was compelled to pass along the information. Bill Hodgman and Brian Kelberg conducted interviews of the Fiatos, and their statements were presented to the defense. A joke had found its way into Hollywood's Trial of the Century, but Vannatter wasn't laughing. It was his tenuous credibility, already battered by Simpson's defense team, that promised to take a beating.

Shapiro argued that Vannatter had shown a "reckless disregard for the truth in offering testimony under oath for the purpose of securing a search warrant."

"And in that endeavor the jury now is entitled to know whether or not Detective Vannatter was untruthful to this jury when he said the purpose for going over to the Rockingham estate was to make a notification to Mr. O.J. Simpson and because of the welfare and well-being of the children, that he was a concerned grandfather and he was concerned for the children of O.J. Simpson," Shapiro said.

Deputy District Attorney Brian Kelberg tried to prevent Shapiro from ruining Vannatter's credibility and, in turn, the strength of his testimony in the murder case.

"Mr. Shapiro has his facts somewhat wrong and certainly has the interpretation quite extremely erroneous." Kelberg said. "Number One, the circumstances from the Fiatos' perspective is as follows: And I'm going to quote Anthony Fiato who I think would be accurately characterized as somewhat of a salty figure, so pardon the language. 'This is all a bunch of bullshit. What he would talk to this court about is Vannatter was there at the hotel, but Vannatter was not a part of the Christi investigation because Lange had a different partner for the Christi investigation. Vannatter just came along.' At some point these guys are just, again to use Anthony Fiato's term, just bullshitting, just shooting the breeze, and some statement is made by Vannatter to the effect of Simpson being a suspect, the husband is always a suspect."

". . . Now, when you put all of this in context and you remember the immortal words of Anthony Fiato to Mr. Hodgman and me at the conclusion of our interview, that everybody was making, again the language of Anthony Fiato, a fuckin' big deal out of stuff that was bullshit, what he was pissed off about, his term, was that he made a call."

"I'm glad you qualified that," Ito said.

Ito allowed the defense to recall Vannatter and call Wacks and the Fiato brothers.

Vannatter was made to appear a liar for making what the Fiatos considered a frivolous statement. The detective's March 16, 1995 testimony, in which he had said that Simpson was not immediately a suspect, was read back to the jury.

Wacks was examined by Johnnie Cochran, who attempted to nail down the smoking-deck conversation. In an attempt to impress the jurors and drive home the importance of the apparently contradictory testimony, Cochran rephrased the question and repeated it, and Wacks answered again in the affirmative. Wacks had not reported the conversation he overheard in February until September 11th, and Cochran raised the specter of a failure to disclose important information in a murder case. On cross-examination, Kelberg was again mopping up a mess.

"I thought by what Mr. Fiato had told me that this information was now in the hands of the media and I thought the media was going to make a big deal over nothing, and I thought that it was my duty to tell my supervisor that at least this situation existed and was going on," Wacks said.

In effect, it was Wacks who had made a big deal over nothing. Anthony Fiato's early September conversation with ABC's Vic Walters had been little more than playful banter.

Then it was the Fiatos' turn. As they waited to testify, the brothers, who had put away dozens of criminals for the FBI and had provided the evidentiary bridge leading to two convictions in the Frank Christi murder case, grew angrier by the minute. The credibility they had fought so hard for was on the line and sure to be called into question. After all, they were The Gangster Brothers, Mafiosi-turned-snitches. The fact the United States Attorney successfully argued that their faces not be shown during their testimony was little solace.

Larry Fiato had no intention of adding to the damage inflicted by the re-examination of Vannatter and questioning of Wacks. Larry's memory on the conversations in question was fuzzy to say the least.

"It was not a serious night," Larry Fiato said. ". . . We were laughing and joking and it was like—I think it was when we first got back and we were all, you know, seeing each other again and you know, yeah, yeah, yeah, you know, shooting the breeze."

Vannatter had made some statements, but Larry insisted they were being taken out of context by the defense.

Then Anthony Fiato took the stage.

"When I walked into that courtroom, all the women jurors nudged each other and said, 'Oh, there he is. There he is,'" Fiato recalled. "It was funny stuff, but if they thought they were going to turn me into a defense witness, they had another think coming."

O.J. Simpson was overheard to say, "That guy could have been my brother-in-law."

If Larry Fiato had been minimalist in his answers, his brother was doing his best Marcel Marceau impression with the immensely skilled Cochran.

Cochran: All right. During that conversation do you recall Detective Vannatter making a statement regarding his going to the Simpson residence in the early morning hours of June 13th, 1994?

Fiato: No.

Cochran: You don't recall him making a statement to you?

Fiato: Not saying that, no.

Cochran: All right. You don't recall him making a statement about going to the Simpson house, Mr. Simpson being a suspect?

Fiato: No, he didn't say that.

Cochran: All right. You don't recall—let me ask—listen to my question. Do you recall a conversation wherein the subject matter of Detective Vannatter going to Mr. Simpson's home in the early morning of January 13th came up?

Fiato: No.

Cochran was exasperated.

Cochran: You don't recall that at all?

Fiato: No.

Cochran: All right. Now, do you recall that you gave a tape or a tape-recorded interview with the District Attorney's office in the recent past?

Fiato: Yes.

Cochran: And you were asked questions about this conversation back in January of 1995; is that correct?

Fiato: I believe so.

Cochran: Have you listened to that tape at all, sir?

Fiato: No, I haven't.

Cochran: You have not heard it? Have you seen any transcript of that particular tape?

Fiato: Not at all.

Cochran: Have you read anything prior to your coming here to testify today?

Fiato: Not a thing.

Cochran: Did you get a chance to talk to Mr. Kelberg today prior to your testifying?

Fiato: No, I haven't.

Cochran: That gentleman over there?

Fiato: No, I haven't.

Cochran: You have not talked to him at all today?

Fiato: I would remember him. No.

Cochran: What would you have talked to him about? You talked to him on the tape, did you not?

Fiato: Yes.

Cochran All right. You recall that? He asked you a lot of questions?

Fiato: Yeah. He asked me questions, yes.

Cochran: All right. You have not talked to him today?

Fiato: No.

Cochran: Did you talk to Mr. Hodgman today?

Fiato: Yes.

Cochran: When was that?

Fiato: I think about an hour ago, an hour-and-a-half.

Cochran: During the lunch hour?

Fiato: Yes.

Cochran: Preparatory to your testifying here?

Fiato: No.

Cochran: Well, he talked to you before you testified here, right?

Fiato: Not in relation to my testimony.

As hard as Cochran tried, Anthony Fiato refused to open a door that might lead to damaging Vannatter, the detective who had shunned him, over a harmless conversation. Fiato's memory was so bad that at one point Cochran asked, "You are Anthony Fiato, right?"

He certainly was, and Anthony Fiato was no fish for the defense in a murder case.

Cochran had the benefit of a taped conversation between Anthony Fiato and the prosecution, in which he recalled Vannatter's husband-is-always-the-suspect statement. Fiato said Vannatter was speaking in generalities regarding the Simpson case and related crimes.

Cochran's attack of the reason behind Fiato's call to Vic Walters also backfired.

Cochran: Did you have a conversation with Vic Walters on September 8th?

Fiato: I said so.

Cochran: And at that time were you angry at Phil Vannatter?

Fiato: Yes.

Cochran: And at that time were you angry because Detective Vannatter and some members of the District Attorney's office had said some things about you that you weren't happy about?

Fiato: Yes.

Cochran: It had to do with Denise Brown?

Fiato: Yes.

But when Fiato told Wacks he had called Walters, it changed the dynamics of the conversation. Walters, a respected journalist who for many years has teamed up with investigative reporter Brian Ross for some of the most compelling organized crime stories broadcast on television, was capable of turning a small slice of the Simpson murder case into a huge story. But he had not gained his reputation by regurgitating contextually questionable material. Wacks, in Fiato's mind, had overreacted.

"I saw him [Wacks] being upset and I said I was pimping him and I was kidding," Fiato said. "And then when I said that to him, he said, oh—excuse me. Can I swear in here?"

"Be my guest," Judge Ito replied.

"Excuse me, ladies and gentlemen," Fiato told the court. "He called me—he said it in this vein. 'You prick, you really had me going.'"

"And what was it that you were doing that in your mind was pimping Mr. Wacks?" Brian Kelberg asked on cross-examination.

"I was exaggerating the circumstances to aggravate him," Fiato replied.

Kelberg: Why did you want to aggravate Mr. Wacks?

Fiato: Well, that is what pimping does. You pimp each other and I got one over on you and he has done it to me in all these years I have known him.

Kelberg: And you enjoyed that exercise; is that correct?

Fiato: I was ecstatic with that exercise.

Kelberg: Would it be accurate to say that it did not appear that Agent Wacks shared your enthusiasm for what you had done?

Fiato: The blood drained from his face.

When Anthony Fiato left the witness stand, he glared at the

defense table. The Dream Team diverted its eyes.

In his book, *Journey to Justice*, Johnny Cochran made much of the Fiatos' testimony:

"On Tuesday, September 19, 1995, we recalled Vannatter to the stand, but he persisted in his deceit. Moments later, as the courtroom cameras were turned off to protect the identities of the government's two professional informants, the Fiato brothers made their entrance. In a way, it was a pity the cameras had gone dark because this was the trial's most cinematic moment."

Suddenly, the names of Anthony and Larry Fiato were on the lips of millions of Americans who were entranced by the O.J. Simpson murder case. ABC News reporter Cynthia McFadden conducted a one-on-one interview for "*Good Morning America*" with Anthony, who then appeared as a special guest on "*Larry King Live*" and "*Nightline*" with Ted Koppel.

"Vic Walters didn't do anything," Anthony Fiato said. "The FBI superviser gave the story to Bill Hodgman. It got everyone pissed off at me, especially the cops. It was like the McCarthy hearings with these people; I was guilty and there was no way to prove myself innocent. It really showed me their true colors. And I don't think I'll ever get over the fact that L.A. D.A. Gil Garcetti was willing to risk two murder convictions by having his people attack my credibility as a witness when they knew that I was the one who delivered Betts and Coe for them.

"Those guys would still be on the street if it weren't for me and my brother. On my word, they were all arrested. Lange and McClain didn't have a clue about a motive. I gave them one.

"The horrendous thing about the Simpson case was that Gil Garcetti, who has to be the biggest political opportunist in the history of the city, was willing to tank the Christi murder case for a shot at Simpson. Why? Because of the publicity. Betts and Coe would have been free men if they'd questioned my credibility. That's something a pimp would do.

"The whole atmosphere of the place made me want to vomit. I

mean, Marcia Clark was giddy from all the attention she was receiving. Same with Chris Darden. And Denise Brown. Only the Goldmans stick out in my mind as genuinely sincere people. These prosecutors were going crazy and blamed the decision on the jurors, but they played a big role in losing the case. They were overanxious and way too self-righteous. They smelled the blood and went on the attack. They saw the kind of jury they had and still they weren't careful not to make O.J. into a sympathetic character by beating him up.

"My experience with Vannatter was limited to watching him drink a bunch of beer one night. He was obviously feeling the strain of the investigation. He drank like he had a hollow leg. But what he said was nothing compared to the way the witnesses in the waiting room were allowed to watch the proceedings on television. What a circus. It was a blood feud and the district attorney's office was willing to let murderers like Betts and Coe out—and basically throw away any chance of convicting Norman Freedberg—because their egos got in the way. They had the ambition and arrogance of Caesar. The celebrity went right to their heads. And you know what? They all wound up making a ton of money out of the deal. They probably kneel down at night and thank God for O.J. Simpson. He made them rich and famous."

In the end, Anthony Fiato had his freedom and the knowledge that he had done something right in his life. But that was the problem: By his definition, he no longer had a life.

Was the trade worth it?

"I ask myself that question every day," he said.

Making the transition to life as a citizen has been difficult for Fiato.

"What would you do if you lived my life and woke up one day and found yourself fifty-three years old?" he asked. "I didn't wind up with a wife and kids, and my career has been such that I can't exactly find work fitting my qualifications in the want ads. What am I going to do? Grab a lunchpail and work construction? For a guy like me, what kind of life is that?"

Epilogue

After his testimony in the Simpson case and appearances on
Nightline and *Larry King Live*, Anthony Fiato returned to seclusion. His life in the mob and with the FBI was over.

But what life remained?

He began seeing a psychologist to attempt to answer the questions he'd had about his violent existence.

"I did bad things," he said. "I have to admit it. It's not an easy
thing to admit. At one time I might have bragged about one story
or another, and laughed and joked, but I'm different now. Now,
I'm answerable to people. Before, I wasn't answerable to anybody.
It takes some getting used to."

After their testimony in the Simpson case, the Fiatos were not
asked to testify in the third trial against Norman Freedberg, which
also ended in a hung jury. LAPD homicide detective Enoch
McClain: "I like to think the Fiatos would have made a big difference if they were allowed to give their version in the second
trial. After three trials, the only way we could still bring Norman
Freedberg to justice is if we had additional information."

Short of that, Freedberg lives in Palm Springs.

On the street, the old mob is either in prison, in the ground, or
infirm.

Larry Baioni and Nicky Giso are dead. J.R. Russo died of
throat cancer in May 1998. Vinny Ferrara and Steve Flemmi, a

long-time government informant, continue to attempt to break out of prison by manipulating the court system.

Willie "Floppy" Fopiano, who had passed up the chance to become a made guy because he couldn't kill a man, recovered from the gunshot wounds inflicted by junkie Guy De Prizio. Willie collaborated with journalist John Harney and in 1993 published a book called *The Godson*. Willie, who spent his final years hanging around the poker rooms of Las Vegas casinos, died of pancreatic cancer in 1995.

Guy De Prizio's killers were never caught, but Fiato knows who killed him.

"Larry Baioni, who ran Boston's version of Murder Incorporated, took the shooting personally," Fiato said. "Larry offered Floppy help after the shooting, but Willie refused. He was still embarrassed about not picking up the gun and following Larry into the life, and he felt he didn't deserve the help. That didn't stop Larry. He told Johnny Cincotti to handle the problem. Johnny recruited his long-time associate and boyhood friend, Bobby Luisi, who I'd been partners with in the Las Vegas narcotics deals. They beat De Prizio to death and dumped him in the harbor. Sonny Polosi relayed the story to me from Bobby, who'd told him that he and Johnny Cincotti had done the piece of work. I laughed when I heard that Bobby had helped take care of De Prizio. Talk about ironic. It was Willie who had stuck Bobby Luisi with a blade during a street fight when we were kids. Bobby hated Willie, and yet he went out and did that work for him. That was a testament to the strength and respect people had for Larry Baioni."

Luisi and Sonny Polosi, who had played a role in the Boston mob's none-too-subtle role in the local narcotics trade, were murdered along with three other men in a Charlestown eatery. At the time, they were shaking down drug dealers for Jackie Salemme.

In Hollywood, the story is the same.

Mike Rizzitello's Los Angeles mob family was short-lived, and today he remains in prison on the Bill Carroll attempted murder charge.

Peter John Milano, the official boss of the family, lives in seclusion in Westlake Village and operates a coffee distributorship. Now in his 70s, he continues to watch member after member of his family be convicted of crimes ranging from extortion to murder conspiracy.

On January 6, 1997, Las Vegas mobster Herbie Blitzstein was murdered inside his Las Vegas townhouse. Blitzstein, who Fiato had encountered years earlier in Las Vegas, was a loanshark who had defied the presence of Milano family members who had migrated to Las Vegas.

Law enforcement had infiltrated the Milano crew so deeply that within minutes of Blitzstein's death FBI agents and police had suspects in the murder-for-hire.

By February, 1998, underboss Carmen Milano and two dozen other men were named in federal indictments linked to the L.A. mob's migration to Las Vegas. The FBI, Metropolitan Police Department and Nevada Division of Investigation along with the Las Vegas office of the Organized Crime Strike Force had landed a devastating blow to the family. Among those indicted were men Fiato had helped put away years earlier, including Milano, Steve Cino, Jimmy Caci, Bobby Milano, and Rocco Zangari. Little known was the fact that Anthony Fiato had provided information that eventually helped the FBI turn his old associate Johnny Branco into a key informant in the case.

"Whether some of the guys on the street know it or not, it's all over and has been for years," Fiato said. "The government has too many ways to get you. It's a real mismatch."

Ronald "Ronnie Rome" Romanowski, who had come so close to being murdered, still spends time in Los Angeles. Robert "Puggy" Zeichick, Anthony Fiato's loansharking partner, lives on Abita Circle in Las Vegas and hangs out daily at the city's sports books.

When last seen, Steve Finkel, convicted in the $1 million Manufacturers Hanover Trust bond scam, was a cabdriver in Las Vegas.

Danny Hutton still fronts the Three Dog Night, which plays one-nighters across the country. Comedian Joey Villa's last big gig came as the house comedian for Jeff Kutash's "Splash" show at the Riviera.

In 1998, movie producer Aaron Russo ran for Governor in Nevada on the Republican ticket. For the record, Russo said he recalled meeting Norman Freedberg, but did not remember meeting anyone named Anthony Fiato.

Larry Fiato has made a new career in the computer field and is strictly legitimate. He lives quietly not far from his older brother, whom he speaks to every day.

"In the North End, the Mafia was a way of life," Larry said. "We looked up to Nicky and Paulie the way some people look up to the President. They were just part of the way things were. We tried to do in California what we'd done in Boston, but California doesn't work that way.

"The way my life has turned out, I can't say it was a bad move for me. I can't say the same thing for my brother. He wasn't meant for the straight life. My brother was built to be a Mafia boss. I feel bad about that, but I also know that he'd still be in jail if I hadn't gone to the government.

"However hard it was for me to cooperate, it was several thousand times harder for my brother."

In the end, there are three dreams.

In the first, Anthony Fiato is driving at dusk through a strange town. He has rented an apartment under an assumed name. As darkness descends, he loses his way and is forced to wander alien streets.

"It's where I live, but as hard as I try I can't remember my name," Fiato said. "I have to remember my name if I'm going to find my way home."

The scene shifts to a lounge in Las Vegas, where Anthony Fiato sees familiar faces at the bar. Big Foot Zangari, Luigi Gelfuso, and, at the end of the bar, Robert "Puggy" Zeichick.

"I storm right past the other guys and walk up to Puggy," Fiato said. "I start yelling at him. 'How could you call me a snitch, you lying motherfucker, when you tried the same thing I did after you got convicted? You tried to make a deal with the government, but they didn't want you. And you have the nerve to call me a rat.' He doesn't know what to say and I raise my hand, ready to slap him."

The final scene is a room illuminated by a single light. There is gray-haired Joe Russo, brick-fisted Mike Rizzitello. And Anthony Fiato.

"They're looking at me and shaking their heads slowly," Fiato said. "I'm trying to talk to them, but they're disappointed in me. And I feel ashamed that I've let them down. I start to tell them I did what I had to do, that I had no choice, but they're not listening. These are men I looked up to since I was a kid, men I was willing to kill for, and die for. And I've betrayed them.

"J.R. looks away, and by then I see that Mike has a gun. I don't even try to move. He points it at me and pulls the trigger, and that's when I wake up. Always in a sweat, always questioning what I did to survive. The shot rings in my ears, and I can smell the sulphur in the gunpowder."

Sources and Acknowledgments

I deeply appreciate the assistance of the police officers and FBI agents who helped flesh out the characters of Anthony and Larry Fiato. Among many: John Benino, Bob Hamer, Michael Wacks, Enoch McClain, and Jack Motto. Comments from Wacks and Weichert were quoted from a confidential Bureau training video called "The Gangster Brothers," which highlighted the casework of the agents and the Fiatos.

The work and generous assistance of numerous reporters is much appreciated. Thanks especially to intrepid Ed Becker, Sam Gideon Anson, John Harney, Ken Mayte, Kim Murphy, Ralph Ranalli, Charles Rappleye, Nancy Wride, and Gregg Zoroya.

On the lengthy list of books used to deepen my background knowledge of the subject: Becker and Rappleye's *All-American Mafioso* (Barricade Books, New York, 1995); Johnnie L. Cochran Jr. and Tim Rutten's *Journey to Justice* (Ballantine Books, New York, 1995); Fredric Dannen's *Hit Men* (Random House, New York, 1990); Ovid Demaris's *The Last Mafioso* (Times Books, New York, 1981); Fopiano and Harney's *The Godson* (St. Martin's Press, New York, 1993); John Peer Nugent's *Mickey Cohen: In My Own Words* (Prentice-Hall, Englewood Cliffs, New Jersey); Nicholas Pileggi's *Wiseguy* (Pocket Books, New York, 1987); Vinny Teresa and Thomas C. Renner's *My Life in the Mafia* (Fawcett Publications, Greenwich, Conn., 1973); Marvin J. Wolf and Katherine Mader's *Fallen Angels* (Ballantine Books, New

York, 1986), and Michael J. Zuckerman's *Vengeance is Mine* (Macmillan, New York, 1987).

I am fortunate to have several dedicated editors in my life. They include Sandra Lee Stuart, Kate Cassidy, Tricia Smith, Allan Wilson, Jeff Nordstedt et. al. at Barricade Books. Las Vegas Review-Journal Publisher Sherman Frederick and Editor Thomas Mitchell continue to encourage my growth as a writer by allowing me the freedom to pursue stories beyond my daily column. For that I am most grateful.

As ever, thanks to my friends and literary allies Lyle and Carole Stuart, whose courage is undaunted.